OUTRUNNING THE DEMONS

PHIL HEWITT

OUTRUNNING THE DEMONS

lives transformed through running

BLOOMSBURY SPORT
LONDON · OXFORD · NEW YORK · NEW DELHI · SYDNEY

BLOOMSBURY SPORT
Bloomsbury Publishing Plc
50 Bedford Square, London, WC1B 3DP, UK

BLOOMSBURY, BLOOMSBURY SPORT and the Diana logo are
trademarks of Bloomsbury Publishing Plc

First published in Great Britain 2019

A catalogue record for this book is available from the British Library

Library of Congress Cataloguing-in-Publication data has been applied for

ISBN: TPB: 978-1-4729-5651-4; eBook: 978-1-4729-5652-1

2 4 6 8 10 9 7 5 3 1

Typeset in Caslon by Deanta Global Publishing Services, Chennai, India
Printed and bound in Great Britain by CPI Group (UK) Ltd., Croydon, CRO 4YY

MIX
Paper from
responsible sources
FSC® C020471

To find out more about our authors and books visit www.bloomsbury.com and
sign up for our newsletters

Contents

Foreword by Dean Karnazes   viii

The Start Line: '*And then I did what I have always done. I ran.*'   1

Charlie Engle: '*When I run, I become the absolute epitome of who I am.*'   8

Theresa Giammona: '*I know he was with me every step of the way.*'   16

Isabel Hardman: '*I learn so much about how to cope with life when I go on a long run.*'   23

Jessica Rigo: '*When I need that extra push to finish strong, I think of my fallen running partner . . . my chosen sister.*'   30

Eleanor Keohane: '*I was an absolute mess. . . But I did it. I ran. Three times, sobbing my heart out.*'   38

The Schneider Twins: '*I truly believe that running has saved my family.*'   44

Sandra Laflamme: '*They said there was blood everywhere.*'   51

Dan Keeley: '*You'd be hard-pressed to find a happier, more grateful person than I am right now.*'   58

Caroline Elliott: '*Knowing that I'm always recovering, one small step at a time.*'   66

Sujan Sharma: '*I am so glad now that I had that hallucination.*' 74

Linda Quirk: '*A disease so insidious that it captures the best in everyone.*' 79

James Buzzell: '*Once you have seen dead people, you realise that death is real and that it is going to happen.*' 86

Anji Andrews: '*I remember seeing a solitary robin . . . and thinking it was a sign my dad was watching.*' 92

Emma Malcolm: '*[Running] clears my mind and enables me to think about all the tough stuff.*' 99

Lisa Hallett: '*I ran two of the ugliest miles ever, and it was the first time I accepted that John was not coming home.*' 103

Serena Wooldridge: '*Through running there was light and hope at the end of the tunnel.*' 110

Bryn Phillips: '*I remember thinking we are not going to survive.*' 116

Hanny Allston: '*I have found a way to run for the absolute joy in the freedom it brings me.*' 122

Kate Jayden: '*How could I let anyone steal running from me?*' 129

Don Wright: '*I am exceedingly lucky to be here.*' 137

Daniele Seiss: '*Running long distances . . . creates a sense of oneness that I can't explain.*' 142

Carolyn Knights: '*[He spent] his whole life wrapped in the loving arms of his mum and dad.*' 148

Alastair Campbell: '*I see [running] as my best meeting of the day.*' 154

Liz Dunning: '*I have got children. I am not going to concede their future to a world of guns.*' 159

Danny Slay: '*It gave me an outlet to think, focus and unwind.*' 165

Ana Febres-Cordero: '*I am amazing, I am strong, I am beautiful, I am kind.*' 170

Lisa Taylor: '*Not only am I still here, I now have a lovely baby with my lovely husband.*' 176

Jason Nelson: '*I put the barrel of my pistol in my mouth with my finger firmly on the trigger.*' 180

Amanda Trafford: '*I wish I could scoop them all up and inspire them to run!*' 188

Cherissa Jackson: '*Purging me from my grief and my sadness, my anger and my pain.*' 193

Lynn Julian Crisci: '*In my mind, you win when you reach the start line, not the finish line.*' 201

Paul Shepherd: '*My son would have become another fatherless child.*' 211

Bryn Hughes: '*I was thinking if I allow myself to die, then evil will win.*' 218

Stephanie Foley: '*Then we did as Sarah did – we ran with all our Hart!*' 225

The Finish Line: '*A group of people I have come to admire hugely.*' 233

Postscript: '*Better Things*' 239

Appendix: The Science Behind the Transformative Power of Running 241

Acknowledgements 256

References 259

About the Author 264

Foreword

By Dean Karnazes, ultramarathoner and
NY Times bestselling author

Running has the power to inflict great pain, and running has the power to heal. A famous surgeon once lamented: 'To cut is to heal.' To be alive is to suffer wounds. Such injuries often come at our own hands; they are self-inflicted. Others – such as the loss of a loved one – are a requisite condition of being human. Neither the wise man nor the virtuous man can escape this sentence. All must endure. To live is to suffer.

A monk may seek transcendence from this suffering through quiet meditation. We runners have a different prescription. Running is our remedy, our salvation. We use running to lighten the unbearable heaviness of being, to cope with the unthinkable and to piece together life once more, step by restorative step.

The potent catharsis running delivers remains mysterious. What could possibly compel a human to strip nearly naked and do something that has all but lost its purpose in this modern world? It defies logic. There is no necessity for running; we runners voluntarily seek the pain, the discomfort and the struggle this accelerated form of locomotion doles out. But herein lies the magic. The hardship of running somehow softens the hardship of life. Running turns the madness into music.

The book you are about to read is an inspiring collection of stories about runners who have run through unimaginable adversity to find perspective, resolution and ultimately peace, within themselves and with the universe. These stories are sure to inspire and compel you, whether you run great distances, modest distances or are just discovering the splendour of a spirit in motion.

The Start Line

'And then I did what I have always done. I ran.'

I run my finger along the ugly, jagged scar on my leg. It tingles unpleasantly. It always does. The runner next to me smiles and nudges me. 'You'll be alright, mate,' he says. And I know I will. What he actually means is: 'Welcome back.'

Three minutes to go to the gun now.

I look along the line of runners. Some are jumping up and down. Some have already slipped into their start position, fingers poised on their GPS watches. Others are just chatting, seemingly without a care in the world – despite the 26.2 miles (42.2 kilometres) that lie ahead of us all.

I catch the eye of the runner on the other side of me. There is nervousness in his smile, but there is also determination. I smile back, and despite the chill, I feel warmer. I am home. I can't think of anywhere else I want to be. Or anyone else I want to be with.

For the next few hours, these runners – hundreds of them, complete strangers to me, one and all – will be my sole companions. And that, to me, is the joy of running – and also the beauty of running. I know that as we run, something remarkable is going to happen.

The next few hours will be healing. Sweaty, knackering, bloody-minded and a slog. But also healing, so very deeply healing. And I suspect, as we stand at the start line, that many other runners are thinking exactly the same thing. For the record, it's the Worcester Marathon. But it could be any marathon anywhere. The real drama isn't going to be in the pounding we are about to give our bodies. The real drama is going to be in our minds.

There are plenty of runners who will run untroubled for the sheer love of running. But far more than we'd ever dare suspect are running for much, much darker reasons – just as I am.

This is my first marathon since being viciously mugged, stabbed, punched, kicked and, to all intents and purposes, left for dead. And as I return again and again to the bigger of the two scars on my leg, I know this will be the way I will resolve what happened to me.

I have set the Worcester Marathon a very specific task, a massive task, and I know the event will be equal to it: the marathon is going to move me on from the pavement in Cape Town where I have been stuck now for 15 months, convinced I am just about to breathe my last.

Looking back, I was an idiot. And I do a lot of looking back. Except it doesn't feel as if I am looking back. The past hasn't become past yet, and that's the trouble. It is an endlessly replaying present, and I am condemned to be its sole and reluctant viewer, a spectator at what seems, with every fresh viewing, ever more likely to be my own demise.

It took a year for me to realise that my attacker probably didn't have the slightest intention of killing me. He was a professional. A long slashing cut to the calf and a deep puncturing stab to the thigh; he knew what he was doing. I wasn't going to get up in a hurry, but then he made doubly sure. He followed up the stabbing with a mini frenzy of kicking to stomach and ribs, back and neck as I lay there in my what-the-hell confusion.

Looking back, looking sideways, looking whichever way I want, I was an idiot – and an idiot intent on compounding his own idiocy. It was 14 February, 2016. I had just watched England lose a one-day international at the breathtakingly beautiful Newlands Cricket Ground, a magnificent setting overlooked by Table Mountain and Devil's Peak. Alex Hales scored a century and then so too did AB de Villiers in a relatively straightforward run chase. England lost, but so what? It was a fantastic day in a fantastic place. I'd recommend it to anyone.

But please, make proper arrangements for getting back. I didn't, and that was mistake number one. I thought I'd easily find a taxi or a bus. When I didn't, I started walking. Mistake number two. Before long, I was walking alone. Did I turn round? Mistake number three. Soon, I was walking on the hard shoulder of a busy motorway.

Did I turn back? Mistake number four. And so the mistakes piled up until I found myself walking through Cape Town's District Six. The irony is that I suddenly knew where I was and could see central Cape Town on the horizon. The danger was that I was in a notoriously dodgy place: flat, deserted, open, urban wasteland. And I paid the price.

Is there a formula dictating that when we make a mistake, our next decision is likely to be an even worse one? I suspect so. That day was the perfect illustration.

In my floppy cricket hat, my rather fetching long colonial-style shorts and an expensive camera around my neck, I might as well have been wearing a T-shirt emblazoned with the words: 'Mug me!' I heard the footsteps behind me, I heard the angry demand for my camera and I was felled by what seemed to be two punches to my leg. I pulled my attacker over and we wrestled. He was behind me at first and then in front of me on the ground as we shuffled round in a rather macabre embrace. And that was when I looked down and realised that his punches hadn't been punches at all. My leg was awash with blood. I let go of him. He stood up and let loose a volley of kicks and then legged it.

What remains is a series of impressions. My hand was on a stone. I raised it to throw at his retreating figure and then thought better of it. Thank goodness. I crawled back onto the pavement and watched the blood pool around me. I tried to stand, but all I really wanted to do was lie back and shut my eyes.

But I was lucky. So incredibly lucky.

My saviour Steven arrived. Steven the pizza delivery guy who pulled up his car and bundled me in.

More than Steven, though, I remember the young girl who was his assistant. She couldn't speak. She stared at me, open-mouthed. I'd never seen horror on anyone's face before, and now I was the cause of it. The impact was huge.

And then the traffic lights. Lots of them at red. Steven stopped the car, pulled his pizza sign off the roof, handed it to me in the back and then shot through every subsequent red light he came across. At the hospital, he dashed in and emerged with a wheelchair.

What a hero. How astonishingly brave to stop when it would have been so easy to drive on. Except, of course, it wasn't in his nature to drive on. I will be forever in his debt.

And then the accident and emergency department.

Chatting about his desire to move to Surrey, the doctor stitched up my leg, but it continued to bleed, swelling agonisingly. He unstitched it, put some deep stitches in, stitched up the surface and then leaned against it with all his weight. My leg turned black, but the bleeding stopped. Fifteen stitches in all, including three in my hand. Three broken ribs. A bruised liver. And one very messed-up brain.

But there is a delay in the way these things affect us.

It hit me three weeks later, back home. My lovely wife Fiona was encouraging me to get out. A Sunday afternoon trip to Fareham shopping precinct in Hampshire, the county where we live. What could be gentler, less threatening than that? And yet, within minutes I was so nearly the oddball who blubbed in Boots. I was standing there, fleetingly alone, knowing that if I spoke, if I breathed, if I moved, I would burst into tears. My eyes filled, but thank goodness for surface tension. The tears didn't tumble. I retreated, dignity more or less intact.

I knew what was wrong. Of course I did. I am a man. Men know these things. I booked an appointment with our practice nurse the next morning and told him my wounds were clearly infected and obviously weren't healing properly. He inspected them thoroughly, told me they were fine and asked if I would consider 'talking to someone'. It took a year for me to realise that I should. I am 'talking to someone' now, and it is helping.

But back then, less than a month after the attack, I fell back on a stubborn self-reliance that I have since learned to depend on less. I resolved to adopt my own two-point recovery plan. And I put it into practice the very next day. I started to write down everything that had happened to me, every last detail, every last thought, every last horror, every last indignity.

And then I did what I have always done. I ran.

The broken ribs hurt like hell. The stab wounds throbbed appallingly as I pulled on barely healed flesh. I was wincing, I was hobbling, I was cursing, but I was mobile. It was a warm, early-spring morning. The sky was blue – and so was the air around me as each step seemed to rip through me. But I started to smile.

There was something so reassuring about running, however badly, however lopsidedly. There was something so familiar, so welcoming and so absolutely me. Left-legged stabs and right-sided broken ribs aren't a match made in heaven, and I was roughing them up as they met in the middle. But suddenly there seemed a purpose in the pain. Or maybe a message. It felt like my body was telling me: 'I'm still here! You and I are still alive!' The spring weather did the rest on a morning that was suddenly glorious.

Everything hurt, but I felt an immense lifting of my spirits. I know now that it was not, to borrow from Churchill, the end. Nor was it even the beginning of the end. But it was, perhaps, the end of the beginning. For the first time in three weeks, I was no longer 100 per cent *Phil who has been stabbed*. I was 1 per cent *Phil who has run 30 marathons*, from New York City to Tokyo, London to Paris, Amsterdam to Dublin, via Berlin, Rome, Mallorca and others. I was no longer the victim. I was, fleetingly, the survivor.

I returned from that run more battered than I had been at the start, but I returned from it more me again. Partially, at least. Running defines me positively – and I had started to allow my real self back in. I had started to put space between me and the mugging.

I had turned a corner. And around that corner was the starting point for this book.

I realised in that moment that running is the most astonishing tool at the disposal of those of us with the good fortune to be fit and healthy enough to make use of it. The months since the attack have been difficult, dismal and distressing in so many ways, but the weirdest thing is that I wouldn't change a thing. Post-traumatic stress disorder (PTSD) brings a huge degree of detachment, and in a perverse way, I have actually enjoyed watching *Phil the runner* reclaim himself from the horror of what happened to him. At times, he's done pretty badly. At times, he's done alright.

Running gives us space. It gives us strength. It gives us connection and it gives us peace. It will never give us all the answers, but it can so often be a large part of the solution. And if my attacker gave me anything that day, he certainly gave me a reason to run. I used to run because I loved to run, but suddenly I was running because I sensed all that running could do for me.

I even began to feel an odd sense of gratitude to my attacker.

It is so easy to sleepwalk through life as we hunker down in our patterns and our routines. He shook me out of mine – and invested my 31st marathon with massive personal significance.

And so as I stand at the start line in Worcester – May 2017, 15 months on from my attack – I am conscious that running has never mattered more to me. I am desperate to plonk a mountain of marathon-ness between myself and my trauma.

But just as importantly, my attacker has woken me up to a wider perspective: a greater awareness of my fellow runners. I am a journalist. I have always loved the company of fellow journalists. But suddenly, I find myself waking up to the beauty of other runners. I have always been a self-contained, solipsistic kind of runner. Now I want to share with my fellow runners just what it is that has brought us all here.

At the start of the Worcester Marathon, my first marathon since the stabbing, I start to feel a new present creep in. I am starting to feel safe again. Safe in the company of these runners – hundreds of people, all from different walks of life, from different parts of the country, each running for different reasons, but hundreds of people who for the next few hours will be united by a common purpose. We are going to run a marathon together.

We will barely talk. In fact, we probably won't talk at all. But we will be looking out for each other in our never-to-happen-again convergence, our once-in-a-lifetime random cross section of humanity. We will be bound together in an intoxicating unity of intent. And that's where running gets spiritual for me.

I know instinctively I am not alone. Some of the runners look serene. Some of them look anxious. The rest are chatting still. I wonder what running means to each and every one of them, and I know in that moment what it means to me. This race today will be my way of consigning that day in Cape Town to the past and getting on with the rest of my life.

There are countless happy runners, I am sure, but I suspect far more than we imagine are running through their own dark hinterlands. I have shared mine here in these words. In this book, it is my immense privilege to celebrate the tales of other runners who have been to hell – and found that the surest, quickest way back is to run. This book isn't my story. It is theirs.

I have had the honour to speak to runners who have shown uncommon courage and utter decency in the face of appalling horrors and tragedies. My own ordeal has made them my cherished companions. Their tales matter to me hugely, and I hope they will matter to you. Scratch a runner, and you will often find an extraordinary story. Run with us now through the pages that follow.

The gun goes . . . and we are off!

Charlie Engle

*'When I run, I become the absolute epitome of
who I am.'*

Charlie Engle is one of the world's finest extreme-distance runners,
an athlete with a catalogue of achievements to his name. A modern-
day adventurer, he fuels himself by testing himself, taking his body to
limits most of us couldn't even begin to imagine.

Over the years, Charlie has summited ice-covered volcanoes and
swum with crocodiles. He has also, and perhaps most famously, run
across deserts. Charlie's Running the Sahara expedition from November
2006 to February 2007 was an odyssey stretching across more than 4500
miles (7240 kilometres) of hostile terrain – a journey that seems ever
more astonishing every time you think about it.

More astonishing still, though, is the fact that Charlie's life could so
easily have ended in a hail of bullets 14 years earlier, the grim finale
to a six-day drink and drugs binge in Wichita, Kansas. Charlie was
driving in a neighbourhood he should never have been in. Someone,
somewhere, thought he had money, and the shots rang out, three of
them hitting his car. Charlie remembers them 100 per cent. One of the
bullets lodged in the driver's door without passing through.

But it was what happened next that proved the turning point in
Charlie's life – an incident which underlines both the cruelty of
addiction and the absurdity of addiction. An incident which is actually
a definition of addiction itself. Charlie laughs now as he tells it. But the
truth behind it is grim.

*I remember sitting on the ground watching the police looking through my
car. I will always remember one officer reaching under the driver's seat and
pulling out a glass pipe. Any moderately sane person would have thought:*

'Man, I am in trouble now.' But all I could think was: 'So that's where it is. I wonder if there is anything still in there.' That's the kind of thinking that's difficult to explain. That's what addiction is. You can explain it physiologically, but you really can only explain it emotionally. But really it was the craziness of the moment that did it. In that moment I decided I was done with drugs.

Charlie's life has since been about channelling his addictive personality into purpose-driven pursuits. He has done it through running – something he simply couldn't do without. Certainly, there is a physical element to it, but far more important is the psychological.

Charlie, who lives in North Carolina, was born an addict. Not born *to be* an addict, but born an addict, he says, thanks to a mix of genetic predisposition and the environment he grew up in. If he had been uprooted to a different family, then maybe things would have turned out differently – and then again, maybe not. The sad reality is that he was a fourth-generation addict.

Science has proved the predisposition. People have a tendency not to believe it when you are talking about an addict, but they will believe it about Alzheimer's or cancer. Addiction is often still perceived as a weakness or a choice, something that afflicts people who are weak in character, and that's a narrative that speaks very loudly to addicts themselves. It is what we believe about ourselves. The insecurity, the need for a substance . . . no one would choose to live that way. Why would you choose that kind of hell for yourself? But I did choose it because I thought it would help me somehow, to mask some emotion or to eliminate some feeling.

There was a short time when the drink and the drugs were fun, but more significantly, Charlie was socially awkward. Going to college at the age of 17, he quickly discovered that he didn't feel quite so awkward if he had a few beers inside him. Most of his classmates knew when enough was enough. Charlie didn't. *Enough* was a concept that baffled him. Some classmates suggested he cut back, but Charlie didn't think there was a problem. He didn't consider himself an addict. He considered himself a partier – and inevitably he surrounded himself with people who saw themselves the same way.

Hindsight tells him that it was a question of denial. Charlie knew that alcohol caused his problems, but he didn't see alcohol itself as the problem. If there was a problem, it was just bad luck or simply that he was overdoing it. In his early to mid-20s, he wasn't yet at the point where he could see what was happening. He didn't have the insight. Charlie was an only child. His parents were 19 when they had him, and he didn't have the guidance.

I grew up surrounded by drugs and alcohol, but not by bad people. My mum was awesome. She was a free-spirited artist. She drank hard and she wrote for 35 years. She was incredible, but she planted this seed that creativity could come from drugs and alcohol.

Whenever Charlie tried to quit, he didn't follow through. As he progressed through his 20s, Charlie epitomised the old addicts' joke: 'Quitting is easy. I have done it 100 times'. Charlie had been there – repeatedly. As he says, it wasn't like he was lacking in self-awareness. He was a binger. He would disappear for days on end. He would empty out the bank account. But always he would come back, determined to quit. And every time he did, he would put on his running shoes. A keen runner as a child, he saw running as his penance, his solace and his punishment all rolled into one. He also ran because he knew running always made him feel better.

Running was certainly always there for me during those 12 years of addiction. Running absolutely saved my life time and again. I was the binger. I would go two months without drinking or drugs, determined to change, and then I would fall off and spend the next two months in a deep, deep hole I couldn't get out of.

Time and again, Charlie would offer what he calls the foxhole promises of addiction: 'If you get me out of this, I will quit.' Promises he was never going to keep. Charlie's wife was becoming increasingly tired of his behaviour, and he knew it, but still he managed to balance it all out in his own mind. Charlie became the top salesman. He bought a house. He bought cars. He lived an above-average life – and allowed himself to reason that those were precisely the things that addicts didn't do. Therefore he wasn't an addict. If he overachieved in some areas of his life, he believed he could carry on with the drink and the drugs.

But the crunch was coming. Something changed when Charlie's wife was expecting their first son, Brett. Charlie had grown up in a house filled with alcohol. He didn't want to see history repeating itself with his own children. But his thinking went further still. Charlie, then 29 years old, became convinced that his newborn son would be his saviour, his way out of his addictions.

And so it seemed – for just one week, an amazing week during which Charlie revelled in being a dad. Holding Brett, he felt emotions he never thought he'd feel, emotions he didn't even know existed. Charlie was convinced he had turned the corner, that this was it.

But after a great week, he dropped his family off, drove into the worst area of Wichita and spent the next six days smoking crack and binge-drinking on a downer that ended with those three bullet holes in his car, put there just for him.

I was in a terrible neighbourhood. I had been up for six days doing drugs, and the assumption was that I was someone who had money, which I didn't have. I put myself in a conflict zone and I fed off the energy. I loved the craziness of it and the razor's-edge danger of it. And I still seek that today . . . with my running.

It was 23 July, 1992, and Charlie has been clean ever since: 'That night in Wichita, I made a decision.' With those bullets and the police search, Charlie finally broke free from his vicious circle of addiction and failed promises.

Charlie, who tells his tale in his book *Running Man*, went to an Alcoholics Anonymous meeting that night, and the next morning he went for a run. As he says, he barfed on the sidewalk, he barfed in the bushes and he probably barfed in the bathtub back home. But on that run he knew he had finally had enough. He knew if he didn't quit, he was going to die. He knew he was an extreme drug user in a way that just wasn't sustainable.

Meetings followed and so did treatment, but Charlie is convinced that running was what made the difference. Meetings and treatment would never have been enough.

Running saved my life and then actually gave me a life. I went to a meeting every single day for three years without missing a day. There was no in-between for me. I needed to fully commit to the lifestyle, but my first sponsor, an AA old-timer, gently hinted that I spent too much time running and that I needed to focus on the 12 steps (of the AA programme). I told him I understood, but that for reasons I couldn't put into words just yet, I absolutely had to run.

Charlie has since gone public with the story of his addiction, the tale of his sobriety and the extremes of his running, and finds that he is frequently challenged: hasn't he simply swapped one addiction for another? In reality, the relationship is far more complex:

When I did drugs, I had one goal and that was to be invisible. I wanted to disappear. I wanted to have no feelings. I didn't understand the feelings I had. All I wanted to do was to hide. But when I run, there is absolutely no hiding. There is nowhere to go. When I run, I become the absolute epitome of who I am. I am the ultimate Charlie Engle for better or worse. And that's the difference. There is nothing real about the person who is doing drugs or drinking. They are being manipulated or altered by a substance. All I wanted to do as an addict was to live in the dark. But running shines a bright light. For me, running is bright light and clarity.

The clarity is the key. It is precisely what Charlie seeks when he runs.

I don't know if it is my addict's brain, but I am a jumbled mess of thoughts and feelings. My brain feels like it never stops. That's the way I am built. It feels like a roulette wheel, but a roulette wheel where there is a ball for every single roulette slot. Usually it feels like the balls are just pinging around my head all the time. But when I run, when I reach maybe mile five, it is almost like I can feel all the balls landing in the slots, finding where they belong. When I run, my brain becomes focused, my thoughts become clear, my ideas are amazing. Maybe it's like writing down your dreams in the middle of the night. In the morning, you look at your notepad and you think: 'What on earth was that all about?' But the thoughts feel amazing at the time, and it is the same with running. When I am running, it feels like all my thoughts are brilliant.

Even so, it was still a question of proportion, something he struggled to find in his first few years of sobriety. Charlie ran 30 marathons in the early years – as he says, he was running like an addict, running as hard as possible every time, starting off fast and finishing fast. He realises now his drive was simply to become depleted. His instinct told him that if he did it often enough, he would 'beat' the addict out of himself.

It took time to realise just why exactly he was running – and how best to harness it.

> *I needed to realise that the personality traits associated with addiction are the best traits. The drive, the energy, the obsession, the obsession that becomes passion . . . those are the things that mean we achieve. I realised that I needed to nurture my inner addict, not crush him. I realised I had to make friends with him . . . but never trust him.*

The mistrust is vital. Charlie realised that his inner addict's goal will always be to lull him into a false sense of security and convince him to have a drink.

A crucial moment came around five years into Charlie's sobriety. He was watching a game of football on television with friends when someone accidentally handed him an alcoholic drink. Charlie was halfway through it before he realised. He felt the alcohol hit his chest and warm his stomach: 'It was almost like the monster came crawling out of the cave. I could hear it rumbling.' In that moment, Charlie's thinking was clear. The first drink was an accident, but sitting there with the glass half-full in his hand, he realised that a second drink would be choice. He got up, walked out, got into his car, drove to a beach, got into his running kit and ran. And ran. And ran until it felt like his chest was going to explode: 'I wanted to purge my body.'

So no, the battle isn't ever won. And that's why Charlie remains in tune with addiction recovery. And that's why, when it comes to running, Charlie will always prefer the ultras. They give him the opportunity, especially on a 100-miler, to empty himself completely.

> *I know for absolute certain that you can't run 100 miles without wanting to quit a few times, without questioning not just your sanity, but your very existence. You think: 'What is so wrong with me that I want to*

punish myself in this way?' But what is so beautiful is that you are in a controlled situation. You are putting yourself through controlled hell. That's the difference.

It's life on a razor's edge again, but this time with purpose.

Charlie maintains that marathons are the hardest races because of their intensity, but ultras appeal because they are puzzles. You can get round marathons if you do the training and have the right mindset on race day.

But with an ultra, you know that you are going to run completely out of all fuel and energy and desire. The gift is that you know you are going to suffer. Comfort is very overrated in our world. No one ever learnt shit from comfort. No one ever says, 'I had such a happy childhood, and I learned so much from it!'

The point is that through our suffering, ultras show our potential. Charlie hates the cliché, but there's no other way of saying it. Ultras give hope, and that's precisely what Charlie and his fellow runners set out to do when they embarked on one of his proudest achievements, the Icebreaker Run, a 3100-mile (4990-kilometre) relay across America in May–June 2016.

Six runners, all in recovery from some type of mental health issue, took turns running for 24 hours a day for 24 straight days. Their goal was to underline the need for better access to mental health treatments for those suffering from depression, post-traumatic stress disorder (PTSD), bipolar disorder or addiction – all at a time when, as Charlie says, opiate abuse in the States is reaching the levels of a national emergency.

Charlie makes the point: most people in prison have been convicted of a drug-related crime, but prison does nothing for them. It doesn't help and wrecks any chance of recovery. With the Icebreaker Run, he wanted to encourage new dialogue and new thinking in – quite literally – a running conversation from one side of the States to the other.

Icebreaker gave us as a group a chance to show what recovering addicts look like. Between us our stories were about as fucked up as you can get. We had everything – addiction, PTSD, sexual assault issues, every manner of issue – and we wanted to show that it didn't destroy us, that we can still be what we want to be, that we can still realise our potential. We wanted to offer hope to people who can't see a way out of their own problems.

For Charlie, it was a unique double, simultaneously selfish and selfless. He was helping others by doing exactly what he wanted to do: 'And when you get the chance to be selfish and selfless in doing exactly the same thing, that's the best.' More importantly, it gave Charlie, his friends and those in need a huge sense of connection – and again, that's a central part of running's great appeal, as Charlie sees it, just as his Running the Sahara adventure had demonstrated 10 years before.

When Charlie decided to run across the Sahara Desert with Ray Zahab and Kevin Lin, he knew it would be a life-changing expedition. He didn't realise it would also be life-defining. But again, it wasn't just the running that made it so memorable. Equally cherished are his memories of the cultures they encountered along the way. Again, it was about connection.

When we ran through the villages, you'd have little eight-year-old boys or girls come out. They didn't know we were coming or who we were, but they would run 15 km down the road with us and then leave us, smiling, laughing and high-fiving us. There was such a joy in them running with us. The boys and girls ran with us to make themselves feel happy, and it made us feel happy too. It was the most beautiful experience. That's what running is about.

Theresa Giammona

'I know he was with me every step of the way.'

Ask Theresa Giammona what her husband Vinny was like, and she will tell you of the day they spent together at Brooklyn Aquarium, just a couple of days before his 40th birthday.

Money was tight. Vinny was a New York City firefighter and worked long shifts, but to make ends meet, he'd always work some more, bartending wherever he could. But he would never willingly forego the chance to spend time with his family. Vinny had a long night ahead of him on 9 September, but when Theresa told him she was taking their two younger daughters, Nicolette and Daniella, to the Brooklyn Aquarium, Vinny's instant response was that he was coming too. Theresa urged him to get some sleep before going to work that night, but no, Vinny was coming with them.

And they had a great day. Not that Vinny was finished with it yet.

Theresa was anxious to get back for their older daughters, Francesca and Toni-Ann, but Vinny spotted the historic Coney Island Cyclone, a landmark wooden rollercoaster dating back to 1927. It wasn't even open, but with that 40th birthday just a couple of days away, Vinny decided he was going to go on it to celebrate. Theresa insisted they didn't have time, but Vinny was having none of it, and so instead of heading home, they went to the Cyclone.

There was no one on it. It was shut. But Vinny went up to the booth, flashed his fire department badge, told them he was 40 next Tuesday and asked to go on. They let him, and he loved it. As Theresa recalls, it was just Vinny all over.

Vinny was just amazing. He lived life to the fullest. I was always the worrier. I worry about everything. He would say: 'We have only this one life. You have to enjoy it!'

With a Kodak throwaway camera, Theresa took photos of him relishing every second on the Cyclone – photos that were soon to become infinitely precious. Theresa was far from realising their importance in that moment, though.

I didn't even appreciate it. I was so annoyed that we were going to miss the bus. But Vinny just enjoyed life. He never regretted anything. He packed a lifetime into his years.

Inevitably, it was an approach that he took with him to work in a job he adored and in which he won respect and promotion.

He loved the fire department, and the guys loved him. His nickname was Lieutenant Fun. He just made every tour fun. He loved the guys, and they had such camaraderie. It was a risky job, but to tell you the truth, I just never thought about him losing his life in the fire department. I was more fearful of him bartending and being out late and getting robbed and something happening like that.

Vinny had been in the fire department for 18 years. His father Vincent M. Giammona, who died in June 2016, was a New York City firefighter before him, retiring as a captain in 1990. Vinny's goal was to emulate his father and work in Lower Manhattan – a goal he achieved.

He was also, it seemed, about to achieve a very different goal. To celebrate his 40th birthday, he was going to run the New York City Marathon for the first time. He secured his place in the February and was working steadily towards the big day on 4 November. Vinny was in excellent physical shape.

When he was younger, I think it was the competitiveness of running that he loved, but as he got older, I think it was something to do with keeping his sanity. It was part of his workout, just something he loved doing.

Vinny worked a 24-hour shift on Monday, 10 September, and then, on the morning of his 40th birthday, Tuesday, 11 September, he went for a run. And then it was time to go home and enjoy himself. The family had a great day planned. Their oldest daughter, Frankie, had an ice-hockey try-out for an all-girl team Vinny had found for her, and then they would celebrate. Everything was sorted, right down to Vinny's birthday dinner.

None of it happened. Instead, the world changed forever. The year was 2001.

Out of clear blue skies two hijacked passenger planes were flown into the twin towers of the World Trade Center. After the first plane struck the North Tower, a friend phoned Theresa and told her what had happened. Theresa immediately called the firehouse and spoke to Vinny before he headed out with his fellow firefighters from Engine 24 and Ladder 5.

> *I said: 'Are you coming home?' He said no, he had to go. I told him I loved him, and he told me he loved me, and then I said: 'See you later.' He was off duty and responded as a volunteer. I told him to be careful and never thought these would be the last words that I would say to my husband.*

Vinny was never to return. His body was never found. On 11 September, 2001, Vincent Giammona made the supreme sacrifice along with 342 colleagues from the Fire Department of the City of New York, 37 officers from the Port Authority Police Department and 23 officers from the New York City Police Department.

For 10 days, Theresa held out hope for Vinny. It was just possible he was one of a number of people believed to have been trapped underground and somehow still alive. But then shatteringly, all doubt evaporated. On the second Friday after 9/11, Theresa, her parents, her parents-in-laws, Vinny's brother and his two sisters travelled by boat to Ground Zero.

> *When we got there, it felt like we had walked into a war zone. It was still burning 10 days later. There was so much debris flying around. That's when I realised that nobody could be alive there.*

Theresa, who lives on Long Island, was a widow. Francesca, Toni-Ann, Nicolette and Daniella – respectively eight, six, three and two – had lost their father. Vinny had always wanted a boy. Instead he gave his girls boys' names: Frankie, Toni, Nicki and Dani. Boys they weren't, but they meant the world to him – as did Theresa. And now he was gone.

For Theresa, life became a complete blur, a seemingly endless round of wakes and funerals. Always Theresa clung to the hope that Vinny's body would be found. Those of all his immediate colleagues who perished were recovered, except Vinny's and that of 31-year-old Gregory Saucedo, a 10-year FDNY veteran based with Vinny at Ladder 5. All Theresa could do was struggle with her grief.

> *I feel so proud of Vinny now, but at first I was just absolutely devastated for a very long time. There was the anger. Why did this happen? If he had come home, he would still be here. And then I would be thinking what had happened to him, the fact that he just disappeared. It was very, very hard for a very, very long time, but now I know he is a true hero. I think I always knew he was a true hero, but it was very hard to accept that he was gone.*

In the immediate rawness of Theresa's loss, however, friends and family realised there was something very concrete they could do to honour him. As the 2001 New York City Marathon approached, a race Vinny had been so set on completing to celebrate that 40th birthday, it became crucial to Theresa that the number he would have worn should cross the finish line. Vinny's friends from the State University of New York at Binghamton joined with fellow firefighters from his firehouse and his sister to run a tag-team marathon wearing Vinny's NYC marathon registration number – 13 people strategically positioned along the route, each running just a few miles to take the number on to the next in line on its journey to a finish so cruelly denied Vinny. It mattered hugely to everyone.

> *He worked so hard for it. He so much wanted to run that marathon. I just wanted to make sure that his number crossed the line – and it took 13 people to do it because none of them had trained for it. And I was so happy that night that they did it. Did it help with my grief? I don't know . . . because my grief lasted for years, and there are still to this day moments when I am up and down. But I so much wanted it for him that day.*

However, the family wasn't done yet with the New York City Marathon. In 2009, Theresa's brother-in-law, Steven Giammona, turned 40 and ran the entire NYC Marathon wearing Vinny's running shoes.

As the years passed, Theresa realised that she too had unfinished business with the event. She realised it was a race she needed to run herself – a challenge completely out of the realm of all her life's experiences. Theresa hoped to do it for her own 40th birthday. That wasn't to be; she wasn't ready. Instead, she tackled it in 2015 for her 45th birthday.

The final spur came from Answer The Call, the New York Police and Fire Widows' and Children's Benefit Fund. The charity exists to support the families of New York City police officers, firefighters, Port Authority Police and emergency medical services (EMS) personnel who have been killed in the line of duty. It is a charity Theresa believes in passionately. When they emailed Theresa saying she could have automatic entry to the marathon if she fundraised for them, it was too good an opportunity to miss.

It was also a monumental undertaking – first because Theresa insists she absolutely isn't a runner, but second and more worryingly because obstacles soon appeared on her journey to the start line.

Steven's wife Marilou is what Theresa considers a proper runner, and it was Marilou who helped get Theresa up and running on her marathon journey. However, Theresa promptly ran into trouble, fracturing her knee – apparently through running. 'Don't ask me how I did it!' The doctor was adamant: she had to let it heal before running again. Marilou came to the rescue. She calculated just how long Theresa's recovery would take and worked out that she would be ready to resume just in time to embark on a 16-week marathon programme.

Theresa launched into it at the start of July and was back on track until she was hit by a car on 3 September while out cycling in preparation for a bike race.

I didn't break anything, but my leg was really badly bruised, and I had problems with my knees. The doctor told me that if I did the bike race, I would be guaranteed not to do the marathon.

It was the marathon that mattered more. The result was six weeks of physical therapy. Theresa was supposed to be running with Josephine

Smith, a New York City firefighter and good friend who had lost her firefighter father on 9/11, and when they could, the two trained together.

When I did my training with Jo-Jo, she really pushed me hard, but I knew on the day of the marathon I wasn't going to be able to keep up with her pace, and I didn't want to ruin it for her.

Fortunately, Theresa then became friends with a girl called Meg Navatto, who runs at the same pace. They started to train together, but then came the incident with the car. The injuries meant Theresa missed out on the two longest runs of her training. She resumed for a 19-miler (or 31 kilometres), after which it was time to taper down on distance. Nervousness kicked in. Meg reassured her that the crowd on the day would give her all the incentive she needed.

In fact, it was Vinny who got her round.

I know he was with me every step of the way.

And he was with Theresa before the event as well. On the day, as a slower runner, Theresa was supposed to be starting off at 11 a.m., but when she picked up her number, a group of runners from the fire department team got her a place on the fire department bus to the start, along with Josephine and Jessica Martinsen, another FDNY widow running for Answer the Call. It meant that Theresa headed off with the elite runners:

That's how I know Vinny was there. That was Vinny taking care of me from the start. And it was a beautiful day. The weather was perfect. It was not too sunny, not too warm, but it was not too cold. It was just the perfect day to run a marathon.

Theresa started off with Josephine and Jessica, but soon felt them pulling away from her. Jo-Jo was turning around and urging Theresa on, but in Theresa's mind was Marilou's advice to keep to her own pace, particularly important at the start. And that's when Vinny provided again. She found herself running alongside Aima Cotes, a 'lovely cop, half my size'. Aima asked if Theresa would mind if they ran together, and so they did for the next 10 miles until they became separated at a water station by the next group of runners coming through.

After that I was running on my own. But it was Vinny who got me through. I physically felt him with me. I couldn't give up. I felt as if he was carrying me. I felt him saying: 'You have got to keep going.' And he did. He carried me through. I felt his presence with me the entire time. I had never done anything remotely like that before. That medal was for him.

Theresa crossed the finish line in tears. The achievement was 100 per cent in his honour.

I wanted to achieve something for him. It was something I felt he would have been so proud of. I wanted to accomplish it for him. I was so heartbroken that he was never able to do it. It was something I felt I needed to do.

Some people run to process grief. Some people run to heal their pain. Theresa isn't one of those runners. This run was purely symbolic – and hugely empowering. As Theresa says, when she completed the race, she felt she could do anything. Theresa ran the New York City Half Marathon the following year. The full marathon was for Vinny. The half was for her, and there her running journey ended.

Theresa still runs occasionally now, no more than 4 miles (6 kilometres). Instead, she walks every day. Her point is that she achieved what she wanted to achieve.

It was for Vinny and for my girls. Running a marathon was so out of my realm, but I wanted to show them that if you put your mind to something, you can accomplish it.

And even in her celebration, Vinny was there. After the marathon, Theresa was invited to the New York Road Runners club, organisers of the New York City Marathon, for a closed party celebrating 10 runners who would share their stories. Theresa was due to tell hers last, and as the others told theirs, she found herself deeply moved, fearing her own tale would pale by comparison. However, when Theresa shared her experiences, she was met with tears and warmth.

My husband was so out front and centre of everything, and that's just not me. That's not how I am, but there I was telling the story. It was another Vinny moment . . .

Isabel Hardman

'I learn so much about how to cope with life when
I go on a long run.'

Talk of anxiety or depression often conjures up images of people incapable of getting out of bed or sobbing uncontrollably. For Isabel Hardman, assistant editor of *The Spectator* and presenter of Radio 4's *Week in Westminster*, depression took a much more alarming form – a constant fear which left her feeling like the proverbial rabbit in the headlights.

Isabel had known feelings of misery before, but as the year 2016 progressed she felt she was losing control of her mind. This was an awful year, which began with a serious trauma in her personal life. Isabel prefers not to go into the details, but it came at the start of a year that should have been the most fulfilling of her career. The year 2016 offered UK journalists the mouth-watering prospect of the Brexit referendum, which was then followed by two party leadership contests and a new prime minister. It was a year that should have been all the inspiration Isabel needed. Instead, slowly, she found herself sinking into a very dark place indeed, her thinking ever foggier, her reactions ever more anxious and extreme.

I had had a massive personal catastrophe, and normally, I cope with problems by working, but the catastrophe was such a massive strike on my mind, because it had gone on for so many months that I started to fall apart. If I look back on my descent into really serious mental illness, I can see that the way I reacted to things started to change. I could not concentrate. I became paranoid about another catastrophe happening. I was hyper-vigilant about everything. My friends were all having to be massively reassuring or else really feeling the pressure.

Isabel was loving her job at *The Spectator*, but by the autumn she found herself run ragged, sinking into the horrors of rumination, a vicious circle of dwelling and self-blame.

> *It's a pattern of thought that just goes around and around, an obsessive circle where you just never move to a conclusion. I ended up fixating on something, on the bad things that had happened or on situations that might seem a threat. I would think about them over and over again. The best way I can describe it is that your mind just keeps turning like a washing machine on a spin cycle, that noise that you can hear throughout the whole house. I just couldn't think properly because I was stuck in such a horrible pattern.*

And alongside that was the fear. Isabel insists she is not a scaredy-cat in her normal life. She has appeared frequently on television, including a 2017 appearance on the BBC comedy quiz show *Have I Got News for You* – the kind of commitments that would terrify millions, but which Isabel habitually took in her stride. Except in 2016. As her depression deepened, so fear took an ever stronger hold. 'The biggest thing for me was that I was just frightened the whole time,' she recalls. Indeed, fear ate away at her to the point where she couldn't actually write. Isabel's job wasn't the cause of her condition, but her condition was making her job impossible.

On and off, Isabel had to take quite a few days off sick, but everything came to a head at the Conservative Party Conference in October 2016. Isabel knows that everyone around her would have found her enormously on edge, and she admits she can't really remember terribly much about the conference at all.

> *I can remember arriving and recording a podcast and then breaking down in my Airbnb. I was trying to write our evening email bulletin, which would be read by everyone in Westminster from the prime minister downwards, but the ruminations were just so strong. I could not think to write a sentence, and that's pretty fundamental to a writer. I was on my own. My new partner John was in Istanbul at that time. I had been struggling on and off for quite some time with quite bad suicidal thoughts. I called him and told him what was going on. I was supposed*

to be speaking at a dinner that night and then I was supposed to be on Newsnight. *My partner just said to me: 'You need to stop. You just need to go to hospital.'*

As Isabel says, her mind had stopped working. It was as simple as that. She messaged her boss and admitted she couldn't cope. She called 111 and was sedated by an emergency doctor. She went home the next day and was off sick for the next two months.

Isabel had been on antidepressants since June, but they hadn't been working, and she had been alarmed at the weight she had gained in a very short space of time. Isabel went back to her doctor and was switched to sertraline – which has been fantastic, she says. But it soon became clear that her activities would be just as important to her recovery as the medication she was taking. Isabel's GP encouraged her to seek help through counselling, but crucially she also urged Isabel to make sure she got out every single day, ideally to do something active. She urged Isabel to find a personal trainer.

Growing up in Surrey, Isabel had always been sporty. As a child, she had been a member of an athletics club and loved to sprint. The shorter distances were always the attraction; 800m or 1500m just didn't do it for her. She had no confidence over the longer distances, but would always manage a massive kick towards the end.

But then other things took over, and running took a back seat between the ages of 16 and 25, the point at which running re-emerged for other reasons. As she says, it was the classic mid-to-late 20s thing of trying to do up the zip on a size 8 dress and struggling. She decided that she needed either to buy some new clothes or to start exercising. She opted for the latter and found genuine enjoyment in parkrun, the free, weekly, five-kilometre timed runs that have sprung up around the world in recent years. Night-running with a head torch – 'the purest kind of mind tunnel' – also brought pleasure and fulfilment.

But as Isabel lapsed into depression, so the running stopped. As she says, everything stopped. Everything had gone – self-esteem, exercise, the lot. Fortunately, her GP realised the importance of getting back to it – precisely the turning point she needed. It meant digging into her savings, but it was worth it. Isabel sought private counselling and structured her life around seeing her personal trainer twice a week and also riding twice a week.

Running made such a difference. First of all, it was getting me out of the house. I am a very outdoor person. I grew up in the country. My ideal day is going for a walk in the Lake District or riding in the woods. For me, in a way, being outdoors is more important than running. Since being ill, I now have a thing where every day I do something that involves nature, even if it is just taking a photograph of a weed growing in the pavement. Outdoors is so powerful in the buzz it gives us, a real sense of the richness of life. If you look outside, there is so much to discover and running is such a good way to get there.

Isabel was fortunate in her choice of personal trainer. Vanda regularly works with women suffering from depression. She was hugely inspiring and always checked how Isabel was doing mentally.

She just encouraged me to believe in myself. I think running is actually all about self-esteem, but I had lost my self-esteem. I am a great believer in getting to the finish. Running is about the discipline of thinking: I am going to get there in the end. I learn so much about how to cope with life when I go on a long run. I think the internal dialogue that you have with yourself when you run is such a big help. You are saying to yourself: 'I have only got another mile to go and then I am halfway there.' Or you are saying: 'I have already run five miles. There are just two more to go. I can cope with that!' All the talk is you talking yourself round to it.

Isabel always runs for Refuge, a charity committed to a world where domestic violence isn't tolerated and where women and children can live in safety. The charity is the greatest possible motivator. As Isabel says, they help women who are going through the most horrific ordeals. Every week, two women in England and Wales are killed by their current or ex-partner. And every week, another two women escape domestic abuse. Isabel is clear: the women who leave abusive relationships and rebuild their lives and their sense of self are among the bravest women in this country. As she says, she knows that at any point she is running for women who have coped with far more than just the stitch she's battling.

Isabel stresses the importance of never thinking that depression is something you can snap out of or something that can be solved by comparisons. But just thinking about the suffering of those women helps to put the pain of running into perspective – just as running puts life itself into perspective.

When I am just plodding along in a good state of mental health, I find myself thinking about all sorts of things that are in my mind in the background – usually, those drumbeat worries that you don't really realise are there until you find yourself thinking about them as you run along. Running is such a good space to think through those sorts of problems, because when you are running you can't get distressed by them because you are having to think about your breathing, about where you are going. Running keeps dragging you back into the present. It is a kind of mindfulness. Running becomes that personal space where you think of things in an 'Ah, but . . .' kind of way. When I come back from a run, I feel I have tidied my mind.

For a head in a bad place, running offers a similar benefit – though it is, of course, much harder even to start. You have to wait for the benefits to filter through, knowing they surely will.

When I am in a bad place, it is much harder to run, but you can't get worse with running. That's the thing. If you are alone in a room feeling bad, you really can get worse. If I go for a run thinking: I really feel like shit, then I might set out feeling a bit grouchy, and the first mile, I will be moaning to myself, but then I will get into the metronome rhythm of running, and I will be thinking: I have run this far, I am going to keep going. And it starts to feel like an active lullaby.

Isabel spends part of her time in Richmond, south London and the rest on Walney Island, off Cumbria – a great place to become absorbed in nature as she runs. As she says, you just don't realise how much you 'dial down' on a run, though she stresses that running can never offer everything.

It would be wrong to think that running beats antidepressants or that it can transform your mental health, but certainly it does make a hell of a lot of difference. It is physio for the mind.

And in that expression – physio for the mind – Isabel sums up the disconnection which, she feels, besets so many of us.

> *We see the mind as something that can sustain far more than the body can. We push and push and push and push ourselves without realising it. We can accept that even the strongest weightlifter will have a weight they absolutely cannot lift. But we don't see that with the mind. I don't think we understand mental health enough in that way.*

Running – and exercise generally – works by bringing mind and body together, something Isabel found at her local stables. Isabel's instructor remarked just how tense she was as she sat in the saddle. Isabel confessed to stress and told her of her depression. The instructor asked if she minded telling her the trigger. Isabel did so. The instructor observed: 'That makes so much sense. You ride as if you don't have a backbone.' The comment was significant. The instructor had identified the physical manifestation of the 'complete spinelessness' – total lack of self-esteem – Isabel had been feeling in her depression. The apparent spinelessness was mental in origin, physical in expression. And that's where running can help. It comes back to self-esteem again. Isabel knows she will always feel proud of herself at the end of a run.

She knows too that we are living in a much more enlightened world these days. 'Pretty much everyone' has been lovely about her depression, Isabel says.

> *My employers have been fantastic. They have been so understanding. They have genuinely treated me as someone with a physical illness. Effectively they lost me for a year. I tried to come back to work in January 2017 and fell apart by late March. I just needed more time. I came back in a phased way after the snap election, and now I am back full-time.*

Isabel doesn't know when she will stop the counselling. She expects to continue for the next few years at least, but at least she can now recognise the signs if anxiety starts to creep up on her again. If she finds herself clicking through political websites, looking for something to write about, she knows anxiety is guiding her. She can identify it and – much more healthily – simply plunge herself instead into Westminster itself, knowing that inspiration most surely will come.

Looking ahead, Isabel also knows – though she has struggled with plantar fasciitis recently (a connective tissue disorder that results in pain in the heel and foot) – that running will long remain key to her mental well-being. For Isabel, a good runner isn't a fast runner. A good runner is someone in touch with the benefits that running brings.

> *Sometimes I run a parkrun just wanting to run, and then sometimes I want a PB [personal best]. But I just love the races as a special time. People cheer you along the route. Races are great. I love the atmosphere. I love the crowds. I love that sense of running in a pack. You feel the exhilaration as you all set off together.*

And therein lies the benefit. For Isabel running isn't really about running with a friend or her partner. Isabel has run with John, but she admits her preference will always be either to run in a crowd or to run alone. The best run, in fact, is the long solo run in the country, a run where she can stop and look at a wild flower if she wants to. For Isabel, it's about the uplifting aloneness that running can offer.

> *There is something lovely about the solitude of running, but sometimes the solitude of running in a pack is also fabulous, and I get to the last 200 metres and always sprint. I love the fact that you will get these sticky men who look so fit that they can race round it almost without getting out of bed, but I also love the fact some people will take two or three hours to complete a race. You do it for you. That's the wonderful thing.*

Jessica Rigo

'When I need that extra push to finish strong, I think of my fallen running partner . . . my chosen sister.'

Getting back to fitness after the birth of her two children, Jessica Rigo decided in the autumn of 2007 to sign her son up for the preschool programme at the Brandywine YMCA in Coatesville, Pennsylvania. Jessica was familiar with the mission and the values of the organisation. The bonus was that she could use the gym while her son Aidan was in school. Even better, childcare was included for her younger daughter Alexa. It ticked all the boxes.

After a few weeks of working out in the fitness centre, Jessica began to take group exercise classes. And that was when Jacinda Miller entered her life. Jessica was struggling to get to 10 sit-ups when two instructors walked in, both in amazing shape.

> One of them was similar in stature to myself and I remember thinking: I'm going to find out what she teaches and I'm going to take everything she does! That woman was Jacinda.

Jessica joined Jacinda's group power sessions, a choreographed weightlifting class that left her sore but determined. She wanted to be in better shape, and it was easy to get hooked. Jacinda's classes were fun: she was motivating, she was encouraging, and she would tell funny stories to take your mind off the discomfort. Jacinda put everyone at ease.

It was the perfect platform for the deep friendship that soon developed. One evening, Jessica and Jacinda pulled into the parking lot at the same time. Jessica was worried about her daughter, who was scheduled to be tested for possible medical issues. Jacinda sensed something was up.

She gave me a big hug and said she would pray for us. I'm not overly religious, but I believe in the power of positive energy as well as prayer and I was appreciative of it. Looking back, I think this was our first real conversation about our lives.

They grew close. Preschool classes, exercise classes and sitting by the pool with their children repeatedly brought them together at the Y. They talked and they talked. And they talked about their shared passion for running. Previously both solitary runners, they started to run together, and it wasn't long before Jacinda urged Jessica to run a half-marathon. The idea seemed crazy, but Jacinda was serious. Jessica agreed – on condition that Jacinda ran it with her. They signed up for the St Luke's Half Marathon in April 2009 and they ran nearly every step of their training side by side.

What started as a minor friendship solidified into something deeper and stronger. Somewhere in this training, we became running partners, and your running partner becomes a partner in the true sense of the word.

Curiously, and to Jessica's delight and amusement, people started to mistake the one for the other. Jessica remembers walking down the hall at the Y and hearing someone shout, 'Hey Jacinda!' When she turned around, she was met with: 'Oh, sorry Jess, I thought you were Jacinda!'

Completing the transformation, Jacinda urged Jessica to start instructing at the Y. Jacinda saw her potential and 'hammered away at me for months and months'. And it worked. Jessica didn't even have to apply. The wellness director offered her a job on Jacinda's recommendation.

Picture me. Sixty pounds overweight and joining a Y where I knew no one. Within 12 months, I've dropped weight, begun instructing and members are thinking I'm Jacinda. I was tickled pink! And the theme continued. Anywhere we went, people assumed we were sisters. Our own family members couldn't tell us apart from behind. Growing up with brothers and always wanting a sister, we only became closer.

They both caught the long-distance running bug. Their friendship deepened – and deepened still further when Jacinda ran into marital problems: she and her husband divorced. Jacinda was alone with her children for the first time. Jessica's husband, meanwhile, was working two jobs. Jessica and Jacinda began to spend more and more time together, and it seemed inevitable they would one day run a marathon together. In October 2013, they completed the Marine Corps Marathon – sadly, their only marathon together. They completed it in honour of their fathers. Jacinda's father was a marine; Jessica's father had been diagnosed with cancer 11 months earlier.

We ran every step together in honour of our dads, both Vietnam vets. We always had such a blast when running, talking about life events. She was my sounding board, and I believe I returned the favour. Around the Y, we were often called The Evil Twins – because we kicked butt in our classes – or Double Trouble. True to form, many days we showed up dressed the same, down to the capris and tanks. Even our sneakers matched; we didn't even try. Symbiosis is effortless.

However, dark clouds were gathering. Jacinda was dating. His name was Dennis Cassel – a name Jessica hates to say. He'd been working out in the gym, admiring Jacinda from afar. One day he finally found the courage to speak to her, asking her for help with his workouts. A love affair developed, lasting around 10 months.

Looking back, Jessica recalls that no warning bells rang. Everyone trusted him – even the children. Jacinda never feared for her safety and was never afraid of Denny. However, Jessica admits her own thoughts may have been elsewhere. It was a difficult time. On 27 November, 2012 her father Bruce underwent a surgery known as the Whipple procedure, for cholangiocarcinoma (bile duct cancer). One day he seemed fine; three days later he was told he would be dead within six weeks if he didn't have the operation. It was a shattering blow for the family.

My dad was such a force. I can describe it no other way. He scared the shit out of me as a child and inspired fierce loyalty and love forever. I strive to be like him every day. There is nothing he couldn't do. Intelligence beyond measure. Any question I ever had about anything that I couldn't answer myself, I called my dad.

The 18 months following Bruce's surgery were crazy, Jessica recalls. He nearly died from multiple complications multiple times. Jacinda was Jessica's constant support – essential from a practical point of view too because Jessica's parents lived two hours north.

Jessica remembers the day, in the summer of 2014, when she broke down in tears:

> *I was crying, and I remember saying: 'What am I going to do without my dad?' Jacinda took both of my hands, looked me straight in the eye and said: 'You are going to be fine. Do you know why you are going to be fine? Because your dad has taught you everything you need to know.'*

Bruce passed away on 6 September, 2014 with his family at his side. He was at home, as he wished. He was 65. Jessica was devastated. Jacinda was rock solid in her support. She knew exactly when to drag Jessica off for a run.

> *I can still hear her and pray I never ever forget the sound of her voice. She was the glue that held me together.*

As she looks back, however, Jessica can't help wondering whether her grief meant she missed the warning signs elsewhere. While her dad was 'checking out', Jacinda was breaking it off with Denny. She felt he was suffocating her. He had virtually moved in, but didn't contribute. Eventually Jacinda decided enough was enough, a decision Denny couldn't accept. He would call her to say he was suicidal. At some point, he bought a gun.

Jessica and Jacinda were both trying to embark on new lives, Jessica returning to work full-time and Jacinda beginning a new full-time job as the manager of a Target store. Her first day was Monday, 3 November, 2014. Jacinda and Jessica said they would catch up when they saw each other that evening at the Y. Jessica left at 5 p.m. At 5.45 p.m. she had a frantic call from their friend Kim, desperate to check that Jessica was OK. The Y was on lockdown after a shooting. Jessica immediately knew what had happened.

Jessica called Jacinda. She called Denny. She called the Y. No answer. She drove past the Y. There were still ambulances out front.

And then came frantic, separate phone calls from Jacinda's sons, Grant and Mason, aged 17 and 11. Jessica told them to sit tight. Back home, she called everyone she could think of – and remembered an old colleague who was in charge of intake in the ER at Brandywine Hospital. She called him. He wasn't at work, but gave her the back number to the emergency room, a number only employees have. With her heart in her mouth, she dialled it and said she was looking for her sister. Eventually she was told: 'I can't tell you anything except that you need to get here as fast as you can.'

At the hospital, several friends were waiting. The nurse said simply: 'Let's step outside.' Jessica already knew what she was going to say.

I don't even remember how she said it. I think I asked if Jacinda was alive. She told me no. Our three friends had drifted outside to listen, and all of them lost it. The nurse described to me what happened, as reported by the officers. That he had shot her three times and then himself. That she didn't suffer. I took a deep breath and looked at Kim and said: 'We have to go. Right now. I have to get to the boys.'

As Jessica says, she has a 'crazy ability' to remain ultra-calm and collected in a crisis. She knows that losing it will come later. Kim dropped Jessica off at Jacinda's house. The boys were beside themselves with worry, but Jessica felt that telling them the full and horrid truth was a task for family alone. For the moment, all she could do was try to keep them calm, impossible when a police cruiser showed up. Mason became frantic. But somehow, they managed to keep it together, and while one of the officers took care of the boys, the other told Jessica and Jacinda's neighbour Traci what had happened.

How he ambushed her. How he stood over her body and wouldn't let anyone help her, but did yell to a bystander to call 911 but don't come any closer because he had a gun. How the officers arrived on the scene, got out of their squad car and began to approach – and that was when he put the gun to his own head and pulled the trigger. Jacinda died in the parking lot of the YMCA where we met, where she became my mentor, then my running partner, my friend, co-worker and ultimately sister.

Less than two months after losing her father, Jessica had lost her dearest friend, at the age of 41. Back home, she sobbed uncontrollably. Prayer services and vigils dominated the next few days, and then came the funeral. Friends gathered and remembered, and inevitably, they started to discuss just what form that remembrance was going to take. A 5k race was suggested. Jessica insisted it had to be a distance Jacinda loved – a half-marathon. Kim joined her in organising it. By Thanksgiving, a core group had come together and a race date had been set.

We each poured our hearts into making the event a success. We took special care to pour Jacinda into it as well. It is my tribute to my running partner, my sister, half of Double Trouble.

The key was in the detail. Jacinda's favourite colour was purple. It was a no-brainer that purple would be the race colour – the colour, they later discovered, of the Domestic Violence Ribbon. As for the course, Jessica and the team chose roads they had trained on for years, Jacinda alongside them. And for the logo, a horse was the obvious choice. Jacinda was a keen rider, and Chester County is known as horse country. Again, it was a no-brainer.

One day Jacinda had doodled a horse head for one of the children. I called her Mom to see if she still had it. She did! We had another friend who is a graphic artist. What was produced is now The Chester County Half Marathon logo, designed by Jacinda herself!

Another friend, Carlton Langley, put together the entire race website. For Jessica and her friends, in their grief, these were crucial links: The Chester County Half Marathon was created through the community's love for Jacinda – and created in her image.

She touched so many lives. She was a kind and giving person. Jacinda would help anyone who needed it, yet she was humble. She had an infectious laugh. Being around her made people feel good. She loved her family and friends fiercely, and we all returned that love in equal measure.

For Jessica, as for her friends, The Chester County Half Marathon became a channel for her grief – 'something positive to focus on instead of wallowing in sorrow'. Many nights she would work on the race details with tears on her face, but she worked with purpose. She and her friends wanted to play their part in creating something that ensured Jacinda's spirit lived on.

More than 300 people attended Jacinda's funeral. Nearly 1000 people took part in the first Chester County Half Marathon and 5k. By the third running of the event in May 2017, Jacinda's oldest son, her parents, her cousins, her aunts and her uncles and even her grandmother had all participated.

It is a wonderful outpouring of love that her immediate family is able to witness first-hand, year after year. I know they are grateful and amazed, just as I am. On reflection, I am awed by the whole thing. It makes me uncomfortable when people congratulate me or say what a wonderful thing I'm doing. In my mind, it isn't rocket science. Jacinda was my sister in so many ways, and as such I know that, first and foremost, she would want someone to make sure her boys are cared for. The half-marathon provides a way. It is paying for college for her oldest, and when he is finished, it will do the same for her youngest. I am only doing what she needs me to do – looking out for her boys in any way I can.

For Jessica, in those early days, the key was to keep on running. She didn't want to, but she forced herself. She would run and she would cry, and the plan evolved to run St Luke's Half in Jacinda's honour. Suddenly she had a group of friends who wanted to do the same. Even better, Jessica found that if she concentrated, she could feel Jacinda's presence in her usual spot, next to her right shoulder – 'Just for a split second, she lets me know that she is with me.' It was the perfect therapy, and 5ks, 10ks, trail runs, mud runs, Tough Mudders and marathons have followed.

As Jessica says, running is a way 'to unplug, to disconnect, to quiet my mind.' By training for St Luke's and developing the Chester County Half, she has made it back to a point where she can function again. It has been a long road back to a new normal, one she knows she will never get used to, but now Jessica can finally say that she is OK.

Having lost two of the most important people in my life, both events unexpected and horrific, I have learned to take nothing for granted. And so every moment I find joy in the run – even when it sucks – I enjoy it. I laugh at myself for making the choice to run 26.2 miles and paying money to do it! We call it 'embracing the suck'. Running is life. And when I need that extra push to finish strong, I think of my fallen running partner, my best friend, my chosen sister, and I continue on to the finish line.

Eleanor Keohane

'I was an absolute mess. . . But I did it. I ran.
Three times, sobbing my heart out.'

When Eleanor Keohane's world fell apart, she turned to running. It was a devastating blow when her husband Paul was told he had cancer. Running offered Eleanor a way to react that day and a way to cope in the months that followed. With four young daughters to care for, and with Paul enduring the highest doses of chemotherapy, Eleanor had to hold everything together for the sake of everyone. Running helped her do so, offering comfort and strength in the toughest of times.

Ironically, Eleanor was never the sporty one in the couple. She had always loved sport, cherishing childhood memories of watching from the sidelines as her father played rugby. Eleanor went on to play tennis, and after the births of their daughters, she ran a little, simply to lose the baby weight. But she never counted herself a natural runner.

City banker Paul, however, was in another league when it came to sporting ability. Paul was a gifted athlete and an all-round sportsman of distinction. He studied law at Lincoln College, Oxford, and alongside his degree, he picked up three-and-a-half blues – recognition of sporting prowess at the highest level at university.

Sadly, it was while he was playing cricket many years later, for Little Gaddesden against Ley Hill, that it started to become clear something was wrong. Paul was suffering niggling pain around his hips. He was the team's number one batsman, but it was a standing joke among his teammates that he always had a back strain.

A visit to a specialist in April 2010 and an MRI scan revealed nothing abnormal, so Paul took up Pilates and tried to deal with the pain himself. By Easter 2013, however, his health had deteriorated significantly. Finding no solution to his pain became a source of tension between them, Eleanor recalls:

> *Paul was undiagnosed for a good couple of years, which put a lot of pressure on us. I was thinking there was something really wrong, but he was insisting he was fine, in line with what his consultants had told him. It got to a really difficult stage for us. He was saying it was back pain and sciatica, but then he started getting physical issues, more personal in their nature. I started to realise that there was something majorly, majorly wrong. I told him we needed to get a second opinion. I couldn't understand why nobody was doing something more for him, another MRI. In the end, I rang him at work and said: 'I have booked you an appointment with our local GP.' I said: 'You are coming home to have this appointment.' He said he couldn't, he had to be at work. I said: 'You are going to come home now. This is not an ask, it is a tell.' He realised I meant it.*

Paul started to tell the doctor about his sciatica. However, the doctor sensed Eleanor's disquiet and told him he should be scanned properly 'for your wife's peace of mind'. Another MRI scan followed. Paul was at work when the results came through. 'They told him they had found something and that he needed to bring me,' Eleanor recalls. It was the worst possible time. Just two days earlier, Eleanor's father had been diagnosed with cancer. 'My dad and I were so close. It was an awful, tearful conversation.'

Paul's condition was now deteriorating rapidly. Fortunately, Eleanor had the foresight to bring a change of clothes for him and an overnight bag. He was in so much pain on the way to the hospital that they had to stop the car three times.

> *I felt we were losing control of the situation. I said to the consultant I could see that things were really bad. They said they were going to sit down and explain to us why. They gave Paul some pain relief, sat us down and told us.*

The devastating news was that the MRI had revealed a tumour at the base of Paul's spine. It was diagnosed as Ewing's Sarcoma, a very rare form of bone cancer, which usually affects only teenagers. At 50, Paul was the oldest person on record to get it. The care kicked in immediately. Paul was told he was going to need some immediate internal refiguration and that he was going to begin the heaviest possible course of chemotherapy.

> *I know now that Paul had had the cancer for a long time. Paul was a very disciplined man, and his fitness must have kept it at bay for a long time, and then he reached an age where he was not able to exercise quite so much, and that's when it started to take over.*

Their daugthers – Freya, Ursula, Maddie and Cordelia – were aged 11, nine, seven and four respectively at the time. Eleanor recalls biting her lip, forcing herself to be strong, trying to ask all the right questions and writing down the answers, trying to hold it all together. When she left Paul at the hospital, she sat in the car and sobbed: 'My whole being fell apart.' Before getting home, she stopped to wash her face and put some make-up on, steeling herself to tell the girls the grim news. As she says, it was not exactly the kind of conversation she was skilled at having at the time. Tears flowed, but eventually she managed to get everyone settled, her mother-in-law included. Eleanor forced herself to tell everyone that everything would be OK.

And then instinct kicked in. She put on her trainers, got in the car and headed for what she calls 'the cow field' – a sharp, uneven, double hill. She ran up it and down. Up and down again. And then again.

> *I was struggling to breathe. I was still crying. I did it three times. I was exhausted. But it gave me something . . . it gave me a little bit of control. Somehow the pain that you go through when you do something like that just makes you feel a little bit better. I was an absolute mess. I almost collapsed. But I did it. I ran. Three times, sobbing my heart out. And then I got back in the car . . . and I felt a little bit better. I think it is that physical thing . . . the physical thing that helps you work things out.*

Eleanor recalls the weeks that followed as a treadmill of hospitals and treatment in between looking after Paul at home, with barely a moment to herself. Operating on Paul's first tumour would have paralysed him, so instead he had a year of intensive chemotherapy at The Churchill Hospital in Oxford followed by radiotherapy. He seemed to be responding well. As soon as the chemo stopped, however, a secondary tumour developed in his pelvis, part of which was removed in a 16-hour operation in January 2015.

In hindsight, it was probably the beginning of the end, and perhaps he shouldn't have had the operation. He nearly died several times during the operation, and looking back, it would have been harder for us if he had died then, but easier for him, rather than dying six months later as he did.

Back home, the pain was intense, but the Hospice of St Francis – which offers expert care for people living with life-limiting illnesses in West Herts and South Bucks – gave outstanding support. There were regular visits from the district nurses and also from the hospice's specialist community nurses. There was also physiotherapy in the hospice gym, plus psychological support from the hospice's care team. It all meant that eventually Paul was able to move around independently with the help of a frame.

Significantly, the care the nurses offered extended to Eleanor. Paul was on morphine and wanted Eleanor beside him. He would become anxious if she wasn't, but the nurses took over when Paul was asleep. They knew precisely the moment to say: 'Go! Go! Go!'

And I knew I had to go. I had to run. I had to keep up such a brave face for the girls and for him and be so mentally strong and keep smiling because sometimes I could see the panic in his eyes. But I knew I had to run.

Eleanor didn't give up hope until the day the hospice said Paul had two weeks left to live. Eleanor could accept it then, but she remains shocked to this day at the 'sheer brutality' of the treatment he had endured in the hope that he might pull through.

Lots of people go through chemotherapy courses, but this was hard. He had the highest doses pushed through him because he was so strong and he had such a great will to survive. So they put him through a lot, and as his primary carer, I went through it as well. It was such a difficult time. I had the four girls. And the only time off I had was to go for a run . . . and so my running started getting stronger.

Paul died on 22 June, 2015, at the age of 52. The hospice care he received was 'just unbelievable' in every last respect, Eleanor recalls – care which also enveloped the girls. As the end approached, thanks to the children's services team, the girls were well prepared to the point that they knew when Paul was ready to go. Eleanor is relieved to say that Paul died very comfortably and without pain, surrounded by love.

The double tragedy was that the focus then switched to Eleanor's father, Graham.

> *My dad died a year later and chose to die at home, and it was just a different ball game, but in the end Paul really wasn't in pain when he was dying. But I had to be strong for him and for the girls and for my father. It would have been too easy to give in, to stay in bed or have an extra glass of wine or comforts that may not have helped me mentally or physically . . . I needed to find ways to cope that made me feel stronger.*

Running increasingly became Eleanor's solace. The comfort was to run with friends from St Francis Hospice's very own running group, a group started by Berkhamsted solicitor Paul Owen after his own bereavements.

In the months that followed her husband's death, Eleanor chose St Albans for her first half-marathon, a choice that thrilled her father, a veteran himself of the race many times over. Eleanor's father was too ill to be there on the day she completed the course, but he gave her his medals from his own St Albans running days. Running gave Eleanor focus. The half-marathon gave her something to train for properly.

Inevitably, every run was 'emotional' for a long time – and to an extent always will be. But after Paul's death, there was a sense of relief alongside the release running gave her. Eleanor started to see physical exercise as the key to sleep, often running to the point of exhaustion. Through the support of the running group and through running itself, Eleanor started to develop a belief that she could cope with her loss.

> *If I could cope with running for an hour, then I knew I could cope with the rest of the day. In the early days after Paul's death, emotions ran so high and it would take me two hours to take the girls up to bed and to get them to sleep. There would be many tears. The girls were frightened and they missed their daddy so much. I had so many fantastic friends who helped and supported me, but it was a really, really difficult time, trying to deal*

*with my own grief, but also the grief of four little girls. I wasn't eating. I lost
a lot of weight. My girls were saying: 'Mum, you need to start eating!' But
I managed to carry on, and eventually we all righted ourselves.*

There are still days when Eleanor wobbles. People will tell her they
can't believe how strong she has been, how bravely she has coped.
Underneath, she knows that appearances aren't everything. But as she
looks to the future, she knows that running will underpin whatever
lies ahead.

*I don't think anything else would have helped me mentally and physically
in the way running did. Running helped me find the mental strength to
carry on.*

The Schneider Twins

'I truly believe that running has saved my family.'

The Schneider twins are completely dependent in many ways. They cannot be left alone. They will not say when they are hungry, when they are thirsty or when they are tired. They cannot safely cross the road alone.

And yet they are brothers transformed when they run. In the simple act of running, Alex and Jamie have achieved things their parents, Robyn and Allan, would never have dared to believe possible. Robyn has no hesitation in saying that running has saved their lives. Perhaps, it would be truer to say that it has given them a life.

The boys and their parents, who live in the town of Great Neck on Long Island, New York, share running as their common bond – and it is running that has allowed them to function as a united family. As Robyn says, it was an unexpected turn of events that led them first to explore running for Alex and Jamie. Now running has become the focus of their lives. For the whole family, running has been transformational, opening up a world that threatened to remain forever closed.

It's a story that has touched millions of people across the States and beyond. At the 2013 New York City Marathon, Alex and Jamie were featured on ABC's *Good Morning America* and *World News Tonight*. Their story has also been covered in *The New York Times*, *Runner's World* magazine, *USA Today*, *Newsday* and *The Boston Globe* plus countless other publications. The hope that running has brought the Schneiders is a hope that has now been shared around the world.

Looking back, Robyn recalls that she and Allan first suspected something was wrong when the boys were around a year old. They were not speaking and had some unusual behaviours. Watching other toddlers at the park, Robyn noticed that other children of a similar age were already talking and playing with their peers. Alex and Jamie weren't.

At their 17-month check-up, Robyn asked the paediatrician whether the boys were on track. He reassured her that they would speak in their own time. But Robyn's worries deepened. It seemed to Robyn and to Allan that the boys were changing in troubling ways. They had stopped making eye contact. Toys they had loved a month before no longer held any interest for them. Sometimes they were distressed for no apparent reason. They no longer ran towards their parents when their names were called. Alex would shriek and squirm in his high chair at mealtimes, and Jamie's happiness, in his own world while playing in the park, would be shattered by something as simple as sand in his shoes.

Alex and Jamie are their only children, so inevitably, Robyn admits it was impossible for her and Allan to know what was typical and what wasn't, but repetitive behaviour, such as tapping and jumping, became ever more noticeable. The boys were 21 months old when Allan and Robyn decided specialist advice was essential. Robyn vividly remembers the day. Alex was whining and fidgeting under the doctor's desk, and Jamie was repeatedly opening and closing the drawers of the filing cabinet.

The diagnosis was a devastating one. The doctor told them that the boys had 'a language delay with autistic characteristics'. It was an awful moment. This was 1992; autism wasn't generally spoken about or even understood. Robyn freely admits she didn't even know what autism was. She asked. The answer was an explanation along the lines of a neurological disorder affecting their brain development. It was hard to take in. Robyn recalls her overriding desire was to grab the boys and run – as if she could somehow outrun the diagnosis. Her impulse was to protect them from everything that the word *autism* was going to bring.

Robyn labels this as the moment that their lives changed forever. Her maternal instinct took over.

Honestly, I had no time to think. My focus was always to get ahead of the autism, to do all I could for my sons to lift the dark cloud that suddenly threatened them. I consider myself a fighter, a warrior and protector of my sons. My mission in life became clear.

Robyn and her father researched educational programmes for children with autism, and once they discovered applied behaviour analysis, their path was set. It became the foundation for their learning. For years, teaching them skills in small increments and providing reinforcements enabled Alex and Jamie to learn. Aside from academic work, Robyn and Allan also inevitably wanted their sons to be happy and have fun. Recreational activities became just as important as their education.

Robyn's friend Randy, a multi-marathoner and a professional in the field of autism, suggested the breakthrough they craved. After seven marathons, Randy often talked about the ways that running had changed her life. Robyn saw the possibilities. Randy told her that the release of energy would be 'amazing', but there would also be benefits in terms of focus and discipline. Randy also pointed out running's impact on overall wellness, especially when it comes to reducing anxiety. With Randy's words, running seemed to offer new hope. It just became a question of where to start.

The Schneiders found exactly what they needed in a running club for people with special needs. Founded in 1998 by Steve Cuomo, Rolling Thunder Special Needs Program is an inclusive running club on Long Island for all athletes, an organisation dedicated to providing challenged individuals with the opportunity to participate successfully in all levels of mainstream running, walking or wheelchair racing.

Robyn and Allan contacted the club and took the boys to watch a race where the club athletes would be running. Robyn held Alex's hand and Allan held Jamie's as they watched the runners cross the finish line. The thrill of the race struck them all instantly. The Rolling Thunder runners wore white and green singlets, making them easily distinguishable from all the other runners, and Robyn and Allan were amazed by just how many of them there were. Meanwhile, Alex and Jamie were so taken with the atmosphere and the fun that they were jumping up and down in excitement. The boys had found their home, and their excitement was infectious. More importantly, Robyn and Allan realised they had discovered the key to happiness – not just for the boys but for the family as a whole.

Soon afterwards, the Schneiders met up with two of the Rolling Thunder coaches at a nearby park, to see if the boys could run. Robyn and Allan were fearful as they watched the boys run off. Half an hour later, the boys returned, exhilarated and smiling. The coaches, Shaunthy Hughes and Mike Kelly, told Robyn and Allan that the boys were natural runners with unlimited potential. In fact, Alex was exceptionally fast and especially gifted, and he was going to need a coach who could keep up with him.

Another pivotal moment.

Only one of the coaches from the club was faster than Alex. His name was Kevin McDermott, and he now had the challenge of pacing Alex, whose only wish was to run as fast as he could, on every run and every day. First, Kevin tried boxing him in, which didn't work. Then he ran holding a stick in front of Alex as a barrier. That also failed. Next, he tried holding on to the back of his shirt. That strategy ended after Kevin suffered a hernia from straining himself. Finally, he decided to have Alex run behind him, slightly on a diagonal so that he could still see him. It worked. At last he was able to pace him effectively.

Robyn recalls the boys watching her lay out their running clothes on the couch and pinning their race numbers to their running tops the night before their first marathon. She couldn't know what they were thinking, but she knew she was watching happiness. When she thought she had finishing getting their kit ready, Alex then completed the job, smoothing out the wrinkles on each item of clothing. He wanted everything to be perfect. Then he arranged all the running shoes. The family were watching a sense of purpose emerge.

As both Alex and Jamie are non-verbal, it is hard for me to know what and how they feel about running. But when they are getting ready to run, and especially race, they become transformed. Alex especially has become passionate about running and will go from a state of intense anxiety to one of calm, transfixed on every aspect of the racing experience.

Kevin coached Alex for the first 11 years, each year training him to set a new personal record: 18 minutes for a 5k; 59 minutes, 55 seconds for a 10 miler; 1 hour, 20 minutes, 26 seconds for a half-marathon; and 2 hours, 56 minutes, 20 seconds for a marathon. After Kevin moved to Costa Rica, a new coach took over. Boyd Carrington, winner of several national and international championships, set even higher goals. Surpassing everyone's wildest dreams in both his speed and his endurance, Alex ran another sub-three-hour marathon in the 2017 New York City Marathon, with a time of 2 hours, 50 minutes, 5 seconds. Three weeks later he finished the Long Island Half Marathon in an astounding 1:16:30.

The boys have diverged in their running since that first moment of discovery, but running remains the family glue. After 17 marathons, Alex has emerged as a competitive runner who typically runs long distances in negative splits. (A negative split is the strategy of completing the second half of a race at a faster pace than the first.) With eight marathons under his belt, Jamie is a slower runner, enjoying much more the sport's recreational aspect. The contrast between the two is clear. Running brings them together, but they enjoy it in different ways:

> They are very different and get different things out of running. When Alex runs, he is in a state of Zen. Calm and completely focused on the finish line. I doubt he understands the concept of competitiveness. He will run as fast as he can while his coach runs alongside and paces him. His obsession becomes getting to the finish line as fast as he can. Jamie enjoys running at a comfortable pace, listening to his iPod.

Neither of the brothers is able to run alone. Achilles International, an organisation focused on hope, inspiration and achievement for athletes with disabilities, provides guides so that Alex and Jamie can run in the NYC Marathon. But inevitably life's difficulties remain huge and daunting. Several years ago, Jamie was diagnosed with a condition called catatonia, which is part of a slow regression of skills. It meant he developed severe anxiety and self-injurious behaviours. When he runs, both Robyn and Allan try to keep him happy and help him enjoy the moment.

When bombs exploded during the 2013 Boston Marathon, which both the boys were running, Jamie was traumatised. The terrorist attack exacerbated his condition, but Robyn and Allan were determined to help Jamie enjoy the running experience once again. Slowly, with great care and perseverance, they succeeded. Jamie was able to complete three more marathons, and although he is not back to where he was, he continues to enjoy racing once more.

It helps that after more than 400 races between them, Alex and Jamie have both become accustomed to the structure of racing – even if that structure itself is one of the obstacles. As Robyn says, their unique behaviours and early-morning rituals mean that the boys' race preparation at home is a huge challenge. But she and Allan work together to find ways to manage. The sad fact remains, though, that for all the satisfaction and happiness that running can bring, it will never bring independence.

The guides Alex and Jamie run with direct them on the course so they don't get lost, ensure their safety in the crowded field of runners, pace them as needed (especially true for Alex, who is close to elite status), ensure that they are hydrated, shoelaces tight, and redirect any behaviours that may occur (mainly for Jamie).

But again, despite the huge challenges, despite the severity of their autism, the thing that matters most to the family is the unifying power of running. Whatever the future holds, running remains – just as it has been for years – a remarkable source of strength and understanding.

The boys will always need care 24/7. They need help in the shower and the bathroom; they cannot be left alone; they need to hold hands with an adult when crossing the street or standing in a parking lot. And they do not effectively communicate their needs or wants, pain or discomfort. What happens next is inevitably a worry.

We are terrified of the future and what will happen to them when my husband and I are no longer able to care for them. Yet they are lovable, social and enjoy having fun. The running community has embraced them and us as a family, and our sons have become known worldwide from all the publicity they have received. It's been a wonderful journey.

As Robyn says, she hopes and prays they will always be runners. They have become defined by their running, not by their autism, and the distinction is crucial. It's a tale Robyn tells movingly in her book, *Silent Running – Our Family's Journey to the Finish Line with Autism* (Triumph Books, 2015), which describes her sons' journey from the moment of diagnosis through to the finish line of their first marathon. 'I poured my emotions into it and consider it my gift to my sons.' Alex and Jamie will never be aware of the book, let alone read it, but Robyn labels it her legacy to them. The unexpected bonus was that writing it underlined just how far they had come as a family – thanks to running.

> *I truly believe that running has saved my family. Running has had such profound effects on our sons and has brought immense happiness to our family; it has made us stronger and has provided a focus in our lives.*

Sandra Laflamme

'They said there was blood everywhere.'

Sandra Laflamme remembers every last detail: the shouting, the cheering, the noise, the high-fiving and the unbeatable exhilaration of that final stretch on Boylston Street, the last few hundred yards of the 2013 Boston Marathon. She'd trained hard to earn her place at the start and she had the confidence to run strong. And as she ran, she realised she was on course to run her perfect marathon in near-perfect conditions.

The experience was surpassing her every expectation with every step at every turn, and as the finish line came into view, Sandra lapped up every moment, taking every encouragement she could from a crowd that was loud, strong and generous. Buoyed by the thousands of spectators urging her home, she knew she was running towards a time far better than she'd dared hope for on what was proving to be an unforgettable day.

Unforgettable indeed, and for the most ghastly of reasons. This was the day terrorists targeted an event that stood as a symbol of effort, determination, pride, joy and ultimately freedom. In just 12 seconds, thousands of lives changed forever, Sandra's among them. It was a brutal day, one we look back on now as a day on which Boston rallied, showed its strength and won hearts around the world. But for many who were there, the trauma lingers.

Sandra had run a qualifying time of 3 hours 40 minutes to secure her place at the start line. On 15 April, 2013, she stood on that start line in peak form, relishing the prospect of her first tilt at the Boston Marathon in its 117th year. She and her husband Jesse had left their children, Brock and Piper, then aged three and five, back home in

New Hampshire with their grandparents. Sandra was free to run; Jesse was free to support her. Everything seemed right.

> *It was just an absolutely beautiful race day. The weather was just perfect –*
> *or maybe just a little bit too warm for some, but there were blue skies, a*
> *beautiful day, and I was so excited to be there. The nerves were there, but*
> *they were good nerves, and everything was just awesome, standing there*
> *soaking up the atmosphere.*

All seemed set fair for a good time in every sense, and Sandra delivered it – a smart run during which she read the conditions and ran accordingly. The great danger on the downhill is to set off too quickly. You pay the penalty when you crash and burn later – a danger Sandra bore in mind. She knew what to expect. She had discussed the course with her coach. She had developed her race strategy, she knew what she needed to remember. She had also taken on board the lessons she'd learned in her qualifying marathon. As she says, she ran smart.

As she neared the finish, she sensed the reward.

> *I just remember coming down Boylston Street and being so excited because*
> *I was nearly there. Everyone was cheering. I had my name on my arm.*
> *People were shouting out: 'Go Sandra!' There were just so many people.*
> *It was awesome. Everyone was wanting to high-five you. I was high-fiving*
> *everyone. I had a tear in my eye. I remember all the details so distinctly.*
> *They are still very fresh in my mind now.*

Sandra, who lives in Hanover, New Hampshire, crossed the line in 3 hours, 34 minutes. The medal was placed around her neck; she was processed, handed her goodie bag and directed towards the buses that had carried the runners' baggage to the finish. The plan was to meet Jesse in the family area. Sandra hadn't managed to pick him out en route, but she had known he was there – encouragement enough.

Sandra phoned him and phoned her parents. More and more people were coming through with their medals. The atmosphere was cheerfulness undiluted. Looking forward to seeing Jesse and celebrating her run, Sandra was starting to change into clean, dry clothes when suddenly there was a loud boom. She remembers it as 'jarring, frightening'. She was just a couple of blocks away. It was 10 minutes after she had finished.

No one knew what was happening. Everyone stopped talking. Sandra recalls a pause. She remembers the looks on people's faces. Baffled. Concerned. And then they started to talk again. Some people suggested it was a cannon going off to mark Patriots Day, always the day of the race. But the explanation didn't feel right. Sandra started chatting to a woman next to her. They agreed it was odd. Just moments later came the second explosion. By now, it was clear something was seriously wrong. Moments later, a couple of people ran through, shouting that everyone needed to get to the hospital to give blood.

They said there was blood everywhere.

Sandra rang her husband again. He told her he was planning to get on the T, the city's underground, to get to her. He hadn't been able to get to the finish line – it was just too crowded.

By now, people were starting to talk about explosions. Sandra realised she needed to get to the meeting area. Still no one knew what was happening, but worry was spreading among the finishers. When her phone battery failed, she managed to borrow a phone from one of the volunteers. She phoned her husband again, but this time she couldn't get through. She phoned her parents in Pennsylvania, and it was via Pennsylvania that she found out what had happened just a few hundred yards away.

They said: 'You are going to be OK. You need to find Jesse. You need to meet him where he told you to meet him.' My mother said: 'There were bombs that went off.' I said: 'Is everybody OK?' She said: 'People were hurt, but you are OK. Get off the phone and go and meet him.'

But Sandra was also concerned about her friend Lynn. They had started together, but Lynn, carrying an injury, had urged Sandra to run on. The intention was to meet somewhere at the finish. Lynn was still out there. Sandra's only option was to get to her meeting point and wait at the letter L.

But I was just a complete wreck. I remember thinking: 'Why am I here in the middle of all these tall buildings when people are talking about bombs going off?' My mind immediately went back to 9/11. I couldn't stop thinking about it. 9/11 was a series of events over several hours. I couldn't stop thinking something else was going to happen. It was so intense, with the noise of sirens everywhere. People were distraught, myself included.

There was confusion everywhere. Sandra didn't want to stay, but she didn't know Boston well, and didn't know where to go. She was terrified. She managed to make contact with Jesse, who reassured her he was coming while also telling her he was still some distance away. Depleted from the run, Sandra was cold and hungry, but all she could do was wait as the crowds around her thinned. Two other women, also waiting for family, offered Sandra a jacket.

Three hours after her finish, Jesse finally made it through. They were reunited at last, but Sandra's trauma was barely beginning. Her reaction to the bombing was severe, though it took her several months before she saw a doctor and received a diagnosis of PTSD. Instead, in the early days, she tried to deal with it herself, fighting the anger she felt. Blanket coverage of the atrocity meant the headlines were ever-present. Three people were confirmed dead: Krystle Marie Campbell, 29, a restaurant manager from Medford, Massachusetts; Lü Lingzi, 23, a Chinese national and Boston University graduate; and eight-year-old Martin William Richard, from the Dorchester neighbourhood of Boston. A further 264 people were injured. Sandra couldn't get them out of her mind.

I couldn't stop thinking about coming down Boylston Street. I couldn't stop thinking about all the people I had high-fived and wondering if they had been hurt, and I couldn't stop wondering if I had high-fived the little boy who was no longer alive. It made me feel so angry. It was just so unexpected. We were here running a race. This was such a happy occasion.

In the weeks that followed, Sandra found she was hearing the sirens constantly in her head. Haunting her too was the two-mile walk back to the car with Jesse through eerily empty streets, littered with marathon detritus, paper cups strewn everywhere, but no one around.

Tendonitis meant that Sandra couldn't run away the pain after the marathon, but a cruel twist now exacerbated the trauma: the fact that running itself was now was so closely associated with the cause of her increasing disarray. Sandra had known post-partum depression in the past; she also knew that running was the one constant that had always helped her get back to feeling good. As she says, because she wasn't now running and because she hadn't consulted anyone about the way she was feeling, she had no way of working out what was going on inside her mind. She found herself in a 'really deep dark hole'.

Oddly, it was their daughter Piper's anxiety that brought Sandra the medical help she needed. Piper knew what had happened in Boston. She knew her mummy had been caught up in something awful and then, just a few weeks after the atrocity, one of her teachers died unexpectedly. The result was extreme separation anxiety, which in turn heightened Sandra's own anxiety.

> *I was talking to my daughter's therapist, and we were talking about Boston. I was just a wreck. I could not stop the floodgate of tears. My daughter's doctor told me it might be useful for me to talk to somebody.*

Sandra had counselling for a year and has gone back to it several times since. Inevitably, the subject of running came up in therapy. It was agreed she needed to do it. Its promise was somewhere to go to process her thoughts, and as soon as she was able to resume, running started to give her the release she needed. Some runs she would cry the whole way round. Sometimes she would run with friends. It was therapy under another name. She sensed that her healing had begun.

Part of Sandra's recovery was to return to the Boston Marathon one year later in 2014 – a vital step in confronting her PTSD. Sandra recognised that she needed to go back and face it. It was about going back and knowing she could get through it. She was helped on the day by chatting to a woman who had endured pretty much the same experience as Sandra had the year before. There was solidarity in sharing the experience.

Even so, it proved the toughest of challenges. Almost inevitably there were several points where she could barely breathe, let alone run. At around mile eight, Sandra saw people running for a charity set up in memory of the boy, Martin Richard. A wave of emotion overwhelmed her and she had to walk. But Sandra recognised what was happening. She needed to feel those emotions if she was going to come out the other side. As she says, she needed to reconcile herself to what had happened. She felt the terror again, but this time the terror was part of the healing process – a landmark moment in her recovery.

Sandra returned to the Boston Marathon again in 2016 and 2017, the point at which her Boston journey was complete. She had achieved what she had wanted to achieve. Her running adventures now lie elsewhere.

There are still triggers to her PTSD. Recent terror attacks in London brought it all back. But Sandra recognises that she is in a good place now, continuing to run and also enjoying the chance to share her running experiences and thoughts through her Organic Runner Mom website – a place where she explores running as an extension of her organic lifestyle.

As Sandra says, Organic Runner Mom is someone who enjoys family life, someone who enjoys spending plenty of time out there in the real world – away from computers, televisions and screens. Organic Runner Mom is also someone with the keenest interest in sustainable food and organic farming.

Sandra and Jesse run an organic egg-based business, which was started by Jesse's grandfather Leslie Ward after the Second World War in Monroe, New Hampshire. Jesse joined the family business in the year 2000, after graduating from college. Far more than a business, it is a way of life for all of them. As a mum of two, Sandra believes in the organic lifestyle, keen that the food they eat is free from pesticides and antibiotics. Keen too that their business ethos should lie in supporting and working closely with other family-run farms.

And to an extent, Sandra sees her running as an extension of the lifestyle the family has chosen.

She grew up in the Philadelphia area. For a long time, rowing was her sport of choice, but running was part of the training, and when it wasn't possible to go on the water, running was always the first resort. When she moved to Monroe with Jesse, with no team to go on the water with, the running took over completely. With a couple of friends, she savoured the discovery of trail running – perhaps the closest running can ever bring us to nature.

You go through the trees on beautiful trails. I love being in the woods. You hear the birds singing and the trees rustling, and you have got the beautiful solitude of being in the woods. Or you can go on a mountain trail and work your way up and pop out on the top of the mountain. You get that endorphin rush, and you just feel so clean.

Sandra's highest mountain, though, has been her return to Boston the year after the bombing. It was a day she climbed so high she was able to look beyond her pain towards a brighter future. She accepts there will be dips ahead and tough times to tackle, but with her running now, she's finally leaving the atrocity behind her.

For me, it was essential to go back. There were a lot of people who just couldn't, but for me, if I hadn't, it would have left me feeling stuck. Stuck there on that awful day.

Dan Keeley

'You'd be hard-pressed to find a happier, more grateful person than I am right now.'

Ask Dan Keeley why he did it, and the answer is as shocking as it is simple. Dan ran 1250 miles (2012 kilometres) from Rome to London because 12 men under the age of 45 take their own life every single day in the UK. Dan ran because he wanted to help do something about it. And because he was very nearly a statistic himself.

Dan, who now lives in Kent, looks back on a wonderful childhood. He grew up in East Sussex and fizzed with energy, the best kind. Dan was outgoing, optimistic and enthusiastic, and in his mum Carolyn, he had the best possible role model. As he says, her greatest gifts – to Dan and to his brother Toby and sister Samm – have always been her service to others and her belief that, whatever life throws at us, our best days are yet to come. Carolyn taught them all to stay positive and to follow their hearts.

It was the ideal upbringing for Dan to follow his twin passions, being active and being creative. However, as he looks back now, he can see a few warning signs were already there in terms of his mental health. Dan studied sport and leisure management at the University of Brighton from 2005 to 2008. He had a great time, but even during those student years, his mood fluctuated: his energy would be either elevated or lower than normal. He exhausted himself in his first term and was in a state of mild depression by the January, but as he says, the enthusiastic and positive Dan did always return.

After graduating, Dan moved to London as a researcher on a national sports project. He then worked as a sports events manager at an international business park in west London. He also worked as a marketing executive linked to the 2012 Summer Olympics in London. In the meantime, he was working weekends and evenings to save enough money to become an Alpine ski instructor – a dream he'd had since his schooldays.

Things were looking good, especially when Dan secured what he considered his dream job, one he still holds to this day: community manager for a snow sports youth charity that uses skiing and snowboarding to empower inner-city youngsters. As Dan says, it was a job that could have been created with him in mind.

However, after years of seeking a job that impacted positively on society, Dan's mood was reaching simmering point:

Through the first half of 2012, if you had met me, you would have been exhausted. My creative energy started bursting out of me as if a huge weight had been lifted. Friends and family saw it happening but just thought it was a very heightened version of me.

There were times when Dan went three weeks on just two hours' sleep a night. He started thinking about how he could apply to society as a whole the impact he was going to have at the charity. Dan was conscious of the amount of unnecessary suffering going on in the world and decided that it was his responsibility to end it.

Dan and Georgie, his fiancée and now his wife, booked a two-week holiday in Italy in June 2012. The danger signs were becoming ever more apparent in the weeks leading up to the trip.

I could not take my foot off the gas. If I was a Formula One car, then my foot was firmly on the accelerator. I couldn't bear to take any pit stops or change the tyres. I didn't look after myself.

Friends started warning him to slow down, but by now Dan was convinced he was the next Mark Zuckerberg or Steve Jobs, with a worldwide social agenda to fulfil. The irony is cruel. Dan became convinced that it was his job to show the world how to slow down and follow its heart at a time when his own mind was travelling 'at 200mph'.

With his mood escalating, 27-year-old Dan started acting out of character. At the rustic hotel where they were staying, Dan began sharing money he didn't have with all those around him. He secretly bought a bottle of wine for every guest room in the hotel. He wrote what he believed was a New Age bible fit for 2012. He even spent one night fully awake in a dried-out fountain in the courtyard, customised with cushions and parasols from the pool and with bread and wine from the kitchen, all as a demonstration that he was starting to create a better world.

It's a period he looks back on with deep regret: Georgie was petrified. It was clear to her that he needed psychiatric care, and Dan was happy to go along with anything at this point – as long as it didn't obstruct his new-found clarity and his vision to change the world for the better.

The closest hospital was an hour's drive away, and they were soon en route in their Fiat 500. However, during the journey, Dan's mood soared to a new level. If he didn't get out of the car and make a demonstration to the world in the most impactful way possible, he felt as if he was going to explode.

They pulled up on the hard shoulder. Dan scrambled out of the car and started jogging down the hard shoulder, stripping down to nothing but his khaki shorts and raising his hands to stop the slow lane, then the middle lane, then the fast lane. It was 5 p.m. at rush hour with heavy traffic – traffic suddenly at a standstill.

I'd done it. I was standing in the middle of this major motorway, having backed up the traffic for over five miles. I was letting one car go at a time, preaching to each driver to slow down and follow their hearts. I genuinely believed I was the Chosen One and that I had the answer to ease all the suffering going on in the world. I had lost my mind.

Police and ambulance weren't long in arriving, and after a few weeks on a ward in Italy, with Georgie, his mother and his mother-in-law Nicola beside him, Dan was repatriated to the UK, where he spent another few weeks in psychiatric care at the Maudsley Hospital in south London. The diagnosis was bipolar disorder, which Dan and his family accepted. But by now, returning to Dan's F1 analogy, his gearbox and chassis were smashed to bits. For the second half of 2012, his thoughts were never far from suicide.

Dan had gone from believing he was the Chosen One to believing he was now the scum of the earth and a burden on everyone. He lost all sense of purpose. He felt pinned to his bed. The two-metre walk to the bathroom might as well have been climbing Everest.

Dan decided he was going to kill himself and where he was going to do it. Fortunately, Georgie had taken the precaution of hiding the car keys. So Dan found himself face-to-face for a crucial session of talking therapy with his care co-ordinator Grace.

She talked to me about how my actions would affect others. And she just listened. She didn't know it at the time, but she stopped me from taking my own life. I simply wouldn't be here if it wasn't for her.

A turning point came not long afterwards, in January 2013. After weeks of lying in bed, Dan was set the task of buying some milk and cereal from the local shop. After hours of resetting his alarm, Dan made his way to the store, picked up some milk, then turned into the cereal aisle where he froze, for 45 minutes, crying inside, his body paralysed by the colours, the choices, the overwhelming hyperreality of everything around him. Dan couldn't trust his actions or his thoughts any more. He found himself incapable of making even the simplest of choices.

But the experience led to a vital decision as he eventually made the walk home. He resolved to strip back every aspect of his life to the essentials and effectively start again. He needed simplicity and he found it in the concept of minimalism.

It hasn't all been smooth sailing since, but it has been progressive, and today you'd be hard-pressed to find a happier or more grateful person than I am right now, grateful for the people in my life and the life I now lead.

Dan returned to work and started speaking about his experiences. Talking about what had happened wasn't a big decision. It happened naturally, but it struck him that the more openly he spoke about his experiences, the more people responded to his story and to his honesty. Once again, he found himself wanting to help people – but this time, there was no aura of the Chosen One, simply a sense of new-found strength and of the remarkable love and support around him.

And it was from this safe position that Dan started to plot a big adventure – to take on a huge challenge, not only to raise money for a mental health charity now close to his heart but also to share his story. The challenge would link in with Italy, and it would take the form of running.

It was always going to be running. It was never going to be anything else. Running is pure and beautifully simple. You carry with you only what you need, then put one foot in front of the other until you get where you need to be. It couldn't be simpler, with simplicity applied to every aspect of my life now.

It was then that the words *Rome to Home* popped into Dan's mind – a solo run from the Colosseum to the London Eye. Dan knew instinctively that it was perfectly possible. Georgie was by now his wife and he knew that with her support, with the support of friends and family and with sensible solid preparation and due diligence, it was a realisable aim.

Sensitive to those closest to him, Dan built his adventure on a year of planning and nine months of solid training with a backpack. He resolved from the start to be kind to himself. His bipolar disorder had to be factored into the equation. He knew he could probably finish the run in 55 days, but he scheduled 65. He knew he could comfortably average 20 miles (32 kilometres) a day and there would be days when he would run more. Equally, he was ready for days when he ran less.

Dan knew the mental challenge would be bigger than the physical challenge. He was returning to Italy, the country where he had endured his ghastly motorway experience. But he found motivation in deciding to run to raise funds for CALM, the Campaign Against Living Miserably, one of the UK's most innovative charities dedicated to keeping men alive by talking.

As Dan says, talking kept him alive. He understands directly just what a massive difference CALM can make in a country where the statistics are truly shocking. Rome to Home became Dan's way of doing something about it. But again, he was well enough to be clear: he wouldn't be doing it as the Chosen One; he'd be doing it as a compassionate guy who'd been there himself.

Dan's route largely followed the Via Francigena, the pilgrims' route that took the faithful from Canterbury Cathedral to the Vatican – though, of course, Dan would be doing it in the other direction. He would also be adapting it to make it his own pilgrimage, deviating to take in Paris and also crossing to England via East Sussex rather than Kent. This was going to be the route for 21st-century pilgrims. After his experiences in 2012, he knew a powerfully spiritual adventure lay ahead. Indeed it did.

Just as importantly, it was an adventure filled with trust and warmth for his fellow man. Dan didn't book a single hotel in advance. He slept 10 nights in his bivvy bag, and for the rest of the time, he slept in convents, Airbnbs and hostels listed along the Via Francigena. For Dan, the range of the accommodation was all part of the richness of the experience. As for following the route, Dan created a Google Maps overlay on his iPhone. Helping him also were occasional markings along the way.

I wanted to take off as many external pressures as I could and keep the whole thing obsessively simple. I knew roughly where I wanted to finish each day. I never counted the miles. I was purely, purely focused on reaching a safe destination each day and soaking up every second along the way.

Dan set off from Rome on Friday, 25 August, 2017. Simply starting was a celebration of success. Dan's mother Carolyn, Georgie and a few of Georgie's family were in the Italian capital to raise a glass of wine to him. And then he was off.

The longest distance Dan covered in a day was 52 miles (84 kilometres) as he approached Paris. After that he allowed himself two glorious rest days in the French capital, the highlight of which was going to the top of the Eiffel Tower. Most people spend probably 30 minutes up there. Dan was there for at least two hours. As he says, he wanted to 'smell the roses'. He had run the equivalent of an ultramarathon the day before, with no physical repercussions. The feeling was fantastic as he looked out across the city and reflected that he had run there all the way from Rome.

The highlight of the whole trip, however, had come earlier, when he reached the top of the Great St Bernard Pass in the Alps. At a height of 2469 metres (8100 feet), it was undoubtedly a personal summit – very much part of the spirituality at the heart of the whole undertaking. As Dan says, he wouldn't consider himself a religious person – but spiritual, most certainly.

> *I came away from my experiences in 2012 with a deep sense of gratitude for all that I am blessed with. From the moment I set off from the Colosseum, I knew I was so lucky with the people I had supporting me, none more so than my amazing wife and family.*

It all added up to a feeling that someone somewhere was looking after him, perhaps his beloved aunt Sue, who had died tragically young. Sue's mantra had always been *carpe diem*, and at her funeral, Dan resolved that he too would seize the day. He did so as he journeyed 1250 miles (2012 kilometres) from Rome to Home on foot.

Support from friends was outstanding, and alongside his mascot Little Bear, he had company from time to time. For a few days he was joined by Jason and Dexter on their bikes, then his uncle Simon and his girlfriend Gaye, then his friends James and Alex and his cousin Martin. On the home leg, the final five days in the UK, the support grew and grew.

Dan's journey ended at the London Eye on Saturday, 28 October at 1 p.m., his plan delivered far more beautifully than he could ever have dared imagine. The icing on the cake was that he smashed his fundraising aim for CALM, raising not £12,000 but £15,000, and a further £2000 from his Alps stage for snow sports youth charity Snow-Camp. Dan achieved it all without physical injury – not even a blister.

> *I never once didn't want to run. I was craving the running. I had zero doubt that I could do it. It was the most magical, blissful and life-changing experience I have ever had, and it was a spiritual pilgrimage in so many ways. Quietly, I had always wanted to show the world what I could do, and now I'd done it.*

And gratifyingly, fairly early on, the adventure challenge revealed a weakness that Dan immediately knew how to turn into a strength. After 16 days, pushing himself too much, Dan sensed he was entering into a hypermanic state. The warning messages came through from friends and family, suggesting his mood was elevated and needed to be brought back down. He acted instantly: he eased up; he took extra medication; he slowed down, taking off all external pressures and reassessing what mattered most.

As Dan says, he dropped his ego. And he has continued to do so. Through his daily video diaries of his run, Dan found himself constantly humbled by heart-warming messages from people he'd helped with his descriptions of his own experiences. He had wobbled, but he had found the strength to put himself back on track.

There have been no post-adventure blues – and for a simple reason. Reaching London might have been the closing chapter of one adventure, but it was also the opening chapter of an even bigger one – a much more significant journey. Dan's public speaking engagements are taking off strongly. He knows the good he can do simply by telling his story, and he knows his supporters will always be there. He will continue to talk, to share his optimism and to encourage others to talk. He knows that talking saves lives.

It has been the most amazing journey. I ran from Rome to Home to share my story and to keep men alive by talking, and we did it! Something truly powerful someone said to me at the finish line is that by taking on the adventure, I showed men how to slow down and follow their heart. And if that's not something to celebrate five years on from when I lost my sanity, I don't know what is.

Caroline Elliott

'Knowing that I'm always recovering, one small step at a time.'

PE teacher Caroline Elliott was always the little girl who loved to run. And that hasn't changed. But she runs now with a wiser, different head on her shoulders. Caroline looks at photographs of herself before the day she was brutally sexually assaulted, and she wonders whether her smile will ever be that big again. She sees innocence in her eyes; she can see that there is no 'pain in the brain' behind them.

Now there's a pain that is unlikely to ever fully go away.

But there are times when she knows that she is happier now than she has ever been. She loves her life with her partner Liv. She often wonders what true happiness is, but she is confident that she has found it with Liv. Of course, something has changed, pre- and post-attack. Life is vastly more difficult than ever it was, but it is also more valuable. And that's a major compensation.

I look at those past pictures, and I know my brain wasn't aware then of just how much bad things can happen and that they can happen to me. Now my smile shows that. But I know I am happy now.

Caroline was diagnosed with depression and complex PTSD in the months following the attack. She also had the ordeal of two separate court cases, one of which she attended to read her victim impact statement. The following February, she attempted suicide. But she knows now that she is a survivor, not a victim, and that the difference is crucial.

Helping Caroline every step of the way has been running. She was attacked while on an early morning run, but the little girl who loved to run wasn't going to let anyone take running away from her. It was running she turned to in her moment of need, and it has been running that has maintained her ever since, alongside the love she has found with Liv.

Caroline grew up on a cattle farm covering 4180 square kilometres (1614 square miles), 400 kilometres (248 miles) north-west of the closest town, Katherine, in Australia's Northern Territory. As she says, hers is the true Aussie outback. Trips to town were few and far between – and held no interest for Caroline. All she wanted to do was run. She asked her grandparents, Boppa and Nan, to watch her run 'really fast'. Boppa responded by creating her very own running track alongside a fence. Endurance was always part of her DNA, and she ran to her heart's content. As her nan says, Caroline grew up 'strong from the bush' – a background that helped her to become the person she is today.

On one occasion, the family travelled the 400 kilometres into town for a sports day. Six-year-old Caroline asked if she could run in the 1500m. The organisers decided to let her start, just to see how far she got. She started and she didn't stop. No one could believe just how far the little girl in the cowboy hat could go.

What they didn't know was that she was running for the best possible reason – not just for herself, but also for Nonie, her little sister, a year younger, who was born with spina bifida and died when Caroline was two. Caroline's mother recalls that Nonie smiled only once in her short life and that she smiled because of Caroline's smile.

Nonie repaid that gift many years later.

By April 2015, Caroline, now 32, was a PE teacher in a remote Northern Territory community called Borroloola. As she so often did, she went for an early morning run. It was Nonie's spirit, alive in Caroline, which got her through the horror of what happened next – a brutal ordeal lasting 30 minutes and unfurling, Caroline believed, at gunpoint.

Two teenagers pulled Caroline off the road onto the red dirt. One of them said: 'Don't do something stupid or I'll shoot you.' Caroline wasn't to know there was no gun. Her only thought was that somehow she had to negotiate herself out of trouble. Thoughts of Nonie kept her strong. Caroline was alone – her wits were all she had to fight with.

I told them: 'I'm gay. You don't want me. I'm old. Don't do this, boys. I'm a teacher, I know everyone . . .' Then came: 'Well, how about a blow job?' And that was so much safer than what they wanted to do. But it didn't finish there. He dragged me across the road to the dry creek beds, pushed me to my knees and told me to do it. But he didn't like how I did it, so he dragged me by my hair up the road and said: 'Down that dirt road.' I knew only danger was down there, so I negotiated more: 'We have to do it now, the sun is up.'

The second boy joined in and threatened to rape Caroline. Her mind raced. She told them it wasn't what she did, that it wasn't part of the deal. Still she was seeking the alternative. She said she would perform a sexual act on the both of them. Still in her mind was the gun she didn't know they didn't have.

The boys tried to strip her of what they could.

I stopped them from the rest. Thank God for tight sports bras and shorts with attached undies . . . That was too hard for their brains to comprehend, so I just kept saying: 'No, that's too hard, I run, they are tight.' But they took their trophies of what they got off me. It was what the first boy went back for while the second boy was searching through the bushes, looking for my hair tie and saying: 'I can't find your hair tie, miss. I'm sorry, it wasn't my idea.' And I was looking for my water bottle as I knew it had their fingerprints on it . . . then I saw the older boy walking back with my stuff and I thought: 'What the fuck are you doing, Caroline? Run!' And I ran home.

Thirty minutes of horror. Thirty minutes during which Caroline didn't back down. She just kept saying no. Nonie sustained her.

All the things I did, I did for me and Nonie. I felt connected to her. I knew she was always with me. Watching and keeping me safe. Something gave me strength to keep going, to stay focused to negotiate what was going to happen so that I kept myself as safe as possible . . . not to let those boys do to me what they wanted to do. To fight back with my words. I hate what I had to do, but I did it to survive.

Being attacked on a run would have meant an end to running for most people, but not Caroline. As she says, she never blamed running for the attack. Instead, damagingly, in the early days, she blamed herself. She tortured herself with the thought that she hadn't listened to her gut on that fateful day. She heard the boys whistle, but she decided it was safe to keep going. She knows now that she has the right to run and to feel safe in her hometown. She knows she wasn't to blame. But in the early days, she was convinced that it was her own decisions which put her 'in that spot'.

For the first two weeks after the attack, Caroline couldn't face running, partly because of a groin injury she'd sustained during the assault. Instead, she swam – for the first time in almost two years. She did lap after lap. It felt like she was cleansing her body 'of all the bad things on it', swimming safe in her own lane with no one around who knew what had happened. When the flashbacks hit, she would blow out big bubbles and shake her head. Swimming helped calm her brain and cleanse her body.

But after a few weeks, the urge to run started to take over. Her osteopath cleared her to run; her psychologist knew she needed to. It was a turning point.

I didn't speak, I stayed focused on my task and I ran . . . I ran, I cried, I screamed, I laughed and I cried more. I'd never run and cried before. I had always run and smiled. But I ran. And from that day on I was able to do small runs every other day. I was always alert and ready, always on edge, but I didn't want those boys to take running away from me.

A few months later, Caroline moved to the town of Gove, Nhulunbuy, still within the vast Northern Territory. At the time of the attack, she'd been preparing for a race called 3 Marathons in 3 Days. She didn't get to do it. But in her new home, she decided to run and run . . . and managed two marathons in half a day. The town thought she was crazy, but in her mind Caroline had 'beaten the boys'. Just as importantly, she'd got back something that had been taken from her: she'd shown she was still the little girl who loved to run.

The next year, in June 2016, Caroline ran 100 kilometres (62 miles) in Gove to raise money and awareness for PTSD. The whole town turned out to support her. As she crossed the line, 14½ hours later, there were more than 300 people waiting for her. Everyone had a sparkler burning. People were cheering, lights were flashing, car horns were beeping, everyone was smiling. The atmosphere was magical – not least because Caroline's thoughts were now turning towards helping others who had been through their own ordeals. With her run, she wasn't just celebrating running, she was showing what the human spirit can achieve.

> *I helped people know that we can achieve the impossible and that we are there to help support each other – just as they all did for me that day. A day I'll never forget. A day where running brought so many people together.*

Caroline was thrilled that everyone connected with the message she wanted to deliver. She used the attack, she used her recovery and she used her running to tell the world that it is OK *not* to be OK and that we can help each other, and support each other through the hardest times. She wanted to thank everyone who had turned out to support her.

> *Then I was carried away by my partner and closest friend and I held my head high till I knew I was out of sight of the crowd and I cried. I cried so much. Not because of the pain – well, maybe a little bit, as I was in a lot! But because I had done it and I had helped others who have maybe been through something similar or have a mental illness, to see that it's OK to not be OK and hopefully, they can know there are people to talk to.*

Just as important, perhaps, was the run Caroline took six months after her attack: a run that retraced her route. For her, it was a chance to say goodbye to the teachers she had worked with as she embarked on her new life, and also a chance to face her past. She endured the flashbacks. Everything that happened was red raw in her mind. But she knew she had to go through with it.

> *I stopped at the dirt road where I ran home from those boys, and I decided I would turn around and run that run again, this time for the future. I ran it and every step I got stronger. I ran the way to my old neighbour's unit, where I would always see her every morning and smile and she would say: 'How far today, Caroline?' And I would smile and tell her. She would call*

me crazy! That one bad day she saw me at her door banging on it, bent over crying. And as she opened the door, I said: 'Please call the police!', and I went straight to the sink to wash my mouth. But this day she saw the smile she was meant to see that day.

Whether we can ever truly recover from the kind of trauma Caroline suffered is impossible to answer. Her senses remain constantly on the alert for the trigger that will set her brain to danger. The nightmares, the insomnia and the flashbacks continue. 'Every anniversary, every smell, every strange shape in the bush' is a reminder.

Caroline believes she can never go back to being the person she was before. That Caroline has gone.

It took my feeling of safety and trust. Not trust in people, but trust in making plans and knowing that tomorrow will be a good day. I always looked for the positive and I was always telling my fellow staff members, friends and students to live for today because we never know what might happen tomorrow. I was always smiling. People said they came to me to help them smile. My nickname at school was the energiser bunny!

Caroline says she was never naïve enough to think that something awful wouldn't happen to her. In fact, she had often thought what would she do if she were attacked while out running. 'Twist, turn, kick, scream, fight,' she imagined. But she never really thought it would happen. Life was grand. She was happy, she loved her job, she had a race and she had a challenge.

My smile was genuine. Then that day happened. I lost my innocence, my trust, my sense of happy-go-lucky, my smile, my passion for teaching and running. One bad run out of thousands of good runs. And it took away everything. My job, my race, my home, my sense of safety and security. My whole life was taken in that one moment. And those thoughts stayed with me for a long time.

And that's the Caroline who isn't coming back. But she does believe she has emerged stronger – and can now make use of the experience. Running will never again give her the carefree feeling of before; but Caroline knows she is tougher now because of what happened. It took her a long time to understand just exactly what was taken away from her on that day – 28 April, 2015 – but important to her recovery has been to recognise all the things that actually remained intact: 'to see that there are parts of me that are so deep, the things that make me who I am . . . the things that helped me survive that day, the things that could never be taken away.'

Looking back, she realises her way forward was to regain a sense of herself. Tellingly, early on, Caroline's psychologist asked her what her core values were. After long reflection, Caroline told her: 'Honesty, respect, hard work and determination.' Then the psychologist asked: 'What are five great things about you?' Caroline replied: 'I'm kind and respectful, I'm caring, I'm honest, I'm trustworthy, I'm determined.'

The psychologist's response, crucially, was to point out that these were things no one could ever take away from her, an important realisation that enables Caroline to say today a remarkable thing: she wouldn't change anything about the course her life has taken. Without the assault, Caroline wouldn't have met Liv and her children: 'I would never wish it on anyone, ever. But it happened, it has made me the person I am now and it has brought me to my loving family. And I still stand strong with my core values.'

It's the perfect platform from which to reach out and help others. Caroline has learned the hardest lessons imaginable during her months of trauma; she is determined that others should learn those lessons in far kinder ways. On 20 October, 2016 in a lecture entitled *One Step at a Time* at the Vibe Hotel, Darwin Waterfront, Caroline relived her ordeal – with the aim of encouraging us all to seek help when we need it. The video of her talk (*Caroline Elliott Darwin* on YouTube: link provided in the References) is compelling viewing, cathartic for Caroline, empowering for others.

And it's on that basis that she looks to the future:

Trusting in the future and knowing that I may not know what will happen next year, next month or even tomorrow. But trusting and believing that today I am happy, today loved by my family and I love them. Knowing that we are planning a future together even though no one truly knows what that future looks like. Knowing I will be here, with my family beside me, alive, strong, healthy and happy. My partner and I walking the path of life, holding hands and supporting each other over life's hurdles. And me personally, taking each day as it comes and knowing it's OK to not be OK. Knowing that I'm always recovering, one small step at a time. I still battle PTSD and those fears every day, but every day I know I'm getting a little bit better. I'm just happy that I've recovered enough to run again, to smile, to live, to love, to survive and be happy.

Caroline was able to return to work in the autumn of 2017, two-and-a-half years after the attack. In July 2018 she married Liv, the love of her life.

Sujan Sharma

'I am so glad now that I had that hallucination.'

Sujan Sharma believes she was always going to be the black sheep of the family. In fact, she positively revelled in the role. A first-generation Indian growing up in Wolverhampton, she had tattoos, she had piercings, she liked to drink and she invariably picked the wrong boyfriends. It was never going to end well, but at the time she was convinced she was having fun.

Hindsight tells her now that her wild days were all about trying – and failing – to cope with the after-effects of her troubled childhood. Mental health problems were simply something she always had. She regards herself as the product of her upbringing in that respect, the daughter of a father who struggled with his own mental health and with alcohol issues until his death in 2009.

Sujan recalls a tough and cash-strapped childhood, plagued by panic attacks and by anxiety attacks. Now she can easily see why the attacks were happening, but unsurprisingly, she couldn't do so at the time. Panic and anxiety were simply the twin pillars of her existence amid the family turmoil, the twin problems encouraging what was even then her tendency to overthink.

She believes she was about five or six when the anxiety first started to kick in – the direct result of seeing her father's problems and their impact on their shared family life. When he heard voices in his head, violence often followed.

I would run away and hide when things got tough. I would blame my mum. I couldn't see why she stayed. But it was the Indian culture, the Indian way. It was what you were supposed to do. Leaving would have brought shame on the family. My mother is still alive. She's 75.

She coped by going to the temple and believing in God. That's how she managed.

For Sujan, who was born seven weeks premature, being skinny was also a factor in her misery, part of her poor self-esteem – a constant in her teenage years, which worsened as she hit her 20s. As she sees it now, her response was to mask both her panic attacks and anxiety attacks by drinking, by partying and by choosing the wrong boyfriends – part and parcel of the fun she believed she was having.

The panic attacks left her feeling she couldn't breathe, convinced she was going to be sick or collapse. At a lower level, anxiety left her heart racing and her mind besieged by negative thinking. Depression was creeping in – though she didn't recognise it as such. She would lie on the sofa, unable to move. As she says, she would 'zombie out' in front of the TV.

By now Sujan's father was in a nursing home, where he spent the last 15 years of his life until his death at the age of 65. But the damage to Sujan's world had long since been done – and wasn't going away.

I would blame my dad. I went for counselling about my dad and about what happened in our family. I hated what he put us through. When he was in the nursing home, I couldn't forgive him. I wouldn't go to see him . . . or only rarely. But I won't speak ill of the dead now. It happened. I have got to let go of the past . . . otherwise it would just eat me alive.

At the time, it was easier just to drink. In reality, when she drank, Sujan simply became morbid and miserable. Hindsight tells her she was looking for happiness, and failing to find it. The realisation that happiness comes from within was still many years in the future.

It arrived with a terrifying hallucination in 2014. Sujan, who was 40 at the time, was taking painkillers for tennis elbow. She made the mistake of taking them on an empty stomach. After a shower, she was straightening her hair in front of the television when an American model appeared to wink at her from the screen.

It just completely freaked me out. It made me think. It made me realise I didn't want to be like my dad and have mental health problems. I didn't want to start hearing voices. I was on my own and I was scared stiff. But I am so glad now that I had that hallucination. It was the turning point, literally life-changing.

Sujan rang her best friends for reassurance and promised to go to the doctors. She did, and the GP was fantastic. Sujan declined medication. Instead, the doctor recommended Healthy Minds, a free NHS service that provides information and support for anyone experiencing difficulties with anxiety, depression or stress. They helped, but as Sujan says, she's a Sharma: she wanted solutions straight away. 'I am ruthless,' she laughs. 'I always want an instant fix!' And so she followed her instinct. She cut down on salt. She cut down on sugar. She started drinking water and she started eating fruit. In short, Sujan broke her own vicious circle. She was eating rubbish, and she recognised that it was making her feel rubbish. She ate better to feel better – so she was better.

And Sujan took the same ruthless approach to running. By 2014, she was already a regular jogger and starting to see the benefits of exercise. In response to her hallucination, she took the Sharma approach and bumped it up – considerably. Just over a year later, she ran the Wolverhampton Half Marathon.

Running became my goal. It de-stressed me. I don't think about anything at all when I run. I have got asthma, so I have to concentrate on my breathing. I don't think, I just run. And if I have had a stressful day, I just run out the stress. I come home, have a shower and feel calmer.

Not the least of the benefits is that running helps her sleep. Sujan has always been a poor sleeper, but running certainly makes a difference. Sujan has refined her running to the extent that she now no longer runs with music. As she says, she's already got enough happening in her head without adding any more to it.

Sujan knows she will never truly be free from anxiety, but thanks to running, she now considers her life to have been transformed. The point is that running helps to give her the techniques to cope with depression, with panic and with anxiety. And running also helps her realise that she has to remain realistic. Sujan will have good days, but she knows she must accept that she will also have bad days, days when she feels rubbish.

And she knows that running will always give her the lift she needs. It is about knowing the triggers, the balances and the equations. Just as she will always feel down if she gives in and eats a takeaway, she will always feel up if she goes for a run. And she recognises all the signs if she doesn't go for a run or leaves it too long. Her mood lowers. Her self-esteem collapses. Anxiety takes hold, and her sleep deteriorates. Go for a run, and the lift is instant.

Sujan was delighted with her 2 hours, 26 minutes in the half-marathon, and she's planning another. But 10ks are her race of choice. She is also a devotee of parkrunning and loves to help out every week, a key part of her mental well-being. Volunteering at a parkrun is Sujan's way of giving something back – in recognition of all that running has given her in recent years. Adding to the attraction is the fact that parkrunning is free, both metaphorically and financially. Sujan works as a nursery nurse. As she says, her wages aren't huge; she needs to count the pennies.

Parkrunning ticks all the boxes, as does running with the Jolly Joggers in Wolverhampton's West Park, a group of runners set up by Hayley Jarvis, community programmes manager (sport) at the mental health charity Mind. For Sujan, the Jolly Joggers have given her a chance to learn about warming up before a run and cooling down afterwards, aspects she admits she hadn't fully considered.

Something else the Jolly Joggers tell her is that she isn't alone.

I find it just amazing talking to other runners who have got exactly the same things going on in their heads that I have got going on in mine.

Sujan feels almost evangelical about it. She is proud of the number of other people she has got into running. It's a sociable thing, and the sense of community is crucial. Running with her friend Angie is always a chance to enjoy a 'good old gossip'. Sujan's only regret is that she didn't start running years ago.

The anxiety is never going to go away. If she doesn't hear from her boyfriend over a weekend, Sujan will be imagining all sorts of terrible things: he has lost interest, he has forgotten all about her. You name it, she will be thinking it. Negative thinking can still besiege her, but one essential thing has changed. Sujan's running and her improved diet now give her a much stronger platform from which to contend with whatever life throws at her, real or imaginary.

The point is that she has regained a great deal of control. So much so that she has even been able to make peace with her late father. She had never been able to say goodbye to him properly in his lifetime, but she has done so now. She even staged her very own farewell ceremony. She wrote a long letter to him – and burned it.

> *I don't feel bitter any more. I just wanted to burn all the feelings, all the anger, all the pain. I just felt I needed to put it all into the past. I keep saying to myself that I must not think like that, I must not think like my father. I haven't got what he had. I am just Sujan and it is just panic attacks and anxiety. I am not him. I am me.*

Alongside the running and the healthy eating go talking and dancing. And openness. If she is feeling bad at work, she will tell people – just as she is happy now to tell them about all that she has been through down the years. Again, it is important to let people know. All thanks to that hallucination. As she says, it was a sign that she needed to open up.

Sujan has no religion. If there is a god, she argues, why did he put her family through the things they have endured? But if there is one thing she can do, that's to share the problems she has suffered – bravely and in the knowledge that her family will always be there to support her. And so too will running.

> *Running makes me feel good inside and out. Running will always be there to help me. I can't believe I have now got a running-gear drawer! Me, of all people! Never in my wildest dreams did I ever think I would become a runner and love it!*

Linda Quirk

'A disease so insidious that it captures the
best in everyone.'

There can be few things more painful than watching a loved one in the grip of addiction. Linda Quirk has faced it twice. Her response has been to tackle addiction head on in the hope that others will be spared the pain she has witnessed and the suffering she has endured.

Linda set up The Linda Quirk Foundation. Its aim was to 'shift the worldview of addiction' and to change the 'perception of those afflicted from one of disgrace to one of acceptance and hope' – a statement of quite remarkable ambition. Helping her realise it was the most powerful of tools: the forward momentum we gain when we put one foot in front of the other at pace.

Linda's foundation now goes under the name Runwell and has been acquired by Caron Treatment Centers – testament and tribute to its effectiveness. But whoever owns it, Runwell is a word that says it all. It perfectly expresses Linda's belief, learned the hard way, that running and wellness lead one into the other, natural bedfellows helping and supporting each other. Linda knows that where wellness is missing, running may well prove the means to restore it. And when we match the two, we bring communities together and change lives – one footprint at a time.

Linda, who lives in Santa Barbara, California, began running in the mid-1980s at the age of 35. She bypassed the 5ks, the 10ks and even the half to go straight into a full marathon. Partly it was because her brother wanted them to run a marathon together. More importantly perhaps, it was an escape from what she calls a very turbulent marriage.

After completing my first marathon, the Los Angeles Marathon, I felt empowered as well as confident. I was extremely shy but I found that during and after the event people would engage with me. In short, running gave me the confidence that I so desperately lacked. I found the courage to leave my marriage with my two sons.

By then, addiction had already entered her home. Linda's first husband had a substance abuse problem – and life was tough. Linda was brought up in a middle-class family. Her father worked hard and her mother was a homemaker. She'd never encountered alcoholism or drug abuse before and she admits she didn't know how to spot it. She certainly didn't know what to do when she did.

However, she found strength in running, and it was running that helped her escape into the warmth of a strong and happy second marriage. In marrying Randy, she married a kind and compassionate man, her best friend and now husband of 25 years.

But with marriage to Randy, substance abuse entered Linda's life for a second time. Her stepdaughter Katherine became involved in meth at college. Second time round, Linda was much more aware of what was happening and much better versed in what to do, how to react and how to urge Katherine towards treatment. The tragedy was that she was unable to act quickly. The family lost Katherine to the streets of San Francisco for three years before she issued a plea for help. It was an awful time. Linda was forced to walk a terrible tightrope of compassion and firmness.

It was a huge blow to be involved with substance abuse again. I reacted the second time almost as if in shell shock. I was the hardliner in how we both interacted with her. I knew that enabling was not the answer and that playing into her demands would ultimately either kill her or continue to feed her addiction.

But even though Linda played the hardliner, she also had the compassion to spend days and days looking for Katherine, 'days when we were able to find her, walking the streets and talking, just hoping for that window to appear where she would reach out.'

As Linda says, it's so easy to feel that someone struggling with addiction can simply somehow change when you know in your head and your mind how difficult change can be. The point is that for real change to happen, the decision has to come from the user. And that's the point where friends and family become even more important. It's crucial that they are there to support the patient 100 per cent in their choice to begin a life in recovery.

> *The struggle is real. It is not a moral failing, but a disease that is so insidious it captures the best in everyone. Supporting a loved one is difficult because it is about not giving them always what they want, but finding a way to let them know that you are there for them in the positive steps toward their recovery.*

And that's why Linda sees it as so important that treatment programmes incorporate a family component. It is not just about giving the patient the tools to help them change, but also about helping the family – an approach that was crucial to Linda in her own circumstances. Linda knows all the forms of resistance that can emerge, different in each case – which is another reason to offer the patient a treatment that addresses more than just the substance abuse. It needs to get to the inner core of the individual. So Linda created The Linda Quirk Foundation.

> *The Foundation began as a way of giving back for what we as a family had received. Sitting in one of the group family sessions, I heard that some people would not have been there without the help of a scholarship. We were fortunate to be able to afford quality treatment, so I was amazed that there was even a scholarship fund available to assist others. I went home and began trying to figure out how I could use my running to raise awareness. I also set a goal of raising $1 million for the scholarship fund.*

As part of her fundraising, Linda aimed to make it to the Ironman World Championships, always held in Kona, Hawaii. To do so, she needed to qualify via the Lanzarote Ironman – the point at which life threw up the cruellest of obstacles, an accident which now seems in hindsight the catalyst for everything good that has happened since.

Training for the Ironman, Linda was in Santa Inez, California, on a Century bike ride – a non-competitive 100-mile (160-kilometre) fun ride that takes place all over the United States. She remembers little of what happened next. She was later told that she was coming down a hill when her front wheel hit a pothole. She was thrown up in the air and crashed down, headfirst to the ground, her feet still connected to the pedals. Linda broke almost every bone in her head and was in intensive care for three days.

It was the kind of moment that was always going to lead to some hefty soul-searching. Linda knew she should have been dead or at the very least paralysed. She was neither. And that begged the question: 'Why?' The only possible answer was that she was still on this earth to do something for others. For the moment, she didn't know what.

I spent the next few months unable to do absolutely anything, no TV watching, no reading, no exercise. It gave me a lot of time to think and also ask the question why was I here. I was upset a big part of the time and couldn't answer the question until one day it popped into my head. My stepdaughter was in the treatment centre at the time, and that weighed heavily on my mind. Why did addiction come into my life in the way that it did and why more than once? I knew that I was supposed to do something to help.

And help she did. Her work in the field of addiction has been remarkable, raising money, raising awareness and raising hope, exercise so often the means to all three.

Against the odds, Linda made it to the Long Course Worlds in Sweden, part of the ITU World Championships, an event with distances similar to Ironman. Linda was able to compete. The next step was to qualify for Kona. She did. Deciding it was going to be the last time she would ever participate in an Ironman or ride a bike, she was rewarded with 'the most beautiful day' of her life.

But that still left the little matter of the $1 million goal. And that was the point at which running took over – the point at which she sat her husband down and told him of her plan to a run a marathon on all seven continents in one year. Randy felt she ought to be looking at several years. For Linda, one year was precisely the point.

I knew that in order to make any impact at all I had to attempt to do it in one calendar year. So Run7on7 was formed, a website developed and many wonderful experiences happened. My mission was picked up by media and *a contract signed with BP for their Younger For Longer campaign. All the proceeds from that contract went directly into the scholarship fund, helping to push me to the $500,000 mark quickly.*

Between April 2008 and March 2009, Linda ran the Boston Marathon, the Great Wall of China Marathon, the Easter Island Marathon, the Safaricom Marathon, the Reykjavik Marathon, the Melbourne Marathon and the Antarctica Marathon.

Linda and Randy fully funded their own travels. Along the way they connected with treatment centres in each of the countries they visited. They talked about the stigmas that patients faced. They shared best practices and they came to understand that no matter where in the world they were, the issues were similar.

But Linda wasn't done yet.

After completing seven marathons on seven continents, she set her sights on the 4 Deserts Grand Slam, widely regarded as the most prestigious outdoor footrace series in the world. The series consists of the Sahara Race (Egypt/Namibia), the Gobi March (China/Mongolia), the Atacama Crossing (Chile) and The Last Desert (Antarctica). Competitors in the races cover 250 kilometres (155 miles) in seven days over rough country terrain, provided with only water and a place in a tent.

Linda didn't quite become the first woman to complete the 4 Deserts Grand Slam in one year, but she was certainly the second – and also the first American woman and the oldest person. And the connection continues to this day. Run7on7 eventually became Runwell, and there is still a firm bond of friendship between Linda and the 4 Deserts crew.

As Linda sees it, Runwell is about ensuring accessibility of resources to those needing recovery from addiction and mental illness. It is also about helping people live healthy, fulfilling lives. Crucial to that is partnering sports with addiction treatment to help keep patients and their families and friends committed to recovery. Runwell also continues to award grants to fund scholarships to effective treatment programmes. As Linda says, the battle against addiction is seldom won alone – a message she has taken across the States and around the world. Runwell has grown substantially in recent years. True to its mission, it has now gone past the $1 million mark.

By 2017, Runwell had outgrown Linda, and it was acquired by Caron Treatment Centers. She felt it was time to put it in the hands of an organisation capable of taking it to the next level. The name The Linda Quirk Foundation has been dropped, but the name Runwell lives on as Runwell, a Program of Caron Treatment Centers. Linda is thrilled. And she is confident the organisation will become more successful than she had ever dreamed possible. Importantly, its dual focus will remain. Running and fundraising go hand in hand; so too do running and wellness in the Runwell world.

Running was what I did, and it helped me to overcome my own challenges, so I just thought it would be a good way to raise money. It wasn't until I formed Run7on7, ultimately Runwell, that I truly understood how it could be a positive and healthy way to keep someone's focus on a healthy way to live in recovery. There are so many metaphors that can be used to relate running to addiction recovery. Running is absolutely just putting one foot in front of the other, staying the course, believing in yourself and training and sharing with others.

Tragically, Runwell – as part of Caron – is now needed more than ever. The United States is facing one of the largest epidemics of heroin addiction the country has ever seen, caused by the availability of prescription drugs and by doctors prescribing them without checking for addiction issues. History has shown us that alcohol and other drugs can be used safely by many, but those with a propensity towards addiction are playing Russian roulette.

As Linda says, the challenge is to understand that addiction is a brain disease. We must also learn to recognise the signs of someone on the brink – a huge challenge when addiction is something people still find so hard to discuss. They refuse to believe it could happen in their family. Either that, or addiction is dismissed as a moral failing: 'They took the first drink, pill, etc, and so it is their fault.'

Linda's response is to try to bring people together in a positive way. It's all about helping to break down the negative perceptions of those struggling with addiction. And again, that's where running and exercise more generally are crucial. These days, it isn't so difficult to get someone to think about the benefits of exercise within the addiction arena. In the early days, it was simply seen as another way to switch addictions. Research has moved on apace since then.

Treatment centres are now incorporating exercise into their programmes and adopting running as a way to engage their patients. Also because of the wonderful running communities and their acceptance of those dealing with addiction, we are able to use this platform to help break down the stigma and open up the dialogue for change and awareness.

And with that in mind, Linda can quite see why her own running has changed over the years. Initially she ran to escape. Now she runs, quite simply, to 'find the joy in running'. As she says, running has taken her on amazing journeys around the world, given her an understanding of different cultures and brought her countless friendships she cherishes.

Linda hit 65 in February 2018, but there are still plenty more challenges to come. The words *North Pole* have just passed her lips . . .
Runwell has certainly made its mark.

Seeing it become an instrument for so many people to begin their journey into recovery, to live healthy, fulfilling lives and to become the wonderful human beings they and their families always knew they would be is something that one cannot measure. I am just overwhelmed with gratitude that they took the necessary steps to begin – and that Runwell was able to help even in the smallest of ways.

And if you want a measure of Runwell's success, an insight into the possibilities we can realise when we all work together, look no further than Linda's stepdaughter. Katherine's is now a life transformed, a life reclaimed. After those three years lost to the streets of San Francisco, Katherine works in paediatric oncology and is a mum of two.

She is doing amazing and 15 years sober. We couldn't be more proud of her and her accomplishments.

James Buzzell

'Once you have seen dead people, you realise that death is real and that it is going to happen.'

James Buzzell went to hell and back when he went to war. His tragedy was that he brought the hell back with him.

James' parents and two brothers also served their country, but James insists it wasn't out of some kind of family tradition that he joined the Army. He joined quite simply because he was bored and burned out. At the time, James, who was born in Massachusetts in February 1978, was working as house manager in a residential home for abused and neglected children. The job was good, probably the most satisfying job he has ever done, a genuine feeling of making a difference. He lasted three-and-a-half years.

> *But in the end, it was burn out, emotionally and spiritually. You can only have a six- or eight-year-old child that you know and love tell you so many times that they 'fucking hate' you. It's like a cognitive dissonance. You know you love this child and you are doing everything you can for them, but they just cannot see that you are helping them.*

It was time for a new challenge. At the age of 26 in 2004, James secured unpaid leave and walked into a recruiting office. The Marine Corps office was closed; the Army one was open. It was as simple as that. James walked in and told the recruiter he wanted to serve in Iraq – not through any 'kill the terrorist' imperative, he stresses, but motivated by the thought that Iraq was where civilisation started. This was a culture and a place he wanted to experience first-hand. It was a complex country, which intrigued him. Joining the Army was a case of killing two birds with one stone. He would fight for his country, and he would be paid to go where he wanted to go: Iraq.

James underwent 14–16 weeks' training at Fort Benning in Georgia and then moved to Germany with the First Armoured Division at the beginning of March 2005. They deployed to Iraq in January 2006. On James' birthday in February, they moved from Al Asad Airbase to Hit, where they were based in a small school/residential building. Life, just as it had been from the moment they arrived, was scary.

It wasn't a sense of constant threat. It was constant threat. We got bombed, mortars or rockets, every day. When we went out of the wire on missions, there was always either IEDs [improvised explosive devices] or sniper fire or small-arms fire. Basically, we were mortared or rocketed every day.

The response, James recalls, was simply to 'gloss over it'. If you thought about it too much, you would drive yourself crazy, and so you didn't. James doesn't remember his life as pressure all the time. Maybe it was simply that he was part of a squad that was good at not looking scared, a highly capable bunch of people who were not afraid to pull the trigger when required. In retrospect, he says there were plenty of scary moments, but certainly not an overwhelming sense of fear. It was just the way life was.

It wasn't long, however, before James was injured. An IED blew up close by. James emerged with concussion and 'bumps and bruises'. He and his comrades were running night missions because they were told it was safer by night. The first driver in the convoy saw the IED and swerved to avoid it; the second one didn't and James was caught in the blast, just 10 metres (33 feet) behind him. In hindsight, this was the start of the trauma to come.

The way I understand trauma to the brain, like PTSD, is that it can be caused by both individual events and cumulative events. I would say it was cumulative with me. I would say it was that constant state of being near mortal injury. Once you have seen dead people, you realise that death is real and that it is going to happen. And when you see it daily, when you see death and terrible violence all the time, it changes the brain in the way it processes emotions and deals with stress and trauma and heightened emotions like love or hate.

Looking back, though, some incidents emerge as more significant than others. One was the death of his friend Michael Weidemann, killed by an IED in Hit. This was a turning point for James – a tragic end for a cherished comrade who loved the Army and wanted to make it his career. James' fondness for Michael made the grief all the more unbearable. Michael was a soldier who was always happy, always smiling, a practical joker who was, quite simply, a great guy. He never had a bad word to say about anything or anyone. If someone complained, Michael's response was always that things could be worse. They were in Iraq; people were trying to kill them every day. Michael's view was: 'Well, you could be in hospital missing your legs!'

This was the man the US Army lost on 31 October, 2006. It was to be years, however, before the full impact of his death hit James. The reaction was delayed, but it hit hard in the months that followed James' medical discharge in 2012. His ankle had been rebuilt, but hadn't 'healed up to snuff'; he'd also suffered a shoulder injury, a break that hadn't been spotted in the cut and thrust of war. Curiously, his PTSD rating was relatively low on discharge.

The first mistake was to move to South Carolina with his wife Amy. In terms of location and climate, it seemed a smart move, neither of them realising that they were cutting themselves off from a support network they would soon need. In the weeks that followed, it was only running that saved James as he descended into 'a mess about as hopeless and helpless as I could possibly have been in':

> *The Army and the VA (Veterans Affairs) were pumping me full of medication, way more medication than I needed. I don't remember a lot about it. I was on a ridiculous amount of pills – antidepressants, antipsychotics, sleeping pills. I was a zombie.*

Drinking had been part of the Army life, a way of coping, a 'Band-Aid to trauma', but the drinking had escalated. Life became a fog. It's a period from which James has few concrete memories. His early days after leaving the Army were a time of extreme isolation and almost complete withdrawal, punctuated by outbursts of rage.

> *If I did get angry, I would go to 11 instantly. I would yell and scream at a stranger in a grocery store for no reason at all except maybe 'Hey! I want*

that apple!' I don't know how often that happened. I was not often out of the house, but I was a liability to my family at least. Luckily, my wife is a saint. I tell her how much I love her every day, all day long.

But at the time, it was only running that kept him going.

Running is inevitably a huge part of Army life. You run six days a week and then run again on the Sunday. The running, as James saw it, was all part of being the 'best soldier' he could possibly be. It was constant, but during his transition to civilian life, with his injuries and with his medication, James was strongly advised against running – advice that accelerated his decline. He was told that he would damage himself further if he ran. In truth, he was damaging himself by not running.

Fortunately, James realised the need and started to run privately, rare moments of connection amid the deteriorating mess his life had become. As he says, he was running for his mental health and his physical well-being, with benefits he freely admits he struggles to express.

It was my escape. When I was alone in the woods on the trails, there was a sense of peace that you just can't put into words. Everything else drops away. The only way I can describe it would be to paraphrase Buddhist monks or whatever, or to talk about a priest who seeks transcendence. It would be like trying to describe sex to someone who has never had sex. It would be like trying to describe the ocean to someone who has never seen the ocean. You can't; you absolutely can't.

All you can do is revel in the moment and revel in its after-effects. For James, running came to represent a cleansing of the soul, a purifying of the being. It was a chance to self-reflect, as he says, a way to release pent-up anger and anxiety. If he could feel anger or anxiety coming on, he would go out for a run, and without a care for distance, be it one mile or 10, he would run until it went away. And the next day he would do it again.

It's the process of clearing any emotional or mental trauma with physical trauma, just connecting with what was happening. It was something that made sense to me and I knew it to be my truth.

James created his own running mantra: 'Run Tall. Run Strong. Run Straight'. *Run Tall* to make sure your spine is fully extended. *Run Strong* to make sure you are lifting your knees and driving with your hips. *Run Straight* to make sure that shoulder to hip, hip to knee, knee to toe is always straight-lined. It was a question of focusing on running technique and by doing so, silencing the demons.

As James recalls, running during the hardest period of his life focused and centred him. But crucially, his wife Amy recognised that things had to change: running was not enough. Running helped James just about hold everything together – a crucial first step in his recovery. But now he needed the second step. It came when they moved back to Massachusetts. Amy realised they absolutely had to have the support network they now knew was so lacking. And it was there that James checked into a VA hospital for a six-week residential PTSD/trauma programme – a mix of group therapy, meditation and one-to-one therapy, during which he made a vital breakthrough. At the outset, he was clear: he wanted to come off all medication, to strip everything back to see just what exactly he actually needed, if anything.

That was the fall of 2013. I have not taken any of those medications since.

James continued to run until 2015, increasing his mileage and getting back to shape, but since then, having done what he needed it to do, running has receded in his life. James' reconstructed ankle simply couldn't take it anymore. He is back now at the point where he can run again, and he may yet do so, but the need is no longer there. Essentially, running has done its job.

As he says, running proved the means to an end, not the end itself. But the point is that without running, that end would never have been in sight.

James is pleased to say that he considers himself 'much better now' – or at the very least 'much more consistently better' than he has been for a long time. It all comes down to the busyness of his life right now. His day-to-day challenge is successfully running a farm comprising pigs, chickens, vegetables and flower gardens. Also keeping him on his toes is being dad to Isabelle, born four months before his medical discharge in 2012.

At last he is finding peace. He knows where to look. His life is back on track.

Running brought me back from the brink. It taught me some valuable lessons. I know that I don't need to run now to achieve serenity and transcendence. Those are internal, and I reach them in other ways. But I have no doubt: running saved me. Life is good!

Anji Andrews

*'I remember seeing a solitary robin . . . and thinking
it was a sign my dad was watching.'*

Anji Andrews is – and always has been – a complete daddy's girl. Her
mum Meg always jokes that Anji is 99 per cent her father's DNA,
1 per cent hers. As Anji says, her dad simply 'got' her, and he 'got' her
running. Between them was an intuitive bond – and it was that bond
that got her through his final illness and the months which followed
his death.

It was typical of Ron that he never let his cancer get in the way of
Anji's sporting activities. In his final months, he continued to encourage
her to run, knowing it would be her strength against grief. Running
has remained a powerful connection between the two in the time since
his passing.

Anji finds comfort and motivation in all the similarities she shared
with her dad and also in the knowledge that he would approve of the
way she now encourages so many others to run – through her work for
Events of the North and its roster of races. Anji, who manages athlete
communications and social media for the company, finds strength in
her resemblance to her father.

> *I look like him, I think like him, and I am proud to say I see the world the
> same way he did. We rarely disagreed on anything. My dad was a brilliant
> businessman who was able to retire at 50 and enjoy an active lifestyle.
> Like me, he wasn't himself unless he was active. He walked miles with
> or without his dog Jimmy and later, Murphy. He cycled to work when he
> could, finding the ride home would help him get rid of the stresses of the
> day – something I understood when I took up running during my years as
> a primary school teacher.*

Ron continued to cycle on old railway paths and trails near his new home in Durham when he and Meg moved there in their retirement. Tragically, the retirement was not to last long. Ron developed severe back pain and was eventually diagnosed with prostate cancer a few weeks before Christmas 2013. Typically, he didn't tell Anji immediately. She finished first in the Middlesbrough Albert parkrun the day after his diagnosis and he didn't want to 'burst [her] bubble'. But that Christmas, they shared close, intense times, 'doing a lot of walking together, doing what we always did and generally putting the world to rights'. Time was suddenly precious.

Anji used to imagine her father dying while she was with him – and while she wasn't. She suffered crippling panic attacks. Living alone at the time following the break-up of her first marriage, she channelled as much stress as she could into her running: 'I seem to remember those first few months becoming very quick over 5k!'

Ron went through various types of treatment and had various good and bad spells, but sadly, his condition deteriorated at the beginning of 2016. He always spoke about fighting it and getting better, but Anji knew deep down they didn't have long. Even then, his concern was to encourage Anji. He knew she wanted to train for a duathlon one day. For her birthday in April 2016 he bought her her 'dream' bike. He had been unable to cycle for about a year by then; for Anji, it felt like he was handing her the baton. It was a symbolic gift. Anji has gone on to complete a duathlon since his death. The bike is now engraved with his name.

Even as the end approached, Ron remained acutely conscious that running was going to be his daughter's coping mechanism.

Anji recalls:

On his 65th birthday [7 June, 2016] I took him to his hospital appointment, where he was told there was nothing more they could do and they would be stopping treatment. I remember I had a mile race that night and he made me still go along, as he knew I would probably channel some of my impending grief into it. I won the race that night and dedicated my medal to him.

The expectation was that Ron had up to three months left to live. The end came within days. On the morning of 11 June, he died peacefully at home with Anji and Meg at his side. Having lost her dear friend Marcus exactly four months before, also to cancer, Anji was devastated, convinced she would never, ever truly feel happy again.

However, just as her father wished, running remained central to Anji's life – more important, in fact, than ever. Hand in hand with the running has gone a growing involvement in race organisation. As she says, both have been key ways of dealing with the mental health challenges that can so often accompany sudden bereavement. Running proved her prop in overcoming the loop of negative and harmful thoughts that followed.

> *To me, running is a natural act of escape. From my problems, from daily life, from mental challenges. I can head out for a run and think about anything or nothing and come back feeling like I have sorted something out in my mind. When my dad died, I suffered months of flashbacks, literally playing his final days and moments over and over in my head on a loop like a broken record. Running gave me a break even for 10 minutes, where I would think about which roads I had to cross, what pace I was doing, where I was going.*

It was the simplest of processes: running calmed anxieties and gave her something else to think about. The healing was underway.

> *The day before my dad's funeral we ran a massive promo event in Durham ahead of the Durham City Run with Daley Thompson, and I took a group of 50 runners out on a training run, allowing myself that much-needed hour to not think about laying my dad to rest. Some people thought it wasn't right of me to do that, but it was exactly the right thing to do. The selfishness of the act of running allowed me to put myself first just when I needed to.*

But it was about far more than just putting herself first. It was also about cherishing the connection she had with her dad. Running in places Ron loved became a foundation of Anji's life in the months following his death.

> *I miss my dad immeasurably, but running helps me to imagine he's alongside me on his bike, pushing me on whenever I need him. I ran*

in the immediate hours following his death and in the hours before his funeral, and in my mind it's what he would have expected. My dad wasn't a runner, but he just got it.

As a walker and cyclist, Ron always knew the good places to go. He would suggest places Anji could run: the coastline of South Shields where she grew up; the quayside streets of Newcastle he walked through on his way to Newcastle United games; the trails and old railway paths of Durham, where he retired. When Anji started taking her running seriously in 2011, it was her dad who bought her first Garmin GPS watch – because she had suggested he get one for his bike.

On a few occasions, I would go to Durham at the crack of dawn and run while my dad cycled alongside, and I often revisit those times in my mind, regretting that we didn't do it more. I think because he was active, because he pushed his body and because he loved the outdoors, he understood why I loved running so much and why it became so important in my life. On visits to my mum now, I always run the same route where he walked his dog Murphy right up until the last few months when he became too poorly. I like to think in some way he is still there with me, enjoying the beautiful views, peace and fresh air.

Ron was always hugely proud of Anji's achievements, and he always told her so. He understood and respected the work she put into training, and he loved the fact that she competed in races he knew, including the Great North Run and the Blaydon Race. He recognised the need to run – and he recognised that the need grows all the stronger when times are tough.

On the day before my dad died, I left work early after a phone call from my mum, saying he was deteriorating. As ridiculous as it may sound to some people, I packed my trainers and parkrun barcode, thinking I would get up and do Durham parkrun the following day to break up a few hours of the emotional stress. As it happened, my dad died that morning at 4.45 a.m., so I didn't make it to parkrun. Instead, I waited until my brother Lee arrived and went out to do my own 5k up on the trails where we used to walk. I remember getting halfway along, stopping, sitting on the ground in the rain and crying before just turning round and running back.

Back home, Anji sensed that one of the nurses, checking in with her mum, thought running was a bizarre thing to do just three hours after her father's body had been removed. Anji has no doubt it was absolutely the right thing to do – a vital outlet and one she turned to again on the day of the funeral, this time with her friend Paul, who is now her husband. Just a few hours before laying Ron to rest, Paul and Anji ran the 5 miles (8 kilometres) to Jarrow and back, where her dad had grown up. Instead of chatting as usual as they ran, neither said a word.

Only once did the running not work. Four days after Ron's death, Anji was determined to take part in the Newburn River Run. However, emotional stress, lack of sleep and the inability to eat properly led to awful stomach cramps in the middle of the 7-mile (11-kilometre) race. In tears, she walked most of the final 2 miles (3 kilometres).

The last thing my dad had said to me as he was dying was: 'Never give up, and I won't either', and I had that going round and round in my head. Determined not to have Newburn as a horrible memory, I went back a week later and completed the run in my club vest, where amazingly, they had left the finish line painted on the ground. I remember seeing a solitary robin sitting on the trail despite it being the middle of June, and thinking it was a sign my dad was watching, proud I had gone back and finished it properly.

It's at times like these that she needs her dad the most. The anniversaries are sad and important, but as she says, the need to speak to him is strongest when it comes to 'the minor achievements that would have meant the world to him'.

Anji, who lives in Boldon, Tyne and Wear, came to running when the gym she was using closed unexpectedly. Her first Great North Run, at the age of 30 in 2011, was the game changer. Anji has long suffered from both anxiety and depression. The Great North Run was the happiest day of her life. She labelled it her biggest achievement ever.

At times, the 'black mist' will make it hard to get out of bed. On what she terms the *Really Bad Days*, Anji finds it hard to function. She regularly suffers panic attacks, often for no particular reason.

However, her spells of depression have generally been triggered by an event – her dad's cancer diagnosis in 2013, and his death in 2016 in particular.

And this is where the running kicks in for Anji.

I have used running as my drug of choice since around 2012. I rarely run with my phone, so it gives me the escape from everything that normally causes me stress in my everyday life. Working in social media you are, and have to be, always contactable and there are often no regular hours. Running even a few miles gives me the chance to completely think about nothing or everything!

Anji doubts whether anxiety or depression can ever really be cured, but she feels she made huge strides in terms of coping in the months after her father's death. She had a long spell of counselling at the end of 2016, following the loss of her dad, her friend Marcus and her job, all within six months. Her therapist agreed that running is her best outlet and better than any medication she could suggest.

I always joke with people that running is the only thing I have actually been good at, so I could never give it up! Running has given me confidence, my husband, my job and quite often my escape. It has taken me to places and introduced me to people I would never have known. I am not me if I don't run and often when I am injured, I am not myself at all.

The move into coaching and race organisation has been as inevitable as it has been natural. After leaving her job as a primary school teacher in 2013, Anji often volunteered at running events. She became someone people recognised. One of those people was Allison Curbishley, who offered her the job of managing social media for the Sunderland City Run, the Worcester City Run, the Durham City Run and the Kielder Marathon. She now manages athlete communications for all the events run by Allison and Steve Cram through their company, Events of the North.

Alongside the job, Anji also has her own coaching business: Team Enigma Running. The buzz is in seeing people grow in confidence, work hard, believe in themselves and achieve their goals. She is also run director at Riverside parkrun in Chester-le-Street, where she and Paul met. Running brought them together. Anji is now also his coach.

However much the grief endures, life is most certainly going in the right direction now. Anji married Paul in 2017. She thinks back to her first marathon in 2014. The training taught her to dig deeper and work harder than she had ever done before. Just as importantly, Anji ran it with Paul after just a few months together as a couple – a great test of future compatibility, she laughs.

> *I honestly knew the shared experience of training and running the marathon together would mean we would end up together forever because he had seen me at my absolute worst!*

Emma Malcolm

*'[Running] clears my mind and enables me to think
about all the tough stuff.'*

For Britain's wartime prime minister Winston Churchill, depression
was the black dog – not a phrase he coined, but certainly a phrase he
popularised. As she contemplates her own long fight against mental
illness, Em Malcolm can safely say she knows exactly what he meant
by it – and just how many different black dogs there are out there, so
many of them ready to bite.

As Em says, on a good day, you will find yourself with a nice, neat
dog on a lead; a black dog that is small, obedient and completely under
control. On a bad day, it will be massive, sprawling, sitting on your chest,
stifling you, crushing you, robbing you of the ability to feel, to think or
even to breathe, disengaging you from everything as it suffocates you
under its sheer weight of blackness.

However, for the past few years Em has had a vital weapon in her
armoury as she attempts to chase that dog away: the simple process
of putting one foot in front of the other and moving forwards, as fast
or as slowly as she wants. Em knows that running will never be the
complete answer; sometimes the black dog will even overtake. But at
its most effective, she knows that running will give her the space to
process all that's happening in her mind. She counts it as no coincidence
whatsoever that since she's started running, she has found it much,
much easier to tell her story – a crucial, if draining, step towards the
goal of greater mental stability.

Em, who worked for the London-based charity Rethink Mental
Illness from September 2015 to February 2018, was first diagnosed
with depression after a breakdown at the age of 22. However, the

diagnosis was immediately backdated 10 years – which came as little surprise to Em.

When she was 13, the family moved from Buckinghamshire to Kent, from a school where she knew everyone to a school where she instantly stood out and where she was soon bullied. Once it became known that she was the child of adoptive parents, she was taunted with: 'Your mother didn't want you'. She was also a musician and carried a big instrument case, the focus for yet more jeers. Punched and kicked and abused, she took to skipping school – not that anybody noticed or seemed to care.

Em hoped to salvage things by going to university. It didn't work. She had a mini breakdown, returned home, retook A-levels and tried again elsewhere. But back home for Christmas during her second year and now self-harming, she chose Christmas Day to take an overdose, convinced that the world would be better off without her.

Em freely – and now happily – admits she hadn't a clue what she was doing. She genuinely didn't want to be alive, but she didn't take enough tablets to end it all. Instead, she was very sick – and 'crawled' to her parents four days later. A kindly GP was reluctant to prescribe antidepressants or hospitalise her. Instead, half an hour later, Betty, a counsellor, turned up on Em's doorstep.

She was amazing. She must have been in her 60s. She had grey hair up in a bun, and literally she just gave me a big hug. I will never forget that.

However, Em's mental health remained problematic for the next 10 years, with a difficult marriage among the challenges. But then the London Marathon took a hand. Working for a number of charities, she seemed to find herself cheering on runners at the event every April. Eventually, in 2011, she decided she would give it a go herself – a moment that coincided with getting divorced and turning 40.

Em hadn't run for 20 years but signed up for the 2012 London Marathon and launched herself into training. Without anyone around to tell her what to do, she read *The Non-Runner's Marathon Trainer*. She soon ran into injury – which is where grim determination took over. With £5500 worth of sponsorship riding on her completion, she gritted her teeth, got on with it, ran-walked and then walked to finish in

6 hours, 40 minutes – delighted to get to the end before they reopened the roads.

Along the way, she was rewarded by friends and supporters waiting at the 23-mile marker, hugely important encouragement along a route that seemed never-ending. None of them was prepared to leave until they had seen her go by. Even so, the day ended in a degree of indignity. She collapsed as she went for her train and had to be helped by a blind runner and his guide. Hardly the marathon of her dreams, but that hardly mattered. It was still a marathon, and crucially, it offered up possibilities. Em sensed something was opening inside her head. On the back of her London experience, running started to emerge as the perfect platform for those endless thoughts that don't go away.

I never switch off. I am always on . . . or I am asleep. Or I am awake with insomnia. But it was odd. In a really calm way, when I am running, I am thinking about stuff that has happened; thinking about the day. Somebody told me to tune your breath to your feet – in for two steps, out for two steps. And that clears my mind and enables me to think about all the tough stuff.

Just as importantly, running is about being outdoors – and in her own space. As she started to run more, Em, who lives near Fleet in Hampshire, started to realise that she ran for herself: not for a time, not for other people and not even with other people but solely for herself. The next step was to embrace the best, the safest and most supported way in which to do that: the great worldwide phenomenon known as parkrun. Em has become a self-confessed parkrun evangelist.

Sometimes the depression will take hold. There will be a day when she cannot get out of bed. A day when she cannot do anything other than stare at the wall. A day when nothing can engage, not even running. But the next Saturday, the parkrun family will be there, unquestioning, unjudging. They won't mind what's been happening in her life. They won't quiz you, and they won't criticise you. But they will certainly welcome you.

It's the most amazing thing. You register for free, print off your unique barcode and you can run any parkrun, anywhere in the world. It's not a race, so it doesn't matter how fast or, in my case, how slow you are. The only person you are running against is yourself. Not only that, but it's also a community. On a Saturday morning, I spend as much time in the café chatting to my parkrun family and sorting barcodes as it takes me to do the run (around 35 minutes). It's not going too far to say that it has changed my life. I think parkrun is so inclusive. I joined a running club for a year, and I hated it. I felt like I was rubbish. Everyone else is lapping you, and you feel like you are crap. But no one will make you feel crap at a parkrun. You meet your people. When my dad passed away, I said to the vicar the parkrun is my religion. I do it every Saturday. It is non-judgemental. They don't care if you didn't get out of bed the day before. They are just happy to see you – and to see you taking part.

Em admits she will never trust the future. She doesn't believe she can or ever will. As she says, she has been through far too many things that have been far too difficult, but she knows it would be a much more uncertain future still without the stability that parkrunning gives her.

She also found fulfilment through her work for Rethink Mental Illness, a charity that believes a better life is possible for the millions of people affected by mental illness. For 40 years through its services, groups and campaigns, Rethink Mental Illness has brought people together to support each other. Em is thrilled to support the charity in turn.

She has even offered herself as a case study, which means reliving her struggles, an exhausting business. But her belief in the charity and her desire to help others by sharing her story are underpinned by the strength and by the increased confidence that parkrunning gives her.

Running gives me so many things, from space to think and process what is going on in my life to a whole new group of friends. It's what keeps me on the straight and narrow and keeps me balanced.

Lisa Hallett

'I ran two of the ugliest miles ever, and it was the first time I accepted that John was not coming home.'

There seemed something different when US Army Captain John L. Hallett III said goodbye to his two boys for the last time in the summer of 2009. His mother Wendy believes that he sensed he wouldn't be seeing them again. His wife Lisa isn't so sure.

Thirty-year-old John was being deployed the next day to Afghanistan with 5th Brigade, 2nd Infantry Division, Stryker Brigade Combat Team in support of Operation Enduring Freedom. Lisa recalls vividly the night before he left. Their sons, Jackson and Bryce were aged three and one. Their daughter Heidi was just a few weeks away from being born.

> *It was the only time I ever saw John cry. He was holding his boys and he was reading them a story and he said: 'You know I love you so much.' That was the hardest part. John had a job to do and he did it well. But I don't think it ever gets easier to say goodbye to your children, saying: 'I will see you in a year.' Saying goodbye to the children for a year became a lifetime. But I don't think he thought it was forever. But it must have seemed like a year of forever. When he saw them again, Bryce would have doubled his lifetime and Jackson would have lived a third more. John found so much joy in his boys. It was just heartrending to see.*

John left on 11 July. Three weeks later, on 2 August, Heidi was born. On 5 August, Lisa and John spoke for the last time on the phone. Lisa remembers she was wrapped up in the details of refinancing their home, a process John talked her through. As she recalls, it was the most mundane of conversations. She was feeding Heidi as they spoke. Suddenly John remarked that he had never heard Heidi cry.

> *And I just brushed him off. I just said: 'You have got a whole lifetime for that!'*

Tragically, just weeks later, Lisa was called aside at the Fort Lewis military base (since renamed Joint Base Lewis-McChord) in Washington state, where they lived. She was taken to a room where a couple of military men were waiting. Lisa was thinking that John needed to talk to her – 'a stupid thought that my warrior husband needed to speak to his wife!' – or that he had been injured, that he had lost his legs. But she kept telling herself that everything would be alright. Nothing was.

> *They have a script that they read to say that the Secretary of Defense regrets to inform you that your husband Captain John Hallett is believed to have perished.*

Lisa clung to the word *believed* – a word soft enough, she says, to give you hope. In reality, there was no hope at all. No possible doubt. John was dead, one of four soldiers in his unit killed on 25 August while returning from a goodwill mission in Southern Afghanistan.

> *I just sat and I just looked at these pictures of John, and your life flashes forward and it is just absolute numbness and disbelief and despair all at once. And I realised this is forever. This hard is forever.*

John and Lisa had grown up together in California. Lisa was five and John was seven when they met at school, a time when they didn't realise that there was a world outside their school walls. It was a small community, their lives interacted, their families kept meeting. John and Lisa progressed to different high schools, but they attended the same church and the same youth group. Each spring the youth group sent youngsters on a ministry to Mexico to help build homes. On one such ministry, John and Lisa worked together. At the end of the day, at the age of 13 or 14, Lisa announced: 'I am going to marry that John Hallett and have his red-headed babies!'

In reality, it was his friends she dated, and their lives diverged, with John going to the United States Military Academy at West Point. However, when he was going to a cousin's wedding in Santa Barbara, where Lisa was at college, he asked Lisa to go with him. At the end of the day, he invited her on a trip to Lake Tahoe the following weekend. Lisa hesitated, worrying about the 'gas money'. After he'd left, she opened the fridge – and there was the gas money sat waiting, placed there by John.

The relationship blossomed, but military life intervened. They planned to marry in 2004 but had to bring the service forward to 27 December, 2003 when John was deployed to Iraq. They had three weeks together before he left for 14 months. As Lisa says: 'It was: *Welcome to military life!*' But even then, there was something romantic about it.

> *You are sending your husband to war. It was still fairly early in the conflict, and we didn't know what to expect. The risk is there. It is part of military service. But it felt fairly abstract. It wasn't your risk. It was someone else's risk.*

In the background, though, Lisa was already using running as a way to cope. Whenever John endured hardship, Lisa ran a race. When John was at Ranger School, a rigorous combat leadership course oriented towards small-unit tactics, Lisa trained for a marathon. The challenge for John was an arduous one. Lisa's response was that if John was enduring hardship, then so too would she. It was a way of staying close to the man with whom she shared a perfect marriage.

> *People will spend a lifetime looking for the love that we had, and we had it all. John was a good person. He would always choose the right over the easy wrong. It was the instinct in his life. And he always worked hard. He always went the extra mile, and it wasn't just lip service. Before he went to Afghanistan, he had this stack of 14 books next to the bed, books about Afghanistan. He didn't want to understand Afghanistan just from a soldier's perspective, he wanted to understand its culture. He wanted the larger picture. He needed to know.*

Tragically, he did not return from Afghanistan alive. Everything changed on that shattering day in late August 2009. For Lisa, it was then that the running kicked in for real. As she says, the first thing she did, as soon as she could, two days after John's death, was lace up her sneakers.

I just needed to feel. I just needed to get out. And I needed control. And running is all of those things. I hadn't been cleared to run by the doctor. I was the mother of a three-week-old baby. But I just needed to run. It felt very primal. It felt very raw, but I needed it.

She met up with a friend, Carrie Parada, and while Carrie's husband Steve looked after the children, off they went. But even the weather seemed cruel. As Lisa says, remember this is the Seattle area of Washington. It rains. And it rains and it rains and it rains.

But it was just the most beautiful late-summer day. The sun was shining so gloriously. I remember tying my shoes under the glare of the sun. And I remember thinking: How dare you! How dare you shine so beautifully and bright when my world feels so dark! And then I ran two of the ugliest miles ever known to man, and it was the first time I accepted that John was not coming home.

Lisa believes it was the physical reality of running that helped her realise the truth.

You have got the wind blowing on your face, the wind in your hair. Before, it wasn't real enough. It was too abstract. John wasn't here, and then one day he is killed, and then he still isn't here. The idea of losing a loved one that you have not seen for weeks is so hard to understand. You just hope that it was a mistake.

And this is where running really did its work – the start of the process of acceptance, one that continued with the return of John's body from Afghanistan. The intangible was becoming ever more tangible. Inevitably, it wasn't a process the boys could understand. On the contrary, Lisa's tears scared them. When Jackson told her so, it was another landmark moment in Lisa's journey.

I needed that reminder that my children had lost a parent to war and it was not fair on them to lose both their parents. They can't lose John and then lose me to sorrow. And so I started to create structures in our lives that could give them as normal a childhood as possible. The flipside, though, was: Where was I going to put my grief? I was a mom of three children under three, I had lost my husband. What was I going to do?

The answer again was running.

Running was the place where I could unfold all those emotions. It was the judgement-free zone, the place where I could be snotty and teary. Grief isn't what you see on the television. Grief is ugly. Grief is drool and snot. It is not a carefully placed tear, it is choking back your tears. It is choking back the drool. Grief is awful.

In her daily life, Lisa felt she had to hold it all back. She had to put on an appearance. She had to be guarded in how she grieved. But her grief desperately needed an outlet, and running provided it. Simple as that.

I needed to run in order to grieve. When I run, there is no one to see me. I could feel what I needed to feel. I could be raw, and I could escape. I had three children. I was changing two sets of diapers. I was trying to do this Mommy routine and put them all to bed. But it is so hard to do all that when your head is whirring. But I needed to get away from that into this space where John is not coming home, a space where I could think: What am I going to do, what does this mean for our family, what is life after death, how are we going to get through? Running gave me that.

The sheer busyness of everyday life could easily have been a mask to sadness, a blur, but Lisa recognised that if she was ever going to experience again the joy of life, she needed to connect with its lowest lows. Again, it was running that gave her the space to do so.

Running is such a beautiful gift. I hurt in ways I had never hurt before. I felt fear and loneliness and loss. But it also gave me the place to move forward, the way to keep going.

It also gave her the means to take a wider perspective. With her friend Erin O'Connor, she founded *wear blue: run to remember*. This non-profit running community, now national, honours the service and sacrifice of the American military. Lisa is the organisation's chief executive officer.

The organisation emerged organically. A need was recognised and met. Erin and Lisa had long been runners – their way, as Lisa says, of dealing with the challenges of military life. They ran together and they enjoyed the benefits of running. The next step was to bring others together to share those benefits, and so, during the deployment, a small group of 5-2 wives (those from 5th Brigade, 2nd Infantry Division) and battalion support staff started to meet weekly to run.

The first time they did so, dressed in their spouses' 'tacky' blue PT shirts, they looked at each other slightly awkwardly and then set off. They did it again the following week, but this time before setting out, they read out the names of their lost loved ones. And so it continued. Some weeks there were just two of them there; other weeks there were 32, but they felt solidarity, and through that solidarity, they started to focus on the Rock 'n' Roll Seattle Marathon and Half Marathon as a common goal.

We had common experiences of pain and grief, but we had a lifeline in the chaos. And running continues to have that power – because of its tangibility. You can't control what is happening overseas, and sometimes words don't seem enough when you are thinking about sacrifice and service. But in running, you don't have to have words.

At the start of the Seattle race, the names of the fallen servicemen were called out. There were 35 women running. A spectator spontaneously shook each and every one of them by the hand. At mile five, 40 flags lined the course, one for each of the soldiers killed that year so far. It was a day of remarkable emotion, and one that Lisa and Erin instinctively knew they had to harness. When they ran again the week after the marathon, their discussion centred on building on the commemoration they had created.

I needed John's death to have meaning and to translate that meaning into my own life. And in doing wear blue, we have been able to provide something tangible.

And so *wear blue: run to remember* evolved, an organisation with the tagline 'For the fallen. For the fighting. For the families'. Today, they run to honour all military members killed in combat. *wear blue* is now recognised as a powerful network of active duty and retired service members, military families, Wounded Warriors, Gold Star families and community members.

Every week, *wear blue: run to remember* athletes meet to honour the fallen and train for endurance events. At the start of their runs, it has become tradition to call out in a circle of remembrance the name of each military member killed on that weekend over the years of war. Then, *wear blue* runners call out the names of those for whom they run personally – their husbands, wives, parents, siblings, battle buddies, neighbours and/or friends.

At official *wear blue: run to remember* events, American flags line the racecourse to honour the fallen, a tribute called the *wear blue Mile;* each flag is hand held, making it a living memorial. Placed in front of these flags are large posters with photographs of the fallen. As Lisa says, the *wear blue Mile* humanises the ultimate sacrifice made by American heroes.

> wear blue *creates the space for families to connect without words and to run. Running is a shared experience. It is healthy. There are so many ways to cope after a difficult experience, but running is something that all levels can do. It doesn't matter if you are running or walking or sprinting, you are going forward.*

John used to long for Lisa to attend military wives' meetings. What would he make of it all now? What would he have said?

> *With John, it wasn't so much about words. John just had the best grin. It wasn't a smile, it was a grin. That's the only word for it. And I know he would be grinning. And I know he would be grateful that I am supporting the soldiers and the families that he cared about so personally.*

Serena Wooldridge

*'Through running there was light and hope at
the end of the tunnel.'*

Serena Wooldridge was a mum of two young boys when she was
diagnosed with breast cancer in October 2006 at the age of 35 – an
aggressive grade 2 carcinoma. Chemo and radiotherapy followed in
2007. She lost her hair, and she lost her strength. She was terrified she
wouldn't see Robert and Ethan grow up. Running got her through.
It gave her a place where she could sob her heart out.

Serena lives in Patterson Lakes, in outer south-east Melbourne,
Australia, and began running in 1999, after the birth of her older son
Robert. She joined a gym and every morning watched another mother
running fast on the treadmill. Serena remembers that the other mother
made it look so easy and so graceful, and so Serena took the plunge,
building up her stamina 10 minutes at a time, longing for the extra
10 minutes to stop, but always adding more.

> *It was still hard, but I loved getting all sweaty and loved the sense of
> achievement that came afterwards. I felt fabulous and ready to take on
> anything throughout the day.*

Serena began to take it more seriously and started seeing a personal
trainer/running coach. In 2005 they started to train for her first 10k.
Serena recalls she loved being pushed to her max. It paid off. She
finished the 10k with an average speed below 4:30min/km. It was a
proud moment – and the moment she became addicted to racing.

Serena's trainer Nicola Childs, now her best friend, told her that
Serena would one day do a marathon. Serena just laughed and said:
'No way!' A 10k was already hard enough.

But then life intervened in the cruellest way, bringing the cancer diagnosis. Running suddenly offered something very different: a chance to process just what exactly was happening to her. The point was that she couldn't simply stop. She had to find a way to carry on, and that's what running gave her.

I was a mum of two young boys at the time when I was going through treatment – a four-year-old and a seven-year-old. I didn't have time to just feel sorry for myself and lie in bed all day. So I would drop the boys at school and then I was fortunate that I didn't have to work. We had our own business, so as long as I did the books from home, I had plenty of time in the mornings to go running. I would just lace up my shoes and head out the door and try not to think about how sick I felt. It became a good distraction.

During the treatment that followed, the doctors said Serena would be lucky to walk, let alone run. Given she was so young, they were hitting her with some hard treatment. The treatment made the running all the more important.

Sometimes I felt so ill I would have to stop by the side of the path or road and dry retch. Sometimes I would sob so loudly, but I didn't care. I had my headphones on. Sometimes I had to jump into a bush to go to the toilet as I had constant diarrhoea. I must have looked like a madwoman running with a bald head and a bandana on. But once you have gone through this sickness, the tests, the probing, it makes you stronger. You don't care what people think. The only thing that mattered to me was how my boys were thinking and feeling. It was my boys and running that got me through. Wanting to run away from the cancer, run away from my problems, the not knowing, I just wanted to run to exhaust myself to sleep so I wouldn't stay up at night sobbing in the wee hours once I knew all my family were asleep and snoring.

Serena recognised the importance of listening to her heart and staying positive. Running helped get her through the sickness and the therapy.

Running became my sanity and calmed my mind from the demons. After my treatment I knew I wanted to do everything, and especially a marathon

and more. I knew, running a marathon, I could look those demons in the
face and tell them not to mess with this bunny!

Running a marathon was nothing compared to the 'ultra' of
chemotherapy and radiotherapy, but it was a great way to set goals –
for Serena a key way of going forward. As she says, she's the kind of
person who hates not having a goal. Not having a goal means becoming
stagnant. Even going backwards. For Serena, life is about making a
decision and seeing it through.

She confesses that the whole experience has made her less patient
than she was before, particularly when it comes to tolerating 'some
people and some issues'. But impatience is a great driver to running,
and she turned it to her advantage – the best approach, she believes
to hardship. Cancer was a grim reminder that life is too short. Serena's
response was a resolve to run it hard, smile, laugh and enjoy.

One year later, in 2008, Serena was back to running 10k races. She
also did her first half-marathon in Bathurst in 1 hour, 44 minutes, which
proved a spur to her marathon ambitions – realised when she completed
Melbourne in 3 hours, 33 minutes. Three years later, Serena completed
South Africa's Comrades Marathon, an annual ultra between Durban
and Pietermaritzburg. Serena completed the Comrades 'uphill' run
(when the race starts in Durban rather than Pietermaritzburg) – just
under 87 kilometres (54 miles) in 8 hours, 29 minutes.

By now, Serena was starting to look at an even bigger picture. The
goals just kept on growing. Her aim became to run 50 marathons before
the age of 50, an aim she realised in December 2017 with years to spare:
she was just 46. Now, the aim is to keep going towards 100 marathons, a
figure she sees as an absolute minimum. As she says, there is so much to
do and see and experience. With her, everywhere she runs, will always
go gratitude for the help running gave her when she needed it most.

Running just simply made me feel better, and when I wasn't running –
or should I say, back then, plodding – I felt depressed. It made me feel
stronger, a warrior. Even when the doctors said I would be lucky enough to
walk, let alone run, because of the heavy treatment they were hitting me
with, it made me more determined to say: 'I can do this! I will show them!'
It's what you truly believe in your heart and mind that you can achieve.

Of course, we must listen to doctors, but Serena believes we shouldn't ever let them or anyone else take command.

Running became my sanity, where I talked to the universe, to God, to my ancestors, and racing is what I did for all of those people who couldn't run and who are not here today and didn't make it.

Running helped clear Serena's head. It helped her think. It freed her to come up with ideas, and still does so to this day. Running gives Serena her best ideas and thoughts and helps set her goals in life.

Through running, there was light and hope at the end of the tunnel. When you're going through something like chemo, you do lose hope. You have a lot of bad thoughts. Will I make it and what happens when treatment finishes? How does one just slot back into normal life? You live each doctor check-up every six months like a noose around your neck, wondering what the result will be, and you have to live with this for the rest of your life. Yet it has become easier over the years. I suppose reaching a 10-year anniversary makes it feel like so long ago.

Helping Serena was the fact that she saw a very direct relationship between running and recovery.

Running was my healing and recovery. To see my times and distances become faster and longer meant I was getting better, stronger and fitter. It was my time for me, my time away from the hospitals, the doctors, time away from the family, time for me to go outdoors and soak up all the smells and sounds from the universe.

Inevitably, the question she kept asking herself was: 'Why did this happen to me?' She was young, healthy and fit, with no family history of breast cancer. The answers started to come more easily once the drugs began to wear off. She realised she needed to change her life, to stop being the kind of person who says yes to everyone and everything. She realised she also needed to nurture herself.

Running gave her that opportunity. But with the passage of time, the running has changed as well. After 10 years of running marathons, Serena has lost the adrenaline rush of trying always to beat her PB [personal best], as much as she would love to break sub three hours. She came close in 2015 with 3 hours, 1 minute. But it is not just about the times any more.

> *I enjoy life and the freedom of now having conquered breast cancer and I enjoy being an advocate to help so many thousands of women go through this horrible ordeal, that we can change our life and turn it around with true friends and family and that anything is possible. Never, ever lose hope!*

Running means something different to Serena now that she is in such a better place. It took 10 years to feel more relaxed about racing, to learn not to be so hard on herself if she misses a day or a couple of days of running.

> *Years ago, my life revolved around my running. People knew I always had to run first thing in the morning. Now it doesn't matter if I want to sleep in or go for breakfast. Now I'm not so hard on myself and I don't make running a priority, but it is still a big part of my life. I was continually looking for a PB. The adrenaline would surge through my veins and body the night before a race, and I would be hard on myself if my times were not always improving, if I wasn't getting faster. I was competitive. I strove to win. Finding the balance to compete and enjoy is the next level in between marathon 50 and 100.*

The worry will always be there when something doesn't feel right with her body. In that respect, as she says, she will always feel like she is living with a death sentence over her head, but it becomes easier. The light at the end of the tunnel becomes brighter each year.

Post-diagnosis, post-treatment, Serena feels she has become a different person. Sickness, treatment and recovery have made her want to be a person who makes a difference. Life is about breaking the boundaries, believing in yourself, being positive and realising you can do anything you want to do. With the realisation that life is short comes an appreciation of every day – and the knowledge that if you love, smile and laugh, the world will do so with you.

> *You become more daring, more assertive, you know what you want and you go after it and you become determined that nothing will get in your way to stop it – which could be a good or bad thing, I suppose! Your mind*

becomes very inquisitive, but maybe you can overthink things. Running brings peace to my mind and somehow puts everything into perspective and the answers do come. You just have to be patient, which is definitely not my forte, but I'm trying!

Serena's marathons have included – and will continue to include – big-city runs, national and international races and small scenic country races, as well as runs where time doesn't count at all. Spectacular ones at humidity and altitude are also part of the plan. It's all Serena's way of saying an almighty 'Not yet!' to death. As she says, we are all scared of death. Her point is that she has still got so much that she wants to do, to achieve, to conquer and to see. She is determined not to die alone. She is equally determined to leave a legacy.

There were days during darker times when she thought about suicide, but those were few and far between – and that's precisely the reason Serena now wants to help others who have been through a similar experience. She wants to give back and to give hope. Serena is planning to write a book detailing her story. The hope is to pass on the strength that she has gained in the years since cancer threatened to shatter absolutely everything.

I feel stronger from the experience and from the relentless hours of long training runs and ultramarathons which have made me more able to look death in the face and say: 'Take me on if you dare!' But if ever I die, maybe it would be nice to go out while doing what I love most, and that is on a run!

Bryn Phillips

'I remember thinking we are not going to survive.'

The cabin crew had served teas and coffees. They had cleared away the evening meal and they were just about to dim the lights. Leaving RAF Brize Norton behind them as they flew out to Afghanistan in February 2014, 140–160 service personnel were just about to settle down for the night.

Everything seemed perfectly normal. And then suddenly, absolutely nothing was.

One moment, everyone was at their most relaxed; the next, the Voyager aircraft was nosediving towards disaster, the plane plummeting 4400 feet in just seconds from 33,000 feet over the Black Sea in Turkey. One moment, passengers were settling down to sleep. The next, they were thrown weightless from their seats, smashing into the cabin ceiling, convinced they were going to die.

As Petty Officer Bryn Phillips recalls, first there was turbulence. Then there was a strange sensation of weightlessness in his stomach. Then there was terror as they hurtled towards seemingly certain catastrophe.

The next thing you knew, there were people in front of you and behind you, all hitting the ceiling, with all their kit and their laptops all flying around and hitting the cabin. We were probably at about a 35- to 45-degree nosedive.

According to subsequent reports, the incident lasted 29 seconds; to those involved, it seemed an eternity. Bryn was convinced he was going to die.

I remember thinking we are not going to survive. And I was wondering whereabouts we were and where we were going to impact. There was a lot of screaming and quite a lot of shouting going on. People didn't know what was going to happen. There were people trying to grab on to things and trying to strap themselves in. There were people trying to cover their faces and trying to double up to brace themselves.

Fortunately, the plane's pilot and co-pilot managed to retrieve control of the plane, and Bryn felt fine once the plane had completed its emergency landing in Turkey. An aircraft engineer himself, Bryn had worked with black boxes day in, day out; he knew what could go wrong; and initially it seemed that his knowledge – and the accompanying pragmatism – would help him process the incident. Some kind of mechanical failure; as simple as that. These things happened. It had been horrific, but at least they were alive – and that was all that mattered.

Up to 48 personnel were left unfit for duty, and the military fleet of six Voyager aircraft was grounded for 13 days while the cause of the nosedive was investigated. Service personnel were left stranded in Afghanistan while they waited for the aircraft to be brought back into service. As their flight resumed, Bryn assumed that a fault had been fixed, and he was fine with that. There were no signposts at all that he was lapsing into post-traumatic stress disorder (PTSD).

The turning point came with the release of an interim report, which changed everything as far as Bryn was concerned. It pointed to massive human error. A court martial was later to hear that the pilot had been 'practising long-exposure photography' and had accidentally jammed the flight controls with his camera. When he moved his seat forward, the camera wedged between his armrest and the side stick, a joystick used to control the plane. He jammed it forward, disengaging the autopilot and causing the plane to nosedive.

In March 2017, the court dismissed the pilot from the RAF and handed him a four-month suspended prison sentence. Bryn doesn't know his name; he has never wanted to find out.

In the immediate aftermath of the initial damning report, Bryn's own concerns were much closer to home. Suddenly, an apparent accident had become a situation impossible to process. The fact that someone 'in such a high position of control and trust' had acted in this way changed everything, and Bryn soon found himself lapsing into flashbacks, sweats and palpitations at the mere thought of aircraft. He was in Afghanistan, he was doing his job, and he simply carried on, but he knew his mental condition was deteriorating.

> *I made a couple of errors in my own work, but fortunately we have the training that if something is wrong with us, we hold our hands up and say we need help. It wasn't easy to do. It is never easy to admit that you have made errors, and it is harder especially as a male to admit that you are not feeling great, especially when it comes down to mental health. I think the majority of men have that bravado. I think it is inbuilt in our DNA from caveman times! We need to be the alpha male all the time and to think that we can cope with anything.*

Bryn realised he wasn't coping at all. Far from it. From afar, his wife Natalie could see it too and urged him to get help. Bryn's response was: 'I will, I will, I will', but working 12-hour shifts made it hard to break out of the rolling cycle. Finally, when he knew he was making 'big errors of judgement' in his work, Bryn bit the bullet – and found himself in the right place to do it. The care and the treatment he received were second to none. 'Our set-up is absolutely fantastic,' he is relieved to say. The Navy has its own medic teams and its own mental health teams. There was no wait to see a GP, no wait for a consultant referral.

While he was still out in Afghanistan, the prime consideration was to reduce the impact pending his return, but Bryn realised – inevitably – that much of his anxiety was centring on flying. He could still carry out his day job, but when it came to sitting in the back of an unserviceable helicopter carrying out tests and diagnostics mid-air, enough was enough. Bryn was struggling to eat, struggling to sleep, struggling to concentrate. He went through trauma risk management (TRiM), an assessment that scores you on points. Bryn's points were sufficient to take him straight to the doctor: PTSD was the diagnosis.

Bryn's initial treatment was eye movement desensitisation and reprocessing (EMDR) – a process that tries to break down the incident into its key situations and file them correctly.

> *I was told the analogy that you have got these two sides to your brain, and if you imagine them as cogs, they should be linked together and working*

together in synch, but what happens in traumatic situations like this is that the teeth become worn. It is almost like a slipping clutch – both sides are working, but they are not engaged. They are not working together.

The other analogy is the filing cabinet. The brain records what happens during the day and then files it while you sleep. When you suffer a trauma, the trauma becomes a red file, which cannot be stored. As Bryn explains it, EMDR throws the red file on the floor and helps you pick up 'the bits and pieces' and file them properly and safely in a way that enables the mind to cope. To Bryn, this was an analogy that made sense – and when an analogy makes sense, the process works all the more effectively. As he says, it was a way of thinking that appealed to his engineer's mind.

Unsurprisingly, the focus of Bryn's anxiety was travel. What began as anxiety centring on aircraft transferred to all modes of transport. Bryn found he couldn't bring himself to get on a train. Or in a taxi, or a bus, or a car – even when he was being driven by his wife. The trauma had stolen his ability to trust, or to cope if he didn't have control, and both losses were now seeping into other aspects of his life.

He fell back on his own means of transport: running. It's a mode of travel in which his control is complete and the only person he needs to trust is himself.

I have always had a love of running, but what I found at that time was that whenever I was starting to become unwell or starting to bring up the anxieties, running would help. When you go out running, especially on training runs, you tend to spend a lot of time on your own, and in Somerset we have got some fantastic country roads, great places to run. It is just you, the elements, the road and your own mind, and it is great.

For Bryn, who is based in Yeovilton, running wasn't about processing the incident. It was about escaping from it. Running was about blocking it out for a few miles. If he knew he was scheduled for a medical appointment, he would feel the pressure and consequently struggle. If he ran beforehand, Bryn gave himself a temporary escape.

You run and you escape from the situation and you have got all the endorphins and the adrenaline going through your body – and that means when you come back to a bad situation afterwards, you are better able to cope with it. But it is not just about trauma. In this day and age, everybody's lives are becoming more and more stressful. There is more stress being added all the time to our lives. If you run, you can just get away and escape and let your mind relax and you come back so much better able to cope.

As a runner already, Bryn went into these runs knowing exactly what he was doing, conscious of exactly what he wanted to get out of them. And as he ran, so he started to change allegiance. Bryn started out as a track runner at school and in his earlier days in the Navy. He was the Navy's number two runner over 800m and reserve runner for 400m and 1500m. Now, however, he was becoming a distance runner.

And with the distance came a goal – one that was crucial to his recovery. The inter-services competition sees the Royal Navy, the Army and the RAF compete against each other. It became Bryn's aim to run the London Marathon for the Navy – despite the transport challenges he would have to tackle. Bryn recalls it was a painstakingly long process to prepare himself mentally and also to train for the race itself, but by pushing himself, he was able to get so much more out of his therapy sessions. The 2015 London Marathon became his aim – and he succeeded.

Travelling on the train and the Tube around London was very nerve-racking. I had my wife with me, who was a massive, massive support, but then when I got to the start at Greenwich Park, you are just you on your own. And I realised I had done all the hard work. All I had to do was run.

And he did so brilliantly, coming home for a glorious sub-three, completing the course in 2 hours, 53 minutes. However, Bryn knew he was on a journey longer than just the one marathon. London was simply stage one. The next stage was to secure his place in Washington's Marine Corps Marathon, in which the Royal Navy and the US Marines pit themselves against each other as part of their friendly rivalry.

The race was to be staged in October 2016. The stumbling block was the obvious and painful one: Bryn would need to fly to get there. To help him do so, he switched from EMDR to cognitive behavioural therapy (CBT), deemed to be the best way to enable him to confront his fear that 'plane = incident'. He needed to see flying in a much healthier way.

And I did it. I went to Washington. My first plane trip since the incident. A few gin and tonics were drunk to help me with the flight, but I did it without any medical help. And I ran 2 hours, 53 again.

These were landmark moments in Bryn's recovery. In the meantime, he was already creating his own race legacy: the Yeovil Marathon, a race he started to plan after returning from Afghanistan in 2014. It ran for the first time in 2015 as a charity road race in aid of the Royal Navy & Royal Marines Charity. It is Bryn's way of giving back, his gratitude for all the support he has received. He expresses that gratitude by setting up a race for others to run so that they too might know the benefits of hitting the roads. The satisfaction of seeing the runners gather is huge.

I think I get just as much of an adrenaline rush when I have got 200–300 runners on the start line and I press the hooter for them to go. And then two-and-a-half to two-and-three-quarter hours later, the first runners start coming back.

It's a race that effectively symbolises Bryn's return to mental health. His next step is to run it himself. His plan is to do so in 2019 to mark not just his 40th birthday, but also his retirement from the Royal Navy after 22 years. The thought of it all makes him feel good.

PTSD is such a broad scope thing. In military medical terms, I am fully fit and fully deployable. But will I never again be anxious about flying? No. I will always be anxious about flying now, but I know now that luckily I am in a place where I can deal with it a lot easier, a place where I can recognise the symptoms and know how to cope.

A place where he can run.

Hanny Allston

'I have found a way to run for the absolute joy in the freedom it brings me.'

Tasmania's Hanny Allston has made her name at elite level in a wide range of running sports, from orienteering to marathons via mountain, road and distance track running. She remains the only athlete outside Europe to have won a world orienteering title, completing the double of a junior world championship and senior world championship in the same year.

In short, at the peak of her competing, Hanny was the epitome of success. And yet it was at the moment of her greatest triumph that she experienced her greatest challenge. Suddenly Hanny's world seemed to be falling apart. Depression, self-doubt and anorexia threatened to engulf her.

But it has been through a sharper sense of what running really means that Hanny has saved herself and reconstructed her life – this time with a keener understanding of the things that truly matter. Hanny now stands as a genuinely inspirational figure when it comes to enjoying the great outdoors – someone who has learned the hard way how best to bring sport and mental health together. As she looks back on her struggles, she knows that she has finally – and healthily – reunited body and mind.

As a child, Hanny was always a dreamer, something she believes she inherited from her parents. Always striving for excellence, they brought up Hanny and her brother on a small hobby farm south of Hobart. Hanny was encouraged to dream, and in her dreams, she mapped out her future.

For the first 12 years of my life there were only ever three goals for me: becoming an Olympian; living at the Australian Institute of Sport; and a career in medicine.

At first, Hanny believed she would realise dreams one and two through swimming, a sport in which she showed strong early promise. However, as puberty began, Hanny's progress started to slow. Self-doubt and pressure swamped her, and eventually she reached a plateau of poorer performances. She found herself on firmer footing when she joined a track athletics group instead, and on firmer footing still when she turned to orienteering.

Hanny dominated the Junior Women's class in her first national competition and soon found herself on her first national team trip to New Zealand. There she also shone. The team coach asked if she would like to try for the Australian team for the Junior World Orienteering Championships in Estonia. Hanny looked at him blankly, nodded her head and whipped out the family atlas when she got home. Her path was set.

Within a year I had quit swimming and thrown myself headfirst into orienteering. For the first three years I had a rapid and steady rise towards the top, resulting in a bronze medal at the Juniors and a podium result in the Senior World Championships in 2005. There to watch me compete overseas for the first time were my parents.

However, Hanny's life took an unexpected twist in 2005 when she returned from two World Championships just two weeks apart: the Junior World Championships in Switzerland and then the senior World Orienteering Championships in Japan. Examinations overwhelmed her in her medical studies, and she was faced with an ankle reconstruction that could have ended her running career. Max Cherry, her 80-year-old athletics coach, stood by her, but sadly, Hanny's personal problems continued to mount. Just as 19-year-old Hanny was recovering from her ankle surgery, a close family member experienced major troubles with their mental health.

Hanny's response was a simple one. She became convinced that the way to sort everything out was to bring home the gold medal from the next Junior World Orienteering Championships, just six months away. Hindsight tells her now that she was wrong to try to use running as a way of coping.

But at the time I honestly believed that such success would help me out of the enormous hole I felt I had fallen into. It never occurred to me that I couldn't achieve my goal, and I dedicated myself to the challenge. Leading up to the events, I would run alone on Mount Wellington, seeing the golden sunrises as a sign that I was heading towards achieving my goals. During those early months, running was what kept me focused, driven and intact.

Sadly, though, she was riding for a fall – despite securing outward success.

When the gold medals were put around my neck at both the Junior and Senior World Titles in 2006, I suddenly felt this huge balloon of confidence inside me pop. I was still the same Hanny with the same – if not growing – troubles to return home to.

Hanny went back to the sale of the family home, to a parental divorce and a panicked decision to change direction away from medical school. Instead, she moved to New Zealand to study to become a primary school teacher. In the midst of it all, she kept on running. As she says, it was easier to keep running than to confront the 'gaping holes' around her, but still her sporting ambitions soared. It was around this time that her goal began to shift from orienteering to the Olympic marathon. Tragically, life intervened again in the saddest of ways.

When my beloved coach Max passed away with a heart attack at training and then my new mentor, Jacquie, also attempted suicide, I suddenly realised that running couldn't save me. I spiralled into a very dark place where anorexia and self-doubt plagued me. I was unable to concentrate on my job as a primary school teacher in Melbourne, struggled with injury, and, despite rocketing results, the love had completely faded.

In 2010, Hanny returned to Tasmania, deeply depressed. When not even running could bring joy any more, she turned at one point to antidepressants. Fortunately, the real answer was closer to hand. Or to foot, perhaps. It was running that pointed Hanny in the right direction – and sowed the seeds for the successful business she now runs with her husband. After some soul-searching, a long cycle tour in Europe and meeting her future husband, Graham, Hanny started a small running group for adults, which she called Find Your Feet.

It was meant to be a hobby to help fund my new paramedical studies and to bide my time whilst I worked out what I wanted to do. I shifted from teaching myself to become a better athlete to teaching others to find strength, joy and friendships through running. I found that I was not the only one struggling to understand the twists and turns in life, and that many individuals were using running as a medium to confront challenges in their personal lives.

Find Your Feet has developed into a highly successful business, providing a range of services to help Hanny's fellow Australians to 'be wilder and to find their feet', all based on a love and respect for the great outdoors.

And therein lies the irony. Find Your Feet helped Hanny to find her own feet. On a summer evening as she wrapped up another session, a member of the group pulled her aside. Quietly, gently, he said to her: 'Hanny, it doesn't matter how beautiful the gift is that you are giving us if all we see is a person who doesn't give gifts to themselves.'

Those words were crucial. He was urging Hanny to take her own medicine, to practise precisely what she preached – and she acted on it. Hanny launched herself into her studies again, this time studying life coaching, which proved to be the first step on a path that was to lead to a job in athlete welfare at the Australian Institute of Sport in Canberra. One of those childhood dreams was now fulfilled.

Completing the circle, those words also eventually led Hanny back into competing – this time with a greater understanding of how to compete in a much more positive, less self-damaging way. In 2012, Hanny was working to support aspiring Olympians and Paralympians in their bids to take part in the London Games that summer. The job fuelled her own sporting ambitions.

A painful conversation with my now husband sparked a realisation that I needed to return to sport and see whether I could be an elite competitor in a more healthy, sustainable and enjoyable manner. It turns out I can!

As Hanny says, she has now found genuine freedom in her mental health and 'with it, absolute unwavering joy in running and exercise'. What she has now gained is a truer appreciation of running.

> *Running and exercise are now a very personal activity for me. I love the simplicity of pulling on a set of shoes and running straight out the door, wherever that may be in the world. I especially love to explore wilder and more remote regions, such as my island home of Tasmania. In that respect, the joy, the freedom, the feeling of health are all very therapeutic. I love feeling the strengthening connection of my mind and body outdoors.*

Self-knowledge is key, based on 'a lot of internal work', especially since she hit her 30s. Hanny believes she'd avoided understanding the choices she'd made earlier in her life, particularly during the turbulent times. She believes she has got that understanding now. Just as importantly, she also believes she now has a greater sense of self and indeed a greater sense of her own womanhood.

> *Competing at an elite level for nearly 20 years, some of which with a very low body weight, can wreak havoc with your femininity. I knew that to overcome the amenorrhea and live in optimal health I needed to change things around . . . urgently. At first, I wanted to do this out of love for my fiancé, but it began to become a very personal journey of finding my feet. It was a new GP who finally gave me the shove I needed. On my first visit to her rooms, she looked me up and down and said: 'Hanny, you need to find your femininity.' Finally, it all clicked into place. In order to further the journey of finding my feet and really thrive, I needed to find compassion and optimal health as a woman, not just as an athlete.*

Putting it all together, Hanny now believes that running is a window into the health of not just our body, but also and equally our mind – a realisation which makes her wish she had been kinder to herself in the past.

> *I just wish I had recognised it at an earlier point and showed more compassion for my body and mind when I saw it was in trouble. Today, when I go out on a run and feel like I could go forever or can cruise the trails completely in tune with the natural world around me, that is when I know that I am living in a state of optimal health.*

Hanny believes she has now learned 'to identify with Hanny' when she peels back the layers of her life – her business achievements, her running results and her mental health. As she says, it has been a question of learning 'to sit' with her strengths and also with her weaknesses; a question of accepting her choices and showing herself compassion in times of high emotion and especially fear. Again, it is about using exercise to bring mind and body together rather than to drive a wedge between them.

> *I have learnt to express my values and look beyond judgement. I have brought the joy fully back into my running because I no longer feel the need to succeed or seek outcomes to define my identity. Running no longer has to be the rock because I am the rock. And with a rekindled joy of running has come optimal health and a willingness to succeed. My new definition of success is a willingness to sit right on the edge.*

Hanny's running is no longer principally about races and medals. It's adventuring, exploring and simply playing that she loves now. And the mental health benefits are enormous:

> *With my stronger sense of self, I now feel an enormous weight released from my shoulders. I have found a way to run for the absolute joy in the freedom it brings me. Running along a trail becomes my sanctuary, a place where I find my mind will slowly quiet over the duration of the run. I find the same sense of quietness when I go climbing, walk, wander or cycle. Exercise is like a massive reset button now that I am embracing for the right reasons.*

Such thoughts are, of course, the perfect foundation for her work as a coach and life coach – the realisation that we are all living a common human experience with the same suite of emotions. Hanny can empathise with the urge to use running to reframe our lives and find our best mental health, but she will also encourage people to look deep within themselves to make sure they are not running away from issues. It is important to find an identity separate from finish lines and training sessions, she believes.

In other words, Hanny's goals have become more and more personal. In the summer of 2017, she finally completed the dream of running the entire south-coast Track of Tasmania, a wild, windswept and muddy trail crossing 93 kilometres (58 miles) of remote terrain, in which the only way out is either to retrace your steps or to fly out via light aircraft.

Two days before she turned 31, Hanny and a friend dragged their bodies out of bed at 3.00 a.m., pulled on head torches and vest packs and set off. Fear seeped through to her bones, but she was exactly where she wanted to be, on the edge, following her wildest dreams – dreams that surpassed all expectations when she realised them.

Hanny swam across a glistening river and ran down a 5-kilometre (3-mile) stretch of pristine beach. The track arced upwards through rooted, eroded trails to crest the famous Ironbound Range at 1200 metres (3937 feet). At this point they were at 65 kilometres (40 miles) into the trail. The nearest civilisation was a remote airstrip 30 kilometres (19 miles) away, which marked the end of their journey. The feeling was magnificent.

Standing up there, with the roaring coast wrapping around to the South and mountains reaching to the North, I felt utmost strength, in my fears, my resilience and even deeper within myself. I had this overwhelming sensation that I was exactly where I needed to be, in place but also in life. Of all the things I have ever done, this was by far and away the most exhilarating and rewarding. Out there on that track I think I may have finally found my feet.

Kate Jayden

'How could I let anyone steal running from me?'

Alone in her flat, coming round after passing out, Kate Jayden had a chilling glimpse of her future. After years of denying herself food, years of trying to subsist on minimal calories, years of being sick several times a day, she suddenly saw the fate most likely to await her. Her fear was that one day she would collapse again, hit her head against the wall and this time not wake up at all.

In that moment, Kate knew she was killing herself, slowly but surely. She was suffering palpitations; her gums were bleeding; she was incapable of sleeping; she was constantly weak. She knew that she didn't have long – unless she changed her ways.

Fortunately, Kate had at her disposal the huge willpower that had got her into this situation in the first place. The willpower she now turned to running – and the willpower she drew on again when she was subjected to a terrifying sexual assault in the pitch-darkness of a lonely 24-hour endurance run, five years later.

It was in her teenage years that Kate's troubled relationship with food deepened. Against a difficult family background, Kate, who now lives in Manchester, remembers 'experimenting' when she was around 14 or 15, holding back on food. This was probably the beginning of her eating disorder, and in hindsight, she explains it as a search for control. After years of doing well at school, she was looking for a different sense of achievement – and found it in denying herself food. She was showing herself that she was in charge.

In other respects, it became a coping mechanism to overcome the stress of her circumstances at that time. She recognises now that her bulimic tendencies became a form of self-harming. Kate says she wouldn't wish an eating disorder on her worst enemy – and yet, in effect, she willed it on herself. As the illness progressed, there would be days when a cup of soup would be her only sustenance, after which she would make herself sick.

Inevitably, her health deteriorated as her condition took over her entire life.

> *I would wake up weak and cold. I felt dreadful every day. My throat would bleed. My gums have receded, and my teeth are still not right even now, but every day, I would feel awful.*

Kate desperately wanted to get better, but she likens the illness to quicksand. The harder she tried to get out, the deeper she sank. She has no doubt that she was slowly killing herself. She struggled to sleep and feared she wouldn't wake up. Then came the miserable day that brought the turning point she needed.

She was alone in her flat. Her throat was bleeding. She could see the blood in the toilet bowl, where she had been sick again. She recalls struggling to get up and starting to walk back to the living room. She passed out in the corridor. When she regained consciousness, she had the frightening vision that next time her body would lie dead – and undiscovered – for weeks.

Just as importantly, there came another realisation: Kate started to dread just what her death would do to her godmother, Linda. She didn't really have a great deal to do with her biological family at that time, but she was close to her godmother. Kate found herself thinking: *I have got to get out of this.* She recognised that change would be the key, a change that came with a change of job. At a work lunch with new colleagues, she ate and then went to the toilets to make herself sick, but this time, back at the table, it occurred to her that if there was a chance that she could tell she'd been sick, then so too would her colleagues. It was a realisation she managed to turn to her advantage.

> *In a way, it was fear of getting caught that made me get better. I started by not making myself sick after some meals, and then I started with simple things like saying yes to things that I thought bad, like yes to a piece of chocolate. I had to readjust my idea of portion sizes, as I'd only ever known too much, which I'd then purge, or too little. It was like starting to learn to eat again.*

By 2011 Kate considered herself recovered. It had been a tough year, but she knew that if she had the willpower to get herself into this position, then she certainly had the willpower to get herself out of it. She began to use her willpower in a positive way.

Then came a crucial next step – her discovery of running. Kate, who was living in Chester at the time, had cycled from London to Paris. She jokingly recalls thinking she was the bee's knees after the ride, and when the pub conversation turned to the Chester Marathon, she said she wanted to do it – to the disbelief of her companions. It was in three weeks' time, and she didn't even know how far a marathon was. She looked it up on the internet. The Chester Marathon was '17 miles through England', so she signed up.

The next day, at church with her godmother, Kate started to wonder just what she had got herself into. 'I think I have just signed up for a marathon,' she confessed. Later came a discovery. She repeated her belief that marathons are 17 miles long. A friend challenged her. She checked. The Chester Marathon website confirmed that it was indeed '17 miles through England', but Kate hadn't read the rest of the sentence: 'and another nine miles through Wales'.

The training began the next day, a slog around Chester racecourse. Slowly Kate built up her distance, reaching 14 miles (23 kilometres) before the big day. Despite palpitations she believes were linked to her eating disorder, Kate gritted out the miles, to finish in 5 hours, 26 minutes. At the start line she'd been convinced that this would be the end of her, but she remembers thinking it wouldn't be the worst way to go. However, her reaction on finishing showed that she was a marathon runner after all.

Instead of thinking I'd got away with that and could go home and stop, I started thinking I would have a go at another one and train this time.

Kate has now done more than 270 marathons and ultras – each and every one of them meeting a very specific need. She isn't keen to go into her 'woe is me' childhood, save to say that it was tough and that her only way to get through it was to be tough in equal measure. Her childhood and teenage years were difficult, but as life seemed to get easier in her 20s, she recalls that she felt at a loss to know what to do with the toughness she had built up during her formative years.

> *I guess that's what running does for me now. It allows me to exercise that toughness; to keep it and to channel that part of my character which I had to build up. It gives me a chance to push myself, set goals and experience life. There is that expression: I don't run to add years to my life, I run to add life to my years. Running makes me feel alive. It has allowed me to channel what you might consider the negative elements in my life into something positive. If I can show that a normal person like me, not a naturally gifted athlete, can run 100 miles, then someone who is morbidly obese in the office or a friend who is perhaps not quite as fit as they want to be can realise that they too can actually change their lives.*

The eating disorder channelled Kate's mental toughness in a damaging way. The running channels it in a positive way – a strength that she drew on when she was sexually assaulted during a 24-hour ultra through the Worcestershire countryside.

The race, in September 2015, comprised loops of 5 miles (8 kilometres). The winner was the runner who had run the most miles when the 24 hours elapsed, from midday on the Saturday to midday on the Sunday. Kate, 29 at the time, was in great shape and confident. At the halfway point of the race, runners pass a checkpoint and their number is recorded. The lap is logged and their distance mounts. It was all going well; Kate was well ahead in her category. The loops were stacking up steadily.

But then terror struck. It was pitch-black, 10 p.m. on the Saturday night. Kate had passed the checkpoint on her latest loop and had followed the route once again, first downhill and then through a cemetery over a field into a disused quarry. She was running alone, head torch on, complete darkness around her, one earpiece in, alert and running well. She was thinking that she hadn't seen her friend for some time since the start. When she heard someone run up behind her and felt someone start to envelop her in a bear hug, she thought for the briefest of moments it was her friend messing around.

I remember laughing for a second, and then I went from laughter to Holy Crap! This is not my friend. This is the opposite of my friend. Shit. All I could think was that my heart felt as if it was going to jump out of me. This man grabbed hold of my chest and ran with me for several steps, still holding on to my breasts.

Kate managed to shake him off, and he ran away to her left, a 'weedy guy' dressed in black jeans and black hoodie. He disappeared into the darkness. It felt like a horror film, she recalls. Her only option was to run on as fast as she possibly could. She had already done more than 50 miles (80 kilometres), almost two marathons, but the survival instinct kicked in, driven by a fear that ran with her.

I remember being so scared that he was going to jump out from around the corner. I just ran and ran for my life. It was the continuous level of adrenaline, where it physically makes you feel sick.

She tried running without her head torch on in the hope that he wouldn't be able to see her, but the result was that she couldn't see to run. It was 1.5 miles (2.5 kilometres), perhaps 18 minutes, before she found another runner. The entire time she'd run in fear, adrenaline rushing through her body.

I stopped as soon as I saw the other runner. She asked if I was OK, and I said no, and it was just floods of tears. She hugged me and was absolutely lovely. I had to wait that entire last mile-and-a-half, running in fear, to meet another human being, and then it was just a bang sort of moment. It all came out.

The runner rang through to race HQ and offered to stay with her, but Kate felt she needed to run still. She reached the HQ, where word was beginning to spread about what had happened. Kate couldn't speak. Words wouldn't come, but tears did. Arriving at the race HQ, the police suspended the race. Kate estimates there would have been around 100 runners out there. Those arriving at the HQ were stopped from proceeding; one of the race officials went out in a 4 x 4 to reel back in those who had already gone past the halfway mark.

After questioning her, the police drove Kate as close as possible to the scene of the attack and then walked with her to the actual spot. Then they went back to the HQ, where the race team decided that the race would resume at 6 a.m. in the light – a dilemma for Kate.

Before I went in, I knew I was winning my solo category. I was caught between absolute devastation and shock and thinking: Hang on, I was winning this! I was caught between the inner runner and going back to this broken side of me that was struggling to comprehend what happened, in shock.

In reality, there was little doubt what she was going to do. As she says, it all comes back to that toughness she had deliberately developed in herself in childhood. She couldn't *not* finish the race. When something awful happens, Kate's instinct is to fight back.

Running keeps me going in life. It is not your circumstances that define you, it is how you react to them. I thought at that moment: This is what ultrarunning is about. Ultrarunning is about hitting rock bottom and bouncing back. You don't expect it to be that particular rock bottom, but it is the same thing, and this is what I do. I don't quit.

And so Kate rejoined the race when it resumed at first light. Other runners were shocked to see her there. She now realises she was still in shock herself, but she completed the race, covered another six laps to take her tally to an overall distance of 84 miles (135 kilometres) – more than enough to secure the winner's medal, which had been hers for the taking until her attacker struck.

It is still one of my proudest achievements. When everything goes against you and your heart is saying: 'Go home and cry', it is so difficult. But I went back and I finished my job, and I still absolutely treasure that trophy. If you stop, the world doesn't stop for you. What else could I do? It's just inherent to how I have always been. When I found running, I found a part of myself.

Inevitably, there was still a price to pay. Kate, who works in finance, tried to go back to work the next day, strolling into the office as if nothing was wrong, wearing an 'everything is fine' face, but she found herself unable to speak. The shock was still intense; so too was the tiredness. She tried to talk but found herself in the grip of a strange out-of-body experience. She was watching herself. Work was impossible. She was signed off with anxiety and stress in the weeks after the assault.

It wasn't long before she started suffering panic attacks, which were debilitating and at times embarrassing, particularly if they happened in public. These continued until the summer of 2016. Kate would be surrounded by friends, but she still felt alone. As she says, her anxiety levels went through the roof: hers was a life lived on tenterhooks, constantly reliving those moments, living with the constant feeling of being on edge. For the first few weeks somebody slept at her house or she stayed at her friend's house as she struggled during the night to cope with the stress of being in the dark.

Inevitably, it was running that brought her back again.

For three weeks after the attack, Kate couldn't bring herself to run. She couldn't even look at her running shoes. She withdrew from a marathon she was due to run the week after the assault, but something kicked in when she contemplated the next 24-hour run on her horizon. She realised it really wasn't something she could duck.

> *I knew if I didn't turn up for that, I would be in trouble. The thing that had saved me in the first place was running. How could I let anyone steal running from me?*

Kate feels great now. She acknowledges that the events have had an impact on her, and certain circumstances or situations still trigger the feelings from that night, but she is no longer having panic attacks and has been free from antidepressants and beta-blockers for more than a year; she chose to end them after seeing a reduction in her panic attacks. She had also become tired of the toll taken by the beta-blockers on her fitness levels. She wanted to run again at a faster pace.

After a year free of medication, Kate started to see her marathon pace come back. Her first milestone was a return to a sub-four marathon, achieved in December 2017. It was the perfect platform to push herself back to full fitness. Just as running helped her overcome her eating disorder, so too it helped her overcome the horror of her attack.

I don't wish it hadn't happened. Even before the assault, I always said that I have never regretted anything at all, not even the 'bad' things because bad is only bad because good is good and if you don't have the bad, you can never have the good. If something bad happens, you can either think the world owes you or you can come out smiling and show courage and show real strength. And that's what I would rather do.

Don Wright

'I am exceedingly lucky to be here.'

Doctors told Don Wright he had five years left to live when he was diagnosed with myeloma. Thirteen years later, he crossed the line in his '100th marathon with cancer'. The word *with* is crucial: he's not running *from* cancer, he's running *with* it.

Don, from Stillwater, Minnesota, was a fast runner as a youngster, but life intervenes and he didn't get back to running until he was in his early 60s. In 2002, about a year and a half before Don was diagnosed with myeloma, his brother-in-law Calvin invited him to run a race. Don admits he did very badly. It was just a 5k, and he finished red-faced and in a disappointing time. But he was already trying to lose weight through Weight Watchers, and there was something about running that just clicked, so Don decided simply to keep on running.

One of his highlights so far has been the Minnesota Distance Running Association Grand Prix, a statewide competition that features 13 races in a year, ranging from a mile to a marathon. Don was the winner in 2006 at the age of 65 – remarkably good going for someone who was already well past the halfway mark in the five years he was told he had left to live in 2003.

Don had gone to the doctor's two or three times with a pain in his back. On the latest visit, the doctor ordered some blood tests. A few days later, Don received an evening phone call. The doctor told him he had scheduled an appointment for Don with an oncologist.

I denied it right away. I told him that runners have very strange blood test results. The doctor told me: 'Not strange like this they don't.'

Don went along to the appointment with the oncologist, who turned out to be a haematologist. The diagnosis was a stark one – myeloma, a type of bone marrow cancer. Don sought a second opinion at the University of Minnesota. The second opinion was effectively a confirmation. Don was told he had three to five years to live – news that brought his remaining years into a very sharp and different focus. As he says, suddenly he could see his bucket list 'a little bit more clearly', and on that bucket list was the Boston Marathon.

Don, variously an attorney and a computer consultant, had run his first marathon three weeks before his diagnosis, but not in a time to qualify him for Boston. That hadn't bothered him; Boston hadn't been on his radar. But now it was – so he ran two more marathons, both of which brought him the sub-four qualifying time he needed. Crucial support in everything came from his family: Ardis, his wife of more than 50 years, and their daughter, Sarah. Both have been his companion on countless trips to clinics – and on numerous marathons too. Don ticked off Boston and enjoyed it. The travel, the marathon, the whole experience was rather fun. Don had already done a number of marathons in his home state of Minnesota. Incorporating the travel now as part of the experience, he decided to look to other states as he added to his marathon tally.

We didn't plan to do a marathon in every state. I couldn't imagine living long enough for that. But what has happened is that I have been pretty fortunate in having novel medication. I have been lucky enough that a new medication has always come along just as I needed it. Myeloma has a way of figuring medications out and it continues to evolve, so you always need a new therapy. I have had five therapies so far. Three of them were studies. One of the studies lasted seven years. It has always been a question of trying to stay one step ahead.

Don feels that running marathons has helped him embrace his disease, rather than be depressed about it. Part of embracing it has been to bang the drum for the continual need for better medication – or, at least, different medication. As he says, we can't hit the wall when it comes to developing new treatments. Cancer is a clever opponent; it works out ways to defeat your medications, which is why Don believes research to develop new medicines is so important.

Through his speaking commitments, Don underlines the hope that drives him forward: the simple fact that what used to be true just isn't true anymore. The prognosis has now expanded from the three to five years he was first given to eight. Thanks to the changing therapies, Don has gone way beyond even current expectations. Every step of the way he has shown others in his position that diagnosis is not necessarily a death sentence.

Yes, Don is surprised he is still here, but above all he says he feels exceedingly fortunate that the pharmaceutical companies have maintained their progress. He is currently on a medication called humanised monoclonal antibody – and so far, so good.

I have felt pretty well the whole time. One of the things that happens is that the myeloma lives in the bone marrow, and it has a way of breaking out that is very destructive to the bone. That's what is called multiple myeloma, where people present to the doctor with broken bones everywhere. I was lucky. They caught mine early. I have never had any broken bones at all.

And so Don's marathon tally continued to grow. In 2012, he completed a marathon in every US state. The 50th state was his 70th marathon in all, and it came in Hawaii – which, as Don says, was a celebration in itself. To mark the achievement, Don created *eRace Cancer*, a social media campaign to let other patients know that cancer treatments aren't 'always your grandfather's chemotherapy'. Things move on. As he said at the time: 'Here I am with cancer and my biggest complaint is runner's knee.' His hope is to urge others to support medical research and innovation, including new clinical trials – the way new treatments are found.

After his 50th state, Don flew back home to a meeting of ASH, the American Society of Hematology. After completing marathons in 50 states with myeloma, he was, as he says, the poster boy of modern American medicine. Just as importantly, he wasn't ready to stop. One hundred marathons seemed possible, and so he pushed on, reaching his century of marathons in Philadelphia on 20 November, 2016 – while still on treatment. Treatment that wasn't available when he was first diagnosed.

As Don headed towards the finish line, his thoughts were with all those cancer patients still in need of more research and newer treatments.

In a way I felt relieved. I am 76. I know I can run another marathon, but I don't know how many more. It was good to stop for a bit. I think I will run number 101 some place, some time, but I have changed my goals. My goal is now to participate in the US National Senior Games – track events, sprints and shorter runs – in 2019 (in Albuquerque, New Mexico).

As a kid Don was one of the fastest on his block and, even in his 60s, he was fast. Now, with his century of marathons complete, Don is returning to his running roots 'with a race measured in minutes and seconds instead of hours'.

Don is clear: the fact that he has reached this point is down to medical innovation. But there is no possible doubt that running has played a huge part too, helping him avoid the comorbidities – the other diseases that can accompany myeloma, including diabetes and kidney failure. Don believes he has steered clear by keeping fit. On top of that, he believes his running has given him the space to think things through positively and constructively. His running space *is* his space.

One of my doctors wears headphones and listens to books as she runs. I think that is admirable, but I would rather think about things. I am pretty good company for myself. I like to sort things out. Running is healing and allows healing to work. Running as an exercise is great. It is good to always be moving on.

Don is in no doubt: he has prolonged his life through running. And running has also brought the family great togetherness. Ardis and Sarah run too. Don's runs are always family affairs.

Looking back, there are two marathons that stand out as particular favourites. One is the New York City Marathon, which Don has now run three times. It's flat – one advantage – but there is also the little matter of two million spectators.

It is just a wonderful experience with so many people there. It is so uplifting.

At the other end of the scale and yet equally a favourite is the Avenue of the Giants Marathon in Humboldt Redwoods State Park in rural northern California – a paved course winding through magnificent giant redwoods.

Except for the half-marathon point where there is a crowd, it is just totally silent. There is nobody out there to support you. It is just you, the other runners and these enormous trees. It is a great marathon.

Don remains an inspiration to countless thousands of people. Myeloma can't yet be cured, but with new drugs and new treatments available and the determination to keep on running, Don has shown that there is most certainly life beyond diagnosis. It comes back to the distinction Don makes: he is not running *from* cancer, he's not running from anything. He runs *with* his cancer, just as he runs with his family – and the road has proved remarkably long.

I am exceedingly lucky to be here.

Daniele Seiss

*'Running long distances . . . creates a sense of
oneness that I can't explain.'*

As a journalist, Daniele Seiss finds herself only too well qualified to
convey exactly what depression feels like. A writer who works for *The
Washington Post*, she describes vividly the crushing weight it brings
down on its victim. As she says, it's something she wouldn't wish 'on
the worst monsters of humanity'.

In its milder forms, depression can be something like grief, Dani
says. There is a feeling of sorrow, but more often a constant sense
of hopelessness, a sense that nothing matters and that nothing can
improve.

> *But in heavier stages, such as when major depression turned into psychotic
> depression for me, there was this feeling of horror as if the world itself and
> everything in it were just completely unbearable. Something as benign as
> the visual contrast of light and dark appeared frightening. I consistently
> experienced voices telling me I was worthless and delusions such as feeling
> that everyone hated me. At one point, I had actual visual hallucinations.*

As Dani says, there is a physical weight to the feelings depression
brings, 'like being submerged in pitch or like wearing a sopping-wet
carpet over one's head and shoulders', making movement difficult and
partially obstructing the view. Just as frighteningly, it comes with a
feeling of dread – a constant in Dani's early years.

Dani admits she can't say for sure when dark thoughts started to
dominate her life, but she remembers a childhood in the mid-70s in
which she cried a great deal. On a daily basis, in fact. She struggled to
sleep and she struggled to eat, grappling all the while with the certainty
that something awful was going to befall the family.

Panic was never far away; and headaches contributed to the misery – a misery compounded by the fact that she felt she was fighting her terrors on her own. Dani's parents and her teachers were on her side, but 40-plus years ago, no one could conceive that young children could fall prey to severe depression – which is precisely what was happening. Painkillers were offered as the cure-all. In fact, they fixed little. But they were all Dani was given as she floundered in her own personal hell.

In Dani's teenage years, the dread worsened, and so did the sense of isolation. Eventually she was told that she had a severe and resilient case of major depressive disorder. Talking therapy and medication were limited in their effects – and came with their own sets of drawbacks. Talking was draining; drugs weren't a cure. Dani's sad conclusion was that normal life was impossible. She was heading for disaster.

Dani lost contact with her family, she abandoned her college course and she fell into the wrong sorts of relationships. Resisting all attempts to help her, she slipped into homelessness and drug abuse as her life spiralled downwards. There were times when she felt that death was the only way out – and when she wasn't actually planning it, she put herself in situations that put her life in peril. With emptiness came recklessness. Dani exposed herself to danger. She played chicken on the roads, and she balanced in high places. With no sense of her own value, she lapsed into vicious circles of behaviour, risking self-destruction.

At its absolute worst, depression was for me more of a lack of feeling entirely. I would sometimes not speak for very long periods of time. Words just wouldn't form. Sometimes I would feel shame or worthlessness, but mostly, there was the lack of feeling. As if nothing mattered. Since fear was also a feeling I lacked, I would often put myself in dangerous situations, not really noticing – things like not wearing warm clothes in the cold or walking out into traffic or being around dangerous people in bad neighbourhoods. There was for me a constant wish for death as if that were the only thing that would make things right, and sometimes I plotted it out and attempted it.

However, even in the worst moments, something held her back: the memory that she had once felt healthy. She clung to the memory. She knew that she had to keep it alive, to keep thinking: *There was a time when I felt good. I just have to find a way back to it.*

Fortunately, help was close to hand. As a teenager, Dani had discovered the escape on which she now bases and balances her life. It was walking, and then running, which offered an answer – and which she discovered almost by accident. She chanced upon it on a day of despair such as only depressives can know.

> *I think people who have not experienced depression first-hand don't understand the sense of desperation we feel. They may see it as simply feeling sad or being self-absorbed in sadness. But there is a terrible blankness. It is just awful, an entire lack of feeling and a quiet, but often severe desperation to bring an end to that blankness by whatever means necessary.*

That day, Dani simply didn't know what to do. Her salvation was that she did the simplest thing.

> *I simply walked out of the house and up the road. In the distance was a mountain, and I walked to the mountain. I didn't know where I was going, but the roads became more and more narrow and rugged as I went. Houses became farm fields until at last I was on these old, dirt tram roads in the forest. Eventually, I turned around and headed home because it was getting late. But that 25-some mile walk I took that day changed my life because it made me feel so much better. Nothing else was having such a positive effect on my mood at the time.*

For Dani, distance seemed to be the key that unlocked the benefits she felt. However, she soon discovered that running – even short distances – also appeared to have a profoundly positive effect. Eventually, she married the two, and between them they offered Dani a route towards the normal life she had been convinced she would always be denied.

Dani lost sight of the benefits of exercise at college first time round, but running eventually helped her return to college. She got a degree, got married and created for herself a new life in which she felt supported. It gave her the platform from which to ease herself off her antidepressants. Running gave her the strength to cut through her own blackness.

Now, if she is feeling down, Dani will go for a run. She soon starts to sense her mood change, again with the distance. At around 4 miles (6 kilometres), negativity starts to recede as something positive takes over. A further 10 miles (16 kilometres), and a kind of euphoria starts to creep in. Run faster, and it will arrive all the quicker. Another 4–5 miles (6–8 kilometres), and Dani will enter into a meditative state. She feels herself becoming one with her surroundings.

The benefits of running filter through into other aspects of life, something Dani particularly noticed after losing her mother to cancer.

I would often run near my home along a nearby river under the vast tree canopy. As an unconscious meditation, I would try to shift my perspective to what I imagined was the trees' perspective. They had been there for over a century. People had been born and died in their time. It was all part of a natural process. It helped take me out of my own head and feel I was part of something larger and more stable.

Dani admits that running has its limits and it is perfectly possible to overdo it.

But overall, running's effects, even after so many years, have been amazing at keeping me on an even keel and depression at bay. I am, by and large, a different person and I am still in a bit of disbelief at how effective running regularly has been for me at maintaining a consistently healthy state of mind.

Over the years, Dani has modified her running routine, trying always to reap the maximum health benefits. Along the way, the simple lifestyle changes brought on by regular running – such as drinking more water and less alcohol plus sleeping better and eating more healthily – have also helped to keep depression in check. As for the running itself, distance remains key, something she puts down to the meditative attributes of exercise – attributes all the more effective over an extended period of time.

Dani cherishes completing the Boston Marathon as a huge personal achievement, something she'd wanted to do for years, long before she was really a runner. It was only the third race she'd ever run, after a half trail marathon and the Baltimore Marathon the year before, which had qualified her for Boston. Dani admits she knew very little about racing, which is what made Boston just a little scary, but the race went well and she ran it again the next two years – before, as she admits, losing interest. Expense was a factor, but just as important was the fact that trying to run faster all the time was never what running was about as far as Dani was concerned. Much more interesting, she believes, is simply to set different goals.

After completing 10 marathons, Dani moved on to ultra-distance trail races instead – for longer-lasting satisfactions. She has completed 29 ultras and six 100-mile (160-kilometre) races, including one of 114 miles (183 kilometres) over 13 mountains. Part of the attraction is that ultra is in effect a lifestyle – given that the training runs can be just as rigorous and as long as the races themselves.

Along the way comes healing. Dani, who lives in the state of Maryland, has noticed that running on wooded trails or in a natural environment, again for extended periods of time, increases the therapeutic effects of running.

> *What I believe I have been experiencing with running ultras is the physical changes to the brain, the regular neurogenesis that takes place from the rigours of the exercise of running itself, but also, the meditative effects of the repetitive motion over a long period of time, and also the physical effects brought on by immersion in a natural environment, which work so very nicely together. Trail racing, at least here in the eastern US, has the added effect of forest bathing.*

Just as important, though, is the sense of togetherness that ultrarunning brings, a warmth and welcome which are key parts of the strong and friendly running community Dani has come to love.

> *The support of a community – of which many members may also be depression sufferers or even former alcoholics or drug addicts – cannot be understated. Running marathons felt like such a solitary experience. With trails, there are more dangers in going it alone, and so long training runs are often done in pairs or groups. Running long distances brings out a selfless aspect in people and an elevated perspective that creates a sense of oneness that I can't explain, but I know I am not alone in this experience.*

A long training run with a group of friends creates such strong bonds. I now belong to several running clubs, but one, The Virginia Happy Trails Running Club, has become family for me.

And again, it all helps with perspective. Again, for Dani, running isn't simply about races and times.

I feel like being able to keep myself healthy and running so that running can keep me healthy in return has been by far my biggest achievement. I'm also very happy to be able to comfortably cover 100 miles in a day on just about any given day of the year – or in around 30 hours on very mountainous terrain. It has taken me places I would never have experienced otherwise, both in mind and body.

Dani knows she is resilient enough now to be able to run in nearly any weather and in nearly any conditions and to know how best to prepare for whatever lies ahead.

I have learned to listen to my body and to monitor my physical and mental health much more closely because of running.

Ultimately, Dani's ambition, for the sake of happiness and mental health, is simply to keep on running. And alongside the running goes openness. She is convinced they are both the best way forward.

It is still difficult for me to share a certain level of detail of my past states. I have experienced the stigma depression carries, and I have, on occasion, experienced a bit of whiplash after sharing. But I have made a commitment to just open up about it as much as possible, because it is the best way to fight stigma, to heal and to help others dealing with the same problems.

Carolyn Knights

'[He spent] his whole life wrapped in the loving arms
of his mum and dad.'

You have to find something special to help you round the Ultra-Trail 100 on Australia's Blue Mountains. Carolyn Knights found something very, very special indeed – thoughts of Hector, her precious grandchild, who lived just a few short hours. With a photograph of Hector pinned to her backpack, she ran the most remarkable run of her life.

Carolyn, who lives in Campbelltown, a city south-west of Sydney, started running in 1975, thanks to a challenge from her husband's hockey club – and she has been running ever since. Trail running is her speciality. She loves training with her 'trail buddies', who offer invaluable advice, companionship and friendship, but she also loves the solitude of hitting the trails alone. It gives her a very particular connection.

> *Trail running is my happy place. I love running on my own as it is solitary and I can listen to the birds and hear the wildlife. Mainly I see wallabies, goannas, koalas, bush turkeys and very, very occasionally snakes – which mainly slither away when they feel feet vibrations!*

The attractions are huge. She loves to get a new PB; she relishes the chance to conquer a new trail; and over the last few years she has consistently been able to beat the rest of her age group across a number of races. In all those respects, trail beats road. As Carolyn says, the competition is still fierce, but the runners usually seem more friendly and relaxed. She also prefers trail from a professional point of view. As a massage and fitness teacher and practitioner, she believes trail is generally more forgiving on body and mind even if it is invariably harder in elevation and terrain. It's a different approach.

I can easily beat myself up on road, but put me on a trail and I can usually find a place to let my mind wander if I need increased stimulation or variety.

Carolyn's love of running means that self-motivation is always there, and by training and competing with a group of fellow trail runners, she has a great time. She particularly relishes the challenge of different distances, from 16 kilometres (10 miles) right up to 100 kilometres (62 miles). 'I adore being fit and active and want to continue forever,' says Carolyn. It's a lifestyle that dovetails with her work as a massage therapist and personal trainer. She teaches three-and-a-half days a week and for two days a week, she runs her own business, working with her son Trent, who is also a massage therapist and a traditional Chinese medicine practitioner. Fitness filters through into work, which filters through into family.

The younger grandkids don't really understand yet, but my eldest grandchild also supports me. When he was younger, he used to say when we went for a walk: 'Are we going our pace or granny pace?', meaning 'Will it be easy or are we going to walk fast?'

Briefly, tragically, Carolyn had an even younger grandchild for just three short hours. She gained and lost a fourth grandchild, Hector William Knights Taylor White on 20 March, 2017. As a result of an infection that wasn't picked up early enough to save him, Carolyn's daughter Brooke gave birth at just 23 weeks.

He was perfect but just too young to survive. We cried, talked, cried, laughed, involved each other and there will always be a gap where he should have been. I am glad he got the chance to spend his whole life — three hours in total — wrapped in the loving arms of his mum and dad, Brooke and Ben. My way of dealing with the whole process is knowing that not many parents get the opportunity to hold their child in their arms for their entire life. A small consolation, but it certainly helps.

When Carolyn found out about Hector, she had just completed a bleep fitness test. During the process, she had a feeling that it was too hard and that she needed to pull out early. Around an hour later, Brooke, who lives in the United States, rang to give her the news. Remarkably, Carolyn soon found herself touched by Hector's presence – confirmation of the deep and special bond she has always enjoyed with Brooke and was now enjoying with the grandson she never had the chance to meet.

> *The following week when out training I ran up a hill and at the top I felt the wind on my face and immediately thought of Hector touching my face. Just a little while later my daughter rang and told me that when she left the hospital and went through the doors to outside she felt the wind on her face and immediately thought: Hector will never get the chance to feel the breeze on his face.*

Hector's life and death came six weeks before the Ultra-Trail Australia 100 (UTA100), for which Carolyn was already training. Brooke is naturally 'the most amazingly supportive person' and had been the most vocal in encouraging Carolyn to enter the UTA run. With Hector's passing, the race began to assume a new significance. He was very much in her thoughts during the training runs that followed. Carolyn invariably felt she was 'taking Hector along' with her.

It was all part of stepping up, quite literally, for Australia's premier ultra-trail run. The race with the highest elevation, it is a gruelling trek between Katoomba and Wentworth Falls with around 4400 metres (14,435 feet) of climbing and descending along the way.

And as if that wasn't tough enough, the race got a little tougher still as the big day approached. Heavy rain in the days leading up to the event meant that the organisers had to change the course overnight. They did an amazing job, but the changes added more stairs: 'But, hey, what are a few more hundred stairs in the mix?'

Carolyn approached it all with a solid training programme, weekly massages and also treatment from her son, all of which helped to keep her injury-free and able to complete all the sessions necessary to get her to the start. From there, she ran with a very special ally: her grandson Hector, his photograph on her backpack.

Carolyn set out in slight drizzle. She laughed and she cried. Along the way, she even managed to phone her daughter in America.

During the race every time I felt a breeze on my face, I had the exact same moment, the thought of Hector being with me. I also had a knocking in my pack at around kilometre 79 and asked a volunteer if he could see what it might be. And there was nothing, everything was tucked in. I then thought of Hector and that he 'had my back', just one more reminder that he was with me.

The second half of the race threw a few curveballs her way, but Carolyn managed to focus on the run, stay positive and deal with whatever came along, including crew glitches, cramps and a couple of niggly injuries. She believes this is where her affinity with Hector really came into play: 'I really believe we had a connection into the dark hours of the night and early morning.'

Four times she heard the knocking on her back. Each time her connection with Hector tightened. Each time there were no other runners within eyesight. Otherwise, it was just running, running, running, up stairs and down stairs. Every so often a volunteer would be there to welcome her in the cold, dark night. As Carolyn recalls, the experience was wonderful, especially with music and dancing to entertain the runners at intervals.

Carolyn ended up with a grade-one calf tear and also behind-the-knee issues, most likely from the constant stair climbing, which slowed her in the final 13 kilometres (8 miles). But she managed to run all 963 of the Ferbur stairs, then the ramp and then three more stairs to the finish line. She never once doubted her ability to finish; she knew it was going to be the most exciting event she had ever completed; and it was. She ran the entire course with a smile on her face. Thanks to Hector.

I believe the bereavement actually became my focus and helped me through, although I could certainly have done without it! Running with Hector's photo became a priority after we held a memorial in his memory on a beach in Queensland, Australia, where my daughter and son-in-law married. I thought about his picture often and it gave me the ability to include him in the race.

And what a race it was. Carolyn started at 6.57 a.m. on the Saturday and finished, just over 21 hours later, at 4.05 a.m. on the Sunday – a performance that placed her first in her age group, the over-60s. No one mentioned the picture during the event, but plenty of people have done so since. As Carolyn says, her family completely understood her need and desire to carry Hector's photo with her along the way.

For the runner in Carolyn, the satisfaction is immense. UTA has three distances: 22 kilometres (14 miles), 50 kilometres (31 miles) and 100 kilometres (62 miles). In 2016, she competed in the 22 kilometres and won her age group. In 2017, she triumphed in the 100 kilometres. She will be competing in the 50 kilometres in 2018, hoping to take out her age group once again and so secure an age-group treble.

For the grandmother in Carolyn, the day offered a remarkable opportunity to connect with Hector in the most powerful of ways. She later wrote in her race diary:

I was especially grateful to my daughter and son-in-law for allowing me to include Hector in my journey and that he will forever remain my ultimate trail buddy and get to travel our beautiful country and the world in this amazing sport.

Carolyn has now completed 14 road marathons; three Ironman triathlons, including Hawaii; numerous Olympic-distance triathlons; and countless fun runs. Her trail runs have also included three Brindabella Ranges (54 kilometres/34 miles), the King of the Mountain twice (30 kilometres/19 miles) and the Wild Earth Coastal High 50 – an epic 50 kilometres (31 miles) in the spectacularly picturesque Gold Coast hinterland. She also took out her age group in the Bandera Texas (26 kilometres/16 miles) in January 2017 in –11°C (12°F): 'Wowser, was it cold – 11 layers of clothing and a frozen bladder [hydration pack] until at 24 km the hose thawed!'

But Carolyn labels the 2017 UTA100 the most challenging and rewarding event in her running career – a race she marked in the most modest of ways with a quick cup of sweet potato soup and then bed. Not that she slept for long. Her legs were too jittery and she struggled to turn over. She managed just half an hour's sleep before the race presentation the following morning. Carolyn picked out a pair of trail shoes – one of her prizes – and then it was the journey back home, job done. Gloriously done, in fact.

A distraction can certainly help people overcome grief, as well as talking about it to other people, including family. I still have Hector's photo on my pack and like to say that he is experiencing the trails with me. I just hope to continue running for as long as my little legs will carry me, to be inspired by other people's achievements and to love the journey.

Alastair Campbell

'I see [running] as my best meeting of the day.'

Alastair Campbell remains best known for his time as spokesman, press secretary and director of communications and strategy for former British Prime Minister Tony Blair.

However, for many, Alastair's most important contribution will always be the way he has helped to make it easier for people to talk about their mental health problems. His high-profile openness and honesty about his own difficulties challenged many of the taboos that used to condemn countless thousands of people to suffer in silence, misplaced shame and isolation.

Recent years have seen a much greater, much more inclusive dialogue about mental health in the UK. Alastair has been at the forefront of the movement. In fact, he has been one of the key figures who have enabled the dialogue to develop – a fact recognised in November 2017 when Alastair was awarded an honorary fellowship by the Royal College of Psychiatrists. The award acknowledged his leadership role in breaking down the stigma surrounding mental illness and also his work fighting for better services. Alastair helped set the ball rolling at a time when many considered the stigma insuperable.

In our new era of increasing openness, Alastair's work has had a huge impact. He was a co-founder of the all-party campaign Equality 4 Mental Health, which was credited in Parliament by the then Chancellor George Osborne with securing an extra £600 million for mental health services. Alastair is also a fervent supporter of the Heads Together campaign headed by Prince William, his wife Catherine and his brother, Prince Harry.

Speaking as someone who 'kind of left the planet for a while' during his own breakdown in the 1980s, Alastair is a firm believer that exercise – running in particular – can be one of our greatest allies when we are fighting depression. The physical exercise of running can set up simple mental exercises which somehow help when we are struggling. Sometimes if he is feeling down, Alastair might make his goal as simple as running to the next lamppost. If he manages it, he will target the next tree, then the next car, then the next corner of the street. Somehow this can lift his mood. The physical translates into the mental.

Whenever I get depressed I find it very hard to summon the energy to exercise. But if I can, and I manage to do the run as planned, it tends to help. On the preventive side, running helps general fitness, which helps general mental health. If ever I feel my fitness dipping, I know it is not helping up top.

Ask Alastair what depression feels like, and he will tell you it is different for everyone: 'For me it is feeling dead and alive at the same time.' At times like these, simply remembering the good that running can do can be a big help. It's a question of trusting in the benefits.

I see it as my best meeting of the day. My mind just ticks around at its own pace. Sometimes nothing happens up there. Other times I get really good ideas. Other times I resolve issues that have been bothering me. I just let the mind go. Sometimes I go with a specific thing to think about – maybe writing a speech or a plot line for a book or a family issue. Other times I just go and my mind can go anywhere. Sometimes you just focus on the next few yards and keep doing so.

Regular exercise – cycling more than running of late – has been central to Alastair in terms of managing his depression. In his Downing Street years, he used to run into work and sometimes back. It was a way of thinking about work in a different way, a way of thinking without actual in-a-room meetings, a way of thinking that cleared the mind.

Running was something Alastair came back to later in life after enduring it at school as an obligation.

I ran at school because we had to. Till I was 11, I was living in Yorkshire and I had a term at Bradford Grammar School, where the cross-country course was brutal and included a Jacob's ladder of steps up a steep hill. I hated it, and being asthmatic didn't help. Then we moved to Leicester,

*and it was all a bit flatter and easier, but I never really felt into it. I was
in my 40s when I started running in a meaningful way. I was on holiday,
and my sons cajoled me into joining them for a run. The next day I decided
to do a marathon.*

However, Alastair soon realised that the best way to make sure he did
actually run one was to commit himself publicly. The 2003 London
Marathon became his target. Adding purpose to the race, Alastair
resolved to run it in aid of the Leukaemia Research Fund, a charity
battling the disease that had claimed the life of his closest friend, John
Merritt, 10 years before.

John, who helped Alastair through his breakdown in the 1980s, died
in August 1992 at the age of 35. He labelled it 'cruelty almost beyond
invention' when John's eldest child Ellie also died from leukaemia, six
years later at the age of nine.

Alastair was one of the coffin bearers for John and also for
Ellie. Their loss was a powerful motivator as he contemplated the
marathon – which would have been beyond his contemplation just
a few years before, he admits. But just as Alastair started to relish
the quiet time to think which his marathon training brought him,
so too did he feel the pressure of having gone public. He struggled
with the thought that he simply couldn't *not* finish. But Alastair soon
discovered that having a reason to run is so often the best way of
reaching the finish line.

As he later wrote in his diary, the night before the marathon he
had his recurring dream about losing his race number – but this time
with a twist. The ink had run and made the number illegible and he
was ruled out of the race. When he woke up, however, he soon found
a good omen – the fact that the radio was talking about him as one of
the day's runners.

Miles 9, 15 and 21 proved to be the hardest on Sunday, 13 April,
2003, but the bands and the crowds were great, terrific inspiration to
keep going. Despite the divisiveness of the Iraq War in the UK at
the time, Alastair didn't get a single critical comment from a crowd
determined to roar everyone on. He remembers too being helped by
other runners in a struggle where everyone is in it together.

Alastair recalls that the last few miles from the Tower of London to the finish were 'hard and exhilarating in equal measure', but by then he knew he was on course to achieve his goal of breaking four hours. As he approached Big Ben, he allowed the emotion to come out. Thoughts of John and of the money he was now raising for the Leukaemia Research Fund were powerful spurs to keep going.

> *When I was in the last bit of the London Marathon I was thinking about the friend whose death led me to my involvement with the charity and I started crying.*

And so he made it across the line in a mix of happiness and pain, his family there to meet him. Despite a massive dehydration headache, the feeling of finishing – in 3 hours, 56 minutes, 3 seconds – was fantastic.

Since then, Alastair has continued to work for the twin causes so dear to him. He is the chairman of fundraising for Bloodwise, Britain's main blood cancer charity. Increasingly involved with mental health charities and causes, drawing on his depression, psychosis and addiction, Alastair is an ambassador for Alcohol Concern and a patron of Kidstime, which supports the children of mentally ill parents.

He is also an ambassador for the Time to Change campaign. The campaign argues that far too many people are still made to feel ashamed or isolated because they have a mental health problem – and that's precisely what Time to Change aims to change, by raising awareness of mental illness and by reshaping how we all think and act about mental health. Alastair fronted the charity's antidiscrimination campaign and co-wrote the charity's report *A World Without*, which highlighted the achievements of five major historical figures who experienced mental health problems.

Recognition of his commitment to fighting mental health discrimination came when Alastair was named Mind Champion of the Year in 2009. Honouring people who have made an outstanding contribution to mental health over the previous year, the Mind Champion of the Year Award is nominated and voted for by the public. Alastair gained more than half the votes.

He admits his attentions have turned rather more to cycling these days, but running will always hold a special place in his affections.

Does he see running as a kind of therapy, rhythmic, soothing and restorative?

I love nice scenery and so a run in the Highlands of Scotland or up in the hills near Burnley is more therapeutic than a run through a busy town. I also find running helps create a lot of the conditions I need for my mind to work properly. Sometimes I need solitude and nobody looks at a runner and thinks, 'Poor guy, must be so lonely'. Also, when I get into it, something happens that really gets my brain working well. Not always. But sometimes.

The marathon remains a highlight, along with loads of Great North Runs.

But at the top would be beating Brendan Foster by a millisecond in the Great Ethiopian Run. That was my favourite ever race.

Meanwhile, he can run – or indeed cycle – knowing that when it comes to mental health, we are finally as a society starting to get it right. The next challenge will be how our future governments respond.

We are heading in the right direction in terms of attitudes and the breaking down of stigma. My worry is that as that happens, more and more people come forward and admit to problems but then find the services are not there. I worry politicians and policy makers see the progress in attitude as a substitute for resources when it should be the impetus for more.

Liz Dunning

*'I have got children. I am not going to concede their
future to a world of guns.'*

In the year 2000, Nancy Dunning staked out five strategic spots
along the route of the Marine Corps Marathon in Washington. She
flitted between them, and at each she shouted: 'Run, Lizzie, Run!',
determined to cheer on her daughter on her marathon debut.

Seventeen years later, 'Run, Lizzie, Run' were the words printed on
Liz's running top when she embarked on her second marathon. Liz's
dearest wish was that the crowds would shout: 'Run, Lizzie, Run', just
as her mum had done. She hoped that the voices of friends, family and
strangers would enable her to hear Nancy's voice once again.

Liz liked the thought of complete strangers shouting: 'Run,
Lizzie, Run' without knowing the tragedy those words now carried.
The words helped her through 26.2 miles as she ran in fond memory
of her mother.

Three years after Liz's first marathon, and 14 years before her
second, Nancy was shot dead at the age of 56 on her own doorstep
in Alexandria, Virginia, a city on the Potomac River, just south of
Washington. Liz dedicated that second marathon to Nancy. She told
her late mother: 'We're connected, you and me, today and always.'

Curiously, it was only after the second marathon that Liz realised
the beautiful symmetry of her achievement. Every mile of the
marathon had been for Nancy. Taken together, those 26 miles
represented the 26 years they had shared before Nancy was murdered,
on 5 December, 2003.

As Liz looks back, she finds consolation in the fact that the final
years they had together were years of particular closeness, years during

which Liz came to appreciate just what exactly made her mother such a special person.

We had just a few years in that last chapter when I was a young adult and I was able to connect and relate to my parents in a different way. I was 26 when my mother was killed. I had been back in the area for about four years, and it was then I think I was able to start to see my Mom as a whole person. She was someone who was always really up for anything, always hungry and thirsty for new experiences. She was not someone who would think: I have done X and Y and I will settle now with what I have done. She was always thinking: Oh! This might be fun! I wouldn't say it was restlessness. She was just someone who was always open to new ideas and new things.

When she thinks of Nancy, Liz says she has never met anyone who was 'so incredibly in their own bones', so grounded, so completely at home with herself. Liz believes it was that level of comfort within herself which made her mother so receptive, so open and so supportive of her children.

She was always a great support for me, and if I wanted to run, that was fine. She was very curious about people. When she was talking to you, you always felt you were the only person in the room. There was nobody in life she loved more than me and my brother Chris, and she knew us in a really dynamic and fluid way. Every time she was with us, it was like she was thinking there was always more to learn about us.

And it was in that spirit that Nancy supported Liz on her marathon debut in 2000. Liz had started running as a teenager as part of her training for rowing – but when she went to college in Ohio, there was not a lot of water, so the running took over. The attraction was that running needed no special equipment. You just went out there and did it – and that was the approach Liz took for her first marathon, a race that Nancy investigated far more than Liz ever did. Always a good listener, Nancy always knew someone who knew what she needed to know. She identified someone who had run the race before and mapped out the five points at which she would be able to see Liz run past.

I was just a typical cavalier 23-year-old. I didn't realise that the marathon was such a big thing, such a long distance. But Mum did. She knew. She knew the significance.

Tragically, three years later, Nancy was murdered.

Liz was at work at the time. Nancy was supposed to be meeting Chris and her husband Jim for lunch, but she didn't turn up. They went back to the house. Chris, just 23, went in and found her body. Jim arrived several minutes later. Chris called Liz at work. By the time she reached home, the house was already sealed off. Liz was spared the sight of the blood at least, but little concrete information emerged during the repeated questionings that followed that day. It wasn't until the evening – when Jim, Chris and Liz were together again, still at the police station – that Jim was able to tell them: Nancy had been shot. 'We knew nothing else apart from that,' Liz recalls.

The news was breaking on television. Friends were gathering to look after Liz. She remembers the confusion – and the pain. Running seemed the right response. In the weeks and years that followed, Liz learned that running and trauma go hand in hand, natural running mates.

There is a connectivity between running and trauma. My brain was not able to process the entirety of what happened because it was all too overwhelming for my small brain. In the couple of months after she was murdered, I could not watch TV, and I had a really hard time following conversations involving more than two people. It was all the typical symptoms of PTSD, and it was helpful to have the diagnosis, to know that I was not going crazy. You go from somebody who very much thinks of themselves as bright and capable to almost immediately having no short-term memory. You just have to find a way to process all those thoughts differently.

Jim, Liz and Chris were lucky enough to have a family friend who said to the three of them: 'OK, I am going to find you a therapist and you a therapist and you a therapist, and I am going to find one where you can all go together.' Liz started counselling within a couple of weeks, and it helped, but running was crucial too. She believes the important fact is the obvious fact: that you are doing something active. And being active opens doors in your brain to ideas and experiences – doors that might otherwise remain shut.

If I am sitting in my office, my brain knows that I need to do my work and think about what I am going to make my family for dinner. But when I get up early in the morning and go for a run, there is nobody about and I can run as fast as I possibly can down the middle of the street. It is not like the trauma goes away. The running lets the trauma in. I can run down the street at 5.15 in the morning as if I am being chased, and it lets in the fact that both my parents have been taken from me. My father died in 2012. I know I am going to meet people during the day who won't know the experiences I have had. When I am running, I have that private time alone first.

Inevitably, as time passes, so the grief changes. Liz believes that over the years and with the help of running, she has reached a level of understanding of her pain, her loss and her trauma. She knows what they feel like. And she knows that running will give her the privacy she needs.

I imagine there are people who go to support groups for similar things, but for me, it has always been a little bit more private than that. Part of the need for privacy is that there were cameras for weeks and weeks after the murder, and people were telling me my own story back to me in ways that felt invasive. When I am running, I get my own story in my own time, my own hurt in my own way. Running gives me something very special.

While others might run to run away from their darkness, Liz runs to embrace it.

Even after all this time, I need to actively manage my pain, trauma and grief. I am not trying to make sense of it or to be at peace with it. That's not the idea. But I have to spend time in that darkness. If I don't give myself time and permission to grieve regularly, it will overwhelm me, washing over me like a tidal wave. My mental health and my ability to be a joyful, present friend, wife and mom depend on finding time on the road.

As she says, if she spends time in the darkness, she knows that when she spends time with her children, she can genuinely spend time in the light. And the fact that she can say so brings her back to her mother. Liz regards herself as a 'pretty reflective' person, something she believes she inherited from both her parents. In the immediate aftermath of the murder, Liz wrote a great deal, a large number of letters to her late mother – again a means by which she coped.

As the years passed, she believed she was coping with something else too – the fact that her mother's killer would never be caught. But then he was, though not before he had killed two more people, in 2013 and 2014. When their murders were investigated, the investigation took the police back to the murder of Nancy Dunning. Eventually, Charles Severance was charged with the murder of three Alexandria residents over the course of a decade.

So much had changed in those years. By now, Liz was married and a mum to two boys, then aged six and two. The looming trial changed things further. As Liz says, when she met new people, there had been no point saying: 'Hi, my name is Liz and my mum was murdered years ago and the killer has never been caught.' With court proceedings on the horizon, however, it was all back in sharp focus. She felt obliged to forewarn her older son's kindergarten, and her running intensified, all part of the mental preparation she felt she had to put herself through.

I think with all the experiences in my life, I have very, very rarely been given the chance to prepare for something hard. Thinking about the trial, preparing for it, I knew I had to spend time running.

Liz didn't have to testify, though her brother did. She made a point, however, of attending every day of the trial.

I wanted to represent Mom at the trial and I wanted the jury to look across and think: 'Oh, that must be Nancy Dunning's girl.'

Severance was convicted of all three murders and a variety of related charges on 2 November, 2015 – All Souls' Day. The trial concluded nearly 12 years after Nancy's death – and it has certainly made things easier. Liz hasn't told her children yet what happened to their grandmother, but she knows the task will be simpler for the fact that she won't have to add 'and her killer was never caught'.

A year after the trial, Liz was ready to move towards a much more positive commemoration of her mother. The spur was the fact that

2017 would see Nancy's 70th birthday in the March and Liz's 40th in the April. Liz recalled a close time they had spent together 20 years before when their 50th and 20th birthdays coincided within weeks. She knew she had to mark 2017 in a significant way.

The world of marathon running provided the answer. Liz realised that the 2017 Washington DC Rock 'n' Roll Marathon was to be staged on 11 March, precisely the day Nancy would have turned 70. Liz resolved to run it in her memory – a decision that also gave birth to Liz's website, which takes as its title those very special words Nancy had shouted at her from those five strategic spectator points 17 years before: *Run Lizzie Run* (www.runlizzierun.com).

> *I realised I was going to be running on my home streets, and the website idea started really the first time I went for a long run after making my decision. I realised that I needed to let my brain work again for a while on the loss and the trauma and the grief. I realised that 26.2 miles is an awfully long way, but I realised it would be an even longer way if I let myself be flooded with those thoughts again.*

Through the website, Liz started to share her thoughts and her grief. She also started to raise funds for gun control advocacy, another way to turn the race into something positive, uplifting and energising. With the help of more than 300 donors, she raised almost $29,000.

> *Is it possible to get to a different place about guns? I hope so. It's really hard to believe it every day. There have been so many horrific things that have happened, but I am not going to concede it. I have got children. I am not going to concede their future to a world of guns.*

As Liz says, the run wasn't about sadness – not entirely, anyway. It was about movement and progress. She hopes one day it might also prove to have been about triumph. Liz puts it simply: 'If we all stand up and act, we can ensure there are fewer of us with this particular hole in our hearts.'

Danny Slay

'It gave me an outlet to think, focus and unwind.'

Nearly 100 firefighters converged on the Atherstone Industrial Estate when fire ripped through a vegetable warehouse on 2 November, 2007. Crews rushed to the former airfield from immediate and neighbouring counties. Tragically, by the time the blaze had been extinguished, four firefighters were dead. The fire had entered the grim annals of firefighting history.

In the thick of it all was Danny Slay, 36 at the time, in a role that exposed him to sights no one should ever have to see. Danny was part of the body recovery team, a ghastly task that marked him deeply – though it was to be several years before he realised just how much it had damaged him personally.

As the years started to pass, Danny noticed that he would lapse into a depressive state around the time of the anniversary – 'really teary and upset'. Personal issues in the background further undermined his mental health. By 2011 he was deep in PTSD, prey to appalling flashbacks. As he says, he was 'literally there' in his mind, back at the scene of the fire all the time.

The fire service was able to give him first-class support, but Danny realises a key moment in his recovery came over Christmas 2011, when he was staying at his father's house in Cumbria. In his depression Danny knew he needed to do something. He was already starting to lose weight, having grown to 15 stone (95 kilos). On impulse, he decided to run. As he ran uphill through the snow, he discovered it was an exhilarating release.

Danny describes the feeling in the simplest terms: relief. It was as straightforward as that. And while he was at the Fire Service College in Moreton-in-Marsh, Gloucestershire, he found the perfect opportunity to pursue it further. The choice was to sit and do nothing or go out of the gate and run. If he went for the run, the choice was again a simple one: a 3-mile (5-kilometre) circuit or an 8-mile (13-kilometre) circuit. Danny opted for the latter and felt his sense of release grow in proportion to the distance. Running immediately offered challenges, and he knew it would be good for his mental health to meet them. This was a case of the further, the better.

> *It gave me an outlet to think, focus and unwind. People start with 5ks or 10ks. I wasn't interested in that, I wanted to do ultramarathons.*

Danny's target became the London 2 Brighton Challenge – a 100k route, Capital to Coast – in June 2012. He limbered up for it with his first ultramarathon in the May, the London Ultra, a 50k race from south-east to north-west London.

At school Danny had always been a team player. His sports were rugby and football. In fact, he continued playing rugby for around 20 years until, as he says, injury and age caught up with him. Suddenly now he was discovering he was a runner. The transition from anti-runner ('just not that interested', he says) to ultrarunner was rapid. The endorphins kicked in, and he enjoyed the challenge of having to do it, with sponsorship money riding on his race.

It became clear: alongside the treatment he was receiving, running was helping to relieve the symptoms of his post-traumatic stress disorder (PTSD). Key too was recognising that there was a problem in the first place. Denial was a huge obstacle to overcome. Danny admits it took him a while to see what others were so clearly seeing: an unhealthy single-mindedness at work meant he was intolerant of suggestions from colleagues. At the time he was living away from his family, navigating a break-up, and again, he couldn't see what others could see: the fact that he was spending far too much time by himself.

It was running that helped Danny to reconnect because one challenge led to another, particularly when he linked up with the charity Hope for Children, which last year helped more than 37,000 children and their families in Africa, Asia and the UK. Danny feels it's a charity that uses its funds wisely. It also offers him precisely the support he needs when he goes that extra mile on their behalf, just as he did when he successfully tackled a race recognised as one of the world's most gruelling: the 'unforgettable' 254 kilometres (158 miles) of the Marathon des Sables. No longer the loner, Danny was part of Team Hope, running alongside five other firefighters – from the Fire & Rescue Services of Devon and Somerset (Paul Cross and Matt Mason) and West Midlands (Pete Drummond, Andy Miller and Ryan Weir).

> *I had struck up a friendship with Pete Drummond, another firefighter who had been at the same Warwickshire fire as me. We had both developed similar issues post-fire. We did the London Ultra together with Andy Miller, and we discussed the Marathon des Sables. It was like a red rag to me! Like me, they just can't turn down a good challenge.*

The adventure took them pretty much to the limit. Danny counts himself a strong guy, but the experience of the Marathon des Sables – the equivalent of six marathons in six days in heat of about 60°C (140°F) with a backpack on – saw Danny and the team discover new depths of resilience. He particularly remembers, his foot 'in tatters', taking half an hour to walk just yards to the medical tent in search of paracetamol, all the while wondering how on earth he was going to run another marathon the next day. He managed it.

> *The MdS was an amazing experience! In the early days, it was a distant dream and as we got closer to the run that dream got closer to reality, but it did not actually sink in until the day we left the UK. Being a team helped us in our spirits, and especially in the low moments the lift we gave each other was really important. There were some extremely low points during the event, but the fact we had not only achieved but smashed our target gave us the motivation to complete the run.*

But there is another legacy too. In support of his Marathon des Sables fundraising, Danny organised Hope24. In May 2014, he and his friends gathered with 196 runners in a mixture of soloists and teams of two, three, five and eight to run a 5-mile (8-kilometre) trail course over a period of 24 hours. It was never his intention to stage the event again, but the feedback from participants was so positive that he decided to give it another go. The event has doubled in size every year since. It has also won numerous awards.

Once again, resilience has been key. Danny looks back to a moment on the London 2 Brighton Challenge in 2012. With 36 miles (58 kilometres) still to go, just as he was crossing the M25, he 'blew up' with a massive blister. He didn't know how on earth he was going to carry on, let alone finish. And yet he did. 'I have never DNF'd anything yet,' he says proudly – referring to that little acronym every runner fears, the dreaded *Did Not Finish*.

In the depths of his depression and his PTSD, Danny says he gave himself a 'kick up the backside' – a kick that has landed him in a world he loves. Again, he stresses that the support of the Fire Service has been second to none, but just as crucial has been the vast running camaraderie which has opened up to him: 'The support within the ultrarunning family is just phenomenal.'

All of this feeds back into his current work within the Fire Service. A station manager based in Plymouth, Danny now works as a defuser, one of the team that talks to the firefighters every time there is a fatal incident. Their aim is to prevent the onset of PTSD.

Danny regrets that conditions meant this was not provided in the immediate aftermath of the Warwickshire fire of 2007. Against that, however, his own experience of PTSD gives him precisely the empathy and understanding needed to see the symptoms of trauma triggered in others.

> *I do think you can do this job if you haven't suffered yourself, but I think having been through it puts me in a good position when we talk about what has happened. What we try to do with the firefighters is to piece together the whole jigsaw so that no one goes home with a piece missing from the picture, which they then stew about. Having gone through it, I do think I have become a good listener.*

Danny has also joined the England Athletics Mental Health Ambassador programme. The scheme aims to establish a network of volunteer ambassadors in running clubs and groups across England to support people who are experiencing mental health problems. The idea is to get them to start running, to get back into running or to continue to run. Its starting point is that physical activity is good for our bodies and our minds, but having a mental health problem can make it difficult to get started for a number of reasons, ranging from a negative body image and lack of self-esteem to more practical reasons, such as having no one to run with or not knowing where to get started.

Danny is well able to help. He knows at first-hand the value of that sense of connection which running can bring. He simply can't say what would have become of him without running, but he doubts he would have found himself in today's strong position: fully connected again to everyone around him. To friends, to fellow runners and, above all, to life itself.

Ana Febres-Cordero

'I am amazing, I am strong, I am beautiful, I am kind.'

One in five Americans will experience mental illness in his or her lifetime. Ana Febres-Cordero, of Boston, Massachusetts, nearly paid for that illness with her life.

Ana is now a proud supporter of Deconstructing Stigma, a campaign that aims to break down the preconceptions and prejudices surrounding mental health. She is proud too to be a suicide survivor – a feat she celebrated by running the Boston Marathon with her father Rafael in April 2017.

Guiding their steps on those 26.2 miles was a shared mission to help trample down the obstacles that discourage so many people from seeking the mental health care they need. For Ana and Rafael, the marathon was also about educating the friends, families and neighbours of people with mental illness. It was about prompting them to find out the ways in which they can support their loved one's recovery.

But maybe above all, those 26.2 miles symbolised the astonishing progress Ana had made in the six months since the black day when she tried to end her life. She realises she will never be the same person again, but knows that this is for the better.

Ana recalls the lowest of low points. On 23 October, 2016, during her freshman year at Dickinson College, Pennsylvania, she wrote goodbye letters to her friends and then tried to kill herself in her college dorm.

During the act, I felt completely numb to what I was doing because I was 100 per cent sure that what I was doing was the right thing. I felt like a complete waste of space. I did not think anything in life was worth it any more. I really tried to convince myself out of it by telling myself there are so many things in life I haven't even experienced: marriage, having kids, getting a job, travelling the world, buying my first house . . . but the tipping point for me was that I did not want to let the kind of person I thought I was go through life.

She was horrified at the thought of having children. She couldn't bear the thought of a child going through what she was going through – all the more so if the child were her own.

I had zero interest in anything in life, I was wasting my parents' money on the education I wasn't getting. I told myself I was ugly and too fucked up to be anything close to successful in life. I had struggled with depression since my junior year in high school. I did not know it at the time, and I had gone two years with thinking the way I was acting was just the person I had become.

Now, Ana feels she can better understand the sheer complexity of the factors that led to her near-fatal decision. She had gone through her first serious relationship, and this too was part of her downward spiral. It was not the only trigger, but it certainly contributed. Hindsight shows her 'all the little things that accumulated during those three years' that led to her state of complete darkness.

Fortunately, Ana's friends were able to intervene, and they saved her life. They took her to hospital, and Ana's mum drove straight from Massachusetts to Pennsylvania. It was the first step on Ana's road to recovery. From that point onwards, Ana – diagnosed with major depressive disorder, social anxiety and an eating disorder – has been a willing participant in all the treatment she has been given.

Ana remains baffled that the signs hadn't been spotted before then, not least by herself. She lists the symptoms of depression, and she knows she had them all. She can tick off feelings of sadness, tearfulness, emptiness and hopelessness. She was prey to angry outbursts, irritability, frustration and a loss of interest and/or pleasure in most or all normal activities. She endured sleep disturbances, tiredness, increased appetite, anxiety and slowed thinking and movement. She also went through feelings of worthlessness and guilt: her focus was on past failures, and her blame fell on herself. She struggled to think and struggled to concentrate, and recurrent thoughts of death assailed her. It was all there.

But how did I not notice? Even all these months later, I am still shocked by how this went totally under the radar for so long. I saw a guidance counsellor at school weekly, along with a therapist for two summers (junior to senior year and senior year to freshman at college). In all honesty, how did they not see the signs? I just look back at that part of my life, just feeling so completely isolated and so different from everyone. I almost knew there was something off about me. I was still just a bubbly and very outgoing girl, but I also shut down after spending too much of a long period with too many people. It is exactly like someone shutting off a switch in my brain. I was completely emotionally numb and not there.

Fortunately, she had a release to hand: the simple act of running. As she says, it was an escape.

My escape, junior and senior year, was running. I could just throw everything out on a run – all my anxiety, insecurities, built-up frustration. You don't need any emotions to run. I felt separated sometimes when I ran. The bottom half of my body was getting fuelled by all of the intoxicated junk that mental illness was putting me through. From the waist up, I sometimes teared up on my runs, just releasing all of my built-up emotions I could not put words to match. The best part, after every run, was I had about three or four hours of clarity in my mind. A sense of relief, a weight lifted off my shoulders.

Inevitably, running played a key role in Ana's recovery following her suicide attempt. As her mental health improved, so she started to exercise regularly again. Her father noticed her revived passion for running and asked whether she was interested in running the Boston Marathon. The answer was yes. They then decided to add extra meaning by running for a cause: Deconstructing Stigma. Their aim was to tell the world that mental illness is absolutely no reason for shame.

Ana speaks now with complete clarity of mind. She has resumed her college career. She is studying at the University of New Hampshire and is proud to be a 'wildcat'. She is happy and confident – and knows that running has helped to get her there. For Ana, running is a way to clear her thoughts and relieve most of her stress and also a way to reassess her cognitive distortions and calm herself down.

Alongside depression, Ana is currently also recovering from an eating disorder. Whenever she felt down or anxious, she turned to food for comfort. But then came guilt, followed by anxiety – a vicious circle that led back to eating 'enormous amounts of food'. She now finds that exercise helps to regulate her appetite, a step towards accepting herself and loving the body she has.

Running also helps directly with anxiety. Ana has noticed that if she goes more than two days without exercise or running, she starts to become anxious for no apparent reason. Worse, as she says, she starts to cave in to those 'contorted scenarios' created by her mind.

Now when I sense that my anxiety is worsening, all I do is go out for a run. It keeps me in the moment, instead of my mind being all over the place. By the end of the run, I feel refreshed. Almost as if I am just starting my day.

Now, as she looks back on the dark days and rebuilds her life with assurance, Ana realises she is running for exactly the same reasons she always has done. The only difference is that she is now conscious of those reasons.

Running is my sanity. It makes sense. It is no chore to me. It is part of me and my life. Running is easy: play some music, put one foot in front of the other and just go. The only thing in my life that is me in the moment, and no one else.

And the same thoughts extended to marathon day in Boston. As she says, she was running with 35,000 other runners, but it was her legs – Ana's legs – which were carrying her through those 26.2 miles.

It was my brainpower and my drive to make it to that finish line that was carrying me through. Running is an escape to another dimension of the mind to me, and every time I feel pain, especially now, I tell myself it is no comparison to the pain I was in on that night of 23 October. The pain is mental. My body is so much more powerful than the block my mind is putting up. Almost like my depression, once I was diagnosed, it was almost like breaking through that wall during a run. Then it's just a runner's high from there on out. I had my diagnosis, and I won't lie. At first, I saw it as a curse. But now, it is my reason to keep going and keep fighting.

How complete the healing can ever be is, of course, impossible to say. Ana believes the healing process is 25 per cent medication and 25 per cent therapy. The other 50 per cent is sheer willpower and acceptance. Add them all up and those pieces in the puzzle have enabled Ana to reach a crucial awareness: not just that she is enough, but that she is more than enough.

> *I am amazing, I am strong, I am beautiful, I am kind, I am intelligent, hard-working and driven, and I have an immense amount of potential that the world has not yet seen.*

As she says, she has made huge steps to becoming 'my best self at this moment', the only moment we ever have. She knows there will never be a time her therapist will look at her and say: 'You are healed from your depression', but she knows the marathon has been vital in that healing process and that she has healed to the extent that she is once again the person she was before her depression set in, almost four years before. She also knows there was great fun in getting there.

> *I loved reintroducing myself to myself. It was an emotional few days for me, realising that this is the real me. I am about to be faced with many more troubles in my life, but as of this moment, I have tackled 100 per cent of the obstacles thrown my way, and I am sure I can face whatever else is coming.*

And in that sense, the question of whether her depression can ever completely disappear becomes almost irrelevant, a question she cannot and will not answer. She's using her energies far more usefully, throwing her weight behind the Deconstucting Stigma campaign.

The project was developed by McLean Hospital, the largest psychiatric affiliate of Harvard Medical School, in partnership with the American Foundation for Suicide Prevention, the International OCD Foundation, Massachusetts Association for Mental Health, the National Alliance on Mental Illness and PROJECT375, a mental health awareness initiative.

The campaign's biggest physical manifestation was unveiled at Boston's Logan International Airport in December 2016 – a series of larger-than-life photographs and interviews with people from across the United States who have been affected by mental illness. The installation, with an accompanying website and book, aims to capture the sheer complexity of living with a psychiatric disorder – a life that involves seeking treatment, navigating America's insurance and healthcare systems and, perhaps toughest of all, facing stigma.

Millions of passengers pass through the airport, and the hope is to tear down the misconceptions of what those with mental illness look like. The volunteers in the project are mothers, fathers, wives, husbands, lawyers, doctors, engineers, musicians and more. Each one has been affected by mental illness, and each one has also faced stigma. Ana will be part of the campaign's second phase – the smiling face of the mental health she now confidently enjoys.

Her strength is that she will never take anything for granted. She speaks with complete candour. She is certain to be a remarkable voice in the Deconstructing Stigma initiative, a voice that was so nearly silenced.

As of this moment, all I know is that I am being treated, and my depression is being managed . . . But why should I focus on this illness going away? Instead, why don't I live in the moment and appreciate that I am alive and enjoy it?

Lisa Taylor

'Not only am I still here, I now have a lovely baby with my lovely husband.'

Lisa admits that she never loved him, but love had failed her in the past and she was in no hurry to look for love again. For the moment, it seemed far more important that Stewart appeared to be kind and that he seemed to understand her world – a world in which she was principal carer to her beloved, vulnerable grandparents. Lisa admits it wasn't the best starting point for a new relationship, but at the time, it seemed good enough.

Stewart had been her boss when they first met some time before. He had made advances, which Lisa rejected: he was married and she had a boyfriend already. Eventually, she left the job, but a while later she bumped into Stewart again. He told her his circumstances had changed. He was no longer married. And just as importantly, he showed her a kindness she needed. She decided to give their relationship a go.

However, it wasn't long before the lies started piling up, fuelling her suspicions. After six months, Lisa told him their relationship had to end. His response was to knock her to the ground and drag her along the floor towards her grandmother's room, threatening to tell her. 'Do you really want to break her heart?' he screamed at her. Lisa said simply no, and the fury that had erupted so suddenly switched off with equal suddenness. Moments later, Stewart was flicking through messages on his phone and asking Lisa what they were going to do for tea. When he went out, Lisa was left alone with the horror of dawning realisation: she was trapped.

For the next six years, her life was perched on a knife edge. On one occasion, she made the mistake of laughing with a couple of young male doctors just after having her appendix out. When she got home from hospital, Stewart punched her in the stomach. She felt constantly, inexplicably poorly throughout their relationship. Blood tests subsequently showed Stewart had been assiduously maintaining her ill health in the vilest of ways – adding tasteless salt to her food and drink.

> *Stewart was clever. He never hit me in the face. But more than the violence, it was messing with my mind. He was always in my head. I used to keep two diaries, one that I knew Stewart would read. I would say things like 'Another happy day with Stewart'. The other was the one I hid, what was really happening. Before Stewart, I was a strong woman and very independent. At the end of the relationship I didn't think I was going to make Christmas, which was only five months away.*

For much of the time, Lisa was convinced she was dying. Indeed, death seemed the only possible outcome – though suicide was something she instinctively ruled out for the simple reason that she couldn't bear the thought of Stewart comforting her mother at her funeral. Lisa had felt unable to tell her mother what was happening because she didn't want her to be hurt in any way. Lisa's assumption was that one day she would try to escape and that Stewart would kill her. She clung to the bleakest of possible consolations: if he did kill her, at least he wouldn't be able to attend her funeral.

Lisa couldn't find the means to get away. However, escape was closer to hand than she knew. She just needed to realise the form it was going to take. The breakthrough was sneaking out of the house for a Pilates class. Crucially, it taught Lisa how to build up body strength. 'But most of all, it gave me a passion again.' It was the turning point she hadn't known how to find.

Lisa began to feel the benefits of exercise, and she began to crave them. Any opportunity she had, she would go for a walk. Swanbourne Lake in Arundel, West Sussex, became a haven. She walked the mile or so round it once, picked up a bottle of water and walked round it again. Before long, she was completing 10 circuits, which is when the urge to run clicked in – a landmark moment, she feels, as she looks back now on the countless little steps which seem in retrospect like giant strides towards freedom.

Fury was another motivation. Anger was what she felt as she started to remember just how strong and independent she had been. Vitally, through running, her strength and independence started to return.

Lisa realises now that without running she would never have found the courage to leave Stewart. Without running, she wouldn't have known the happiness she now cherishes with her husband Timothy and their baby daughter Lydia.

After I left Stewart, I was going to the gym all the time. My goal was to run in between the weights. It was 20 minutes of pure pain, but it just made me feel amazing. There was just nothing like it. And I would run by the river, and it felt like the most fantastic finger up to Stewart. But the great thing was that it was bringing me back to the old Lisa, the Lisa before I met Stewart, the fit, slim and happy Lisa.

Lisa doubts she can ever fully recapture the self she lost. Mentally, she believes she is there, but physically she still has a long way to go. The excess salt and the violence mean that she has endured a long history of deep vein thrombosis, leaving her with very limited blood flow out of her leg. This has been improved by surgery, but for the moment she cannot run. However, this remains the ultimate goal.

I understand how it feels to use exercise and running to help you gain strength at what life sometimes throws at you. There is just nothing like running. It is like my husband getting on his mountain bike, my brother on his motorbike. Running rescued me. When I am running so fast, I feel like I am a child. I am not the most glamorous runner, but I don't care. I just feel like a child, like in those PE lessons at school again that are so much fun that you can't actually believe they are lessons. It's freedom. That's the thing. Running is freedom.

The real pleasure is to run in the cold beside a misty river, the kind of run where you shiver as you step outside, where you relish the haze over the water as you pound out the distance and return home sweaty but reinvigorated – a chance to think about everything and about nothing.

But really the run is two fingers up to Stewart. Before Stewart, I was very sensitive. I couldn't understand how people hurt each other. But Stewart has made me stronger. And I know what matters. I want to be the old Lisa. I don't worry about money, I don't care about what we have got. I just care about health, about my family and about running. Even if I can just run for five minutes a day, I will feel I have conquered everything.

Lisa is now happily married and a mum – and she feels herself largely free of her past. Lisa is not her real name. She still feels she needs a degree of protection as she reinvents herself and holds on to the likelihood of a happy, fulfilled future with her new family. Inevitably, there are still aftershocks. There will always be difficult memories and terrifying flashbacks to negotiate, but she knows now – thanks largely to the impetus which running gave her – that she has set herself on a new and much more certain course.

My life is amazing some days but hard too as I still have health problems because of the past . . . But every time I get low he wins, so I keep that in mind. And I can't believe how much my life has changed! Not only am I still here, I now have a lovely baby with my lovely husband – when I was told I couldn't have children. She is the only painkiller I need.

Jason Nelson

'I put the barrel of my pistol in my mouth with
my finger firmly on the trigger.'

A surge in the number of suicides in the Western Australia ambulance service prompted paramedics Lyn and Ian Sinclair to set up the Sirens of Silence Charity Inc in 2015. Aiming to support 'our triple zero heroes', they soon realised that a broader safety network was needed to protect and support emergency services personnel right across Australia.

As they so powerfully put it, they wanted to help 'save the lives of those who save you' – the people who, armed with strength and expertise, put themselves in the front line and confront what the rest of us would rather not.

The network is all about creating self-help pathways and, by creating a support community, ending the stigma that so often clings to mental illness. The aim is to raise awareness of anxiety, depression, post-traumatic stress disorder (PTSD) and suicide prevention within the emergency services. Jason Nelson can tick pretty much all of those boxes. In Jason, SOS has found no finer supporter, a man who has fought his way back the hard way.

With Jason running in his distinctive kilt, his Rogue Runners Club Australia is proud to put one foot in front of the other for a charity that really can make a difference.

Jason, who has served in both the British and Australian police forces, began running at high school, discovering his aptitude for distance running by accident.

My family and I were taking part in a sponsored walk back in the UK.
It was a 16-mile walk between two RNLI lifeboat stations. As part of

the walk there were two squads of Royal Marine Commando Reserves running the whole distance in squad formation. I decided that I would try to see if I could run it too. I completed the run as a guest of the second squad of marines and from that moment I've been running distance events ever since.

Jason joined Cheshire Constabulary in February 1998 following a career in the Royal Navy. He graduated Dux of his entry and was awarded the coveted Baton of Honour – success that he continued into his early police career. After making more than 150 arrests in his first two years, he was nominated Probationer of the Year. Passing his exams, he became a successful detective constable working on both overt and covert policing teams – for which he received several commendations. And the success continued when he and his wife moved to Australia.

My wife Emma and I were getting itchy feet where we were living and after living in Adelaide as a migrant in the late 70s with my folks and sisters, I'd always had an affinity with Australia. I saw an advert for WA Police recruiting international police officers in August 2005, and 12 months later, we arrived.

Bright hopes for a bright future. Sadly, Jason little suspected the damage that life in the front line was doing him. Dealing with what he terms 'the worst of society', Jason simply kept his 'professional hat' on and worked on through. He would casually debrief colleagues or maybe go for a beer afterwards. Dark humour was a regular resort, a coping mechanism that kept Jason and his colleagues distant from the sights they saw.

At the time, I didn't have a clue what long-term effect it may have on me. I just stored each incident, each short-story trauma, in my subconscious bookshelf and put it away, so to speak . . . or so I thought.

Jason can recite a grim succession of horrors he was dealing with in his professional career.

His job meant delivering death messages to families who had lost loved ones for a range of reasons, from natural causes to accidents and murder. Another ghastly memory was cutting down a young woman from the tree from which she had hanged herself. In front of her family, it was Jason's grim task to attempt cardiopulmonary resuscitation for 20 minutes while they waited for an ambulance to arrive.

Jason was also called on to attend an attempted murder in Cheshire, where the victim had been stabbed repeatedly by her ex-partner in front of her two young children. He was also one of the family liaison officers for the case.

I've never seen so much blood in all my life as I did at that scene. It's quite remarkable that she survived, 27 stab wounds and one that punctured her heart. Sadly, her children, both under five at the time, witnessed the whole attack.

The ghastly list goes on. He worked on murder investigations and attended post-mortems as scribe or exhibits officer. On another occasion, Jason lost a colleague who was killed on duty during a police pursuit. He and the team were badly affected.

In 1998, while off duty, he also experienced the sudden death from a heart attack of his own grandmother. At the time he dealt with it in the way a police officer would deal with it – so that he could help his family through the trauma. Twenty-one years later, he is still only just processing the grief himself. At the time, though, the damage was compounded by the fact that the next sudden death he was called to was that of an elderly lady with the same first name as his grandmother, who had died at the same age in similar circumstances.

All this came on top of suffering sexual abuse during childhood, by a person in a position of trust, and then, in the early hours of his wedding day, the death of his best mate, Pete.

Matters came to a head in 2007–8. Jason, then aged 36, was working on a high-risk covert policing team in Western Australia. This was a sought-after position, and he had jumped at the chance because on first arriving in Australia, he had been returned to uniform. This new role would let him re-establish himself as a specialist investigator, his role in the UK.

As a Pom, however, Jason met resistance from within the force – just as he was still trying to settle himself and his family into the

Australian lifestyle. At work, he believes he was set up to fail – but he succeeded. The pressures intensified. Not wanting to fail and not wanting to let his family down, he spiralled deeper and deeper into depression.

I was tired all the time, angry, irritable. I would isolate myself from my family. I was being very emotional, crying a lot. Plus, there was the suicide ideation. I tried to numb the pain by self-medicating with alcohol.

His depression became a prison, a pain greater than any physical pain he has ever experienced.

Depression has a dark vice-like grip that doesn't want to let go or let up. It is a darkened cell, from which it is very hard to escape.

At first, Jason put it all down to his frustrations at not being able to achieve what he wanted to achieve, but as he descended deeper, he began to realise what was happening. By then, however, it was very nearly too late. The pain was so intense that his only thought was to end the suffering. He believed the only way he could do so was to end his own life. He wasn't the husband or the dad or the person he wanted to be.

I felt useless, and the only option to release myself and my family from that burden was to die. I put the barrel of my loaded service Glock 27 pistol in my mouth with my finger firmly on the trigger. I'd locked the gun away in the gun safe that was in our walk-in wardrobe. I was curled up in the foetal position in the bottom of the shower, sobbing my heart out, when my wife Emma found me. I told her I wanted to kill myself and that she and the kids would be free of me and my pain. She talked to me about our daughters and convinced me to seek help.

Jason was in turmoil. The diagnosis of post-traumatic stress disorder (PTSD) encompassed a raft of horrors: night terrors, nightmares, sleeplessness, hypervigilance, paranoia, irritability, anxiety and flashbacks triggered by smells and noises. Jason struggled on, only to slump again in 2014 when he underwent surgery for a routine hernia repair. Shortly afterwards, he suffered a delayed reaction to the anaesthetic. His heart went from a resting 50 beats per minute in his sleep to more than 160. The crash team was called and worked frantically to reduce his heart rate as they readied the defibrillator. Suddenly every last horror was back with him again.

> *It was the trigger point to all the trauma short stories falling off my subconscious bookshelf and reappearing in the forefront of my mind once more. I didn't understand the symptoms and struggled to cope with what was happening to me, the flashbacks, the sensitivity to noise, the severe anxiety. I tried and failed to deal with it on my own and again became severely depressed and three months later had another major breakdown.*

Fortunately, this time, the horror was to prove a turning point. As he says, this time his suicidal thoughts scared 'the crap' out of him. He didn't want to be that person again. Jason sought professional help, and after 12 months and regular sessions with his psychologist, plus cognitive writing therapy, he was able to desensitise himself to many of his triggers and become happy again. He built on the progress by returning to running.

> *Running has always made me feel good and given me a calming feeling, so I decided to revisit running to help, and the rest is history really. I had run distance events on and off my whole life when I could and always raised money for charity, so I thought I could use it as a focus not just for me personally but also to give back.*

For Jason, it is a mindfulness practice. He concentrates on his breathing rhythm and its relationship with his feet. By doing so, he gets 'into the zone – like listening to a metronome, I suppose'.

> *I think about everything and anything, from positive affirmations about myself and my progress to planning my next charity event. I also practise gratitude about what makes me happy in life.*

Jason is quick to stress that running isn't the be-all and end-all. It can only ever be a part of the overall package, an element of the mindfulness at the heart of his psychological rehabilitation. He uses his experiences to speak in public about mental illness and wellness and also to help educate others to break down the stigma that surrounds the issue. He always stresses that everyone should find what works for them, based on their own strengths and interests.

I'd love more people to run and give it a try, but a recovery journey should always be centred on a person's needs and self-determined by them. But yes, running for me goes hand in hand with daily medication and regular psychotherapy with my awesome psychologist.

Keeping running at the forefront of his recovery is Jason's creation of the Rogue Runners. As he says, he has always been one to look outwards, and for many years has organised running, walking and other charitable events. In some ways, he finds it easier to see the broader picture that exists outside himself.

The difficulty for me, which is still an ongoing challenge, is self-compassion and self-care and the working on the inwards. Sounds back to front. But now doing the community and peer support work is actually part of my self-care.

The Rogues came about in September 2011, when Jason and his co-founders and friends – Cameron 'CamO' Oxford; Arthur 'AJ' Jones, also known as 'The Doctor'; and Peter 'Shinno' Shinnick – were trying to improve their personal fitness. Jason challenged himself to train for the Australian Outback Marathon in 2012 in support of Australia's Leukaemia Foundation and in the process try to raise $10,000. The lads began talking about supporting him, and the idea for the club was born.

We're a free-to-join community running crew that is based on family, fitness, fundraising and above all, fun. And you don't have to be a runner to join. We have members who enjoy walking events just as much as we love running. From the lowly four founding members in 2011, we now have more than 120 members across Australia, New Zealand, the US and the UK. To date we have raised more than $75,000 for various charities.

In 2016, after several years of choosing different worthy charities each financial year, they decided to channel their efforts much more specifically, adopting Sirens of Silence as their long-term ongoing charity of choice. Three of the four founding members of the Rogue Runners – Jason, CamO and AJ – were former police officers, so Sirens was a charity that resonated strongly.

Sirens raises awareness and provides education around suicide prevention, depression, anxiety and PTSD. Importantly, the charity also provides peer support that goes beyond the emergency services' own agencies, including access to psychologists, therapists, lawyers and financial advisors as well as fitness trainers and nutritionists. Additionally, Sirens provides financial assistance to members who cannot afford specialist treatments themselves.

For Jason, the Rogues had found their perfect match.

We'd like the Rogue crew to become the go-to running and inclusive fitness supporting crew for all emergency service workers Australia-wide, filled with members who have lived experience that can help each other through their recovery journeys. We have such a depth of knowledge and experience within the crew that we can help with pretty much everything: training programmes from couch to any distance, nutrition, group runs and informal peer support. After that we'll get working on world domination!

On a personal level, as Jason continues on his path to recovery, he counts the Australian Outback Marathon as a standout achievement, particularly for its proximity to Uluru, or Ayers Rock, the massive sandstone monolith in the heart of the Northern Territory's arid Red Centre.

It was the toughest run because of the terrain, almost all of it off-road, comprising sand, corrugated gravel and some sand dunes. But it is by far the most enjoyable – and spiritual too. Running in sight of Uluru on the red dirt was awe-inspiring stuff. I'm not a religious man at all, but I have a real interest in what being mindful is. Uluru is one of those places where you can certainly practise being mindful. For me I found a real connection with the land while I was there, a kind of warm energy, a calmness.

As for the kilt, Jason confesses it was meant to be a one-off thing. He began wearing it in 2013 in the lead-up to running the Gold Coast

Marathon in support of Blaise Wyatt from Ipswich, who lives with spastic quadriplegic cerebral palsy and needed funds to go to the US for specialist help. Jason's kilt grabbed the attention of other runners and the media. It proved so instrumental in raising awareness that he has run in one ever since. He currently wears the Napier tartan kilt, with the permission of the WA Police Pipe Band.

You need to get a little used to it, as it's about 2 kilos in weight. But it's surprisingly comfortable and airy!

Amanda Trafford

'I wish I could scoop them all up and inspire them to run!'

Amanda Trafford doesn't set out to think about particular things when she goes for a run. It just happens naturally. Everything she has pushed to the back of her mind in the daily bustle of life comes flooding to the front when she puts her trainers on. Then, as she runs, she sorts through it all, processing it constructively and healthily – which is precisely why running has become such a crucial weapon in her battle against depression.

> *I think through it all, through everything . . . and I feel good! Running is my therapy, my headspace, my time to take in the gorgeous scenery I'm so lucky to live around. It's also my time to enjoy those addictive hormones that even chocolate can't beat!*

Amanda, who now lives in Chichester, West Sussex, recalls that running wasn't something she sought out when she was growing up in Warminster in Wiltshire. At school, she was very introverted, didn't have many friends and didn't socialise easily, but she discovered she was a strong cross-country runner. Running didn't give her the feel-good factors it does now, but she was good at it, and being good at it gave her recognition: 'I wasn't over-popular. I was very quiet. But I ran for the school!'

After leaving education, Amanda didn't pursue running. In her early 20s she was much more interested in going out and having a good time, she's happy to admit. However, as she approached the age of 40, running entered her life just as naturally as it had done in her childhood. She was 38, her boys were five and three, and the urge to run took hold. She was working part-time and couldn't afford to go to the gym. As for so many people, the big attraction was that running wasn't just about freedom, it was actually free.

Amanda would return to the gym on occasion, but the boredom of the treadmill was overwhelming. She got her running kicks outdoors – running kicks which developed into a running need when her relationship broke down in 2006–7. Her confidence plummeted. She was becoming a shadow of the person she had been, but it was a while before she realised she was falling prey to depression. Amanda was in denial, and her depression was affecting every single aspect of her life.

I even hated saying the word depression because I just associated it with people staying at home in bed and not working. I wouldn't use the word at all for years. But then I realised what it actually was. Depression and also anxiety. I suffered from low moods and worried about going into big social situations. I would worry and worry. I would be telling myself that I was a bad mother and a bad person, and I would start to believe it and so the anxiety would take over. Your mood lowers more and more and you can't sleep. It's a vicious circle.

Amanda went to the doctor's a few times and was given antidepressants, but she never followed through with the medication, always abandoning it after a few days. But then in 2016, her life hit a new low. She could see the children were suffering with the uncertainty of their home life. Her relationship was still on and off. Amanda resorted to self-harming.

I was literally banging my head against the wall. I was often hurting myself. Or I would be lying on my bed in tears. I would be a very shouty mum and then a very teary mum. And I really would be hitting my head against the wall. It was a cry for help.

Amanda finally listened to her own cry, went back to the doctor and accepted that she needed medication and that she needed to stay on it. Curiously, it was a realisation that underlined just how important her running had been – and needed to continue to be. Without it, she wouldn't have been able to continue at all.

But there was no denying the crisis now. Amanda had taken time off from her job as a carer in a children's hospice: 'You have got to be 100 per cent sound in mind and body to work there at all,' she says.

She wanted to go back, but at the same time she was fighting suicidal thoughts. Amanda recognised that this time she needed to see the treatment through. She accepted the medication and also welcomed a referral to a mental health nurse – 'even though just the words *mental health* sounded so scary.'

> But the lady was my saviour. She said that I needed the medication, but she said that I needed the exercise as well. And I also had some counselling, and I could see that the medication was now making a difference.

Underpinning it, though, and allowing it to work was the running.

> I don't think I realised it, but it was running that was allowing me to be me. I am normally Amanda, the bubbly, happy, sociable person, and I hadn't seen how it was running that was allowing me to be that Amanda by releasing the happy hormones.

And on the back of that realisation, running and medication were soon working hand in hand.

> When I run on my own, I think I process life. You are in the fresh air, and you go to some really lovely places, especially from Chichester. I love to run up Goodwood way or down to Dell Quay. It is so beautiful, and just to run there feels a real pleasure. I am just so lucky to have this beautiful scenery around me that makes me feel happy. The running time gives me that time to enjoy it all. Before I was taking the depression pills, the low mood would come back all the quicker after a run, but it doesn't now. I know I am right now to be taking the pills, but running is even more important.

Not the least of the benefits of running is the way it encourages you to open up to people, Amanda says. It brought the realisation that she was far from alone in all that she was feeling. She saw clearly that the trigger for her depression was the break-up of her marriage, but she now considers depression to be 'just a chemical thing' – and knows that there are thousands and thousands of people going through exactly the same thing every day.

There is a sense of solidarity now, and that solidarity is epitomised by the social aspect of running. Amanda belongs to a running group dubbed the Cake Run, a group that aims to bridge the gap between those who have gone from couch to 5k and those who are already club runners.

A friend sold the Cake Run to Amanda as a 'funny, social running group of like-minded people'. Amanda steeled herself to go along – and loved it. The real test was when her friend was injured and Amanda had to go alone. It was a test she passed with flying colours. Amanda considers joining the group the best decision she has ever made.

> *It's not just ladies, but it is a lot of ladies who have had children and who have come to exercise and socialise. It is not just about the running. We have got such a strong network, and we know we all have ups and downs as runners. Three of us are injured at the moment, and I didn't want to go the other day. But I went along. I said: 'I nearly didn't come today because I have lost my running mojo and I have got an injury', and three of the others said it was exactly the same for them. And it's that spirit that makes you want to come back each week. We meet up twice a week, all the year through.*

Running gives Amanda drive and purpose. In the early days, she threw herself at running – and embraced its challenges. The first challenge was simply to attend the club. Next came the daunting challenge of entering and completing 10ks. Then the half-marathons started.

> *It became a real buzz for me. I'd set myself personal challenges, and you really can't beat that feeling when you've achieved it. All the medical help for depression is a poor second to how running could make me feel.*

Even better, as a runner, Amanda now feels she can be a positive role model for her two boys, Jake and Harry. Just as importantly, she is also a role model for her fellow runners. Amanda was encouraged to gain a coaching qualification. She baulked at first, but her friends in the group pointed out that she was already carrying out a coaching role in the way she instinctively befriended and encouraged new members. Amanda gave in and completed the course, another element now in her well-being.

> *I am proud of it. I am not the kind of person who likes to stand up and talk to 20 people, but when I am doing a session, I will do proper preparation. It is easier because a lot of the people are people I know, but*

it is easy too because it is something I have got a passion for. I deliver the session. I love doing it. And that's what is so great about running. It keeps you fit. You can have chocolate and wine. You can still fit into your skinny jeans. You have got friends. And when I am out running in the countryside, it takes me to euphoric places. It is my headspace.

For Amanda, the coaching is all part of spreading the word. She knows what running has done for her. She now wants everyone to know the benefits it can bring.

Running for me is much more than putting one foot in front of the other. I'm so passionate about the health benefits and how it's totally transformed my life, I want to tell everyone. I wish I was brave enough to stand in front of people and inspire them, particularly if they are suffering with depression and mental health issues. But encouraging people seems to have become natural to me. It's funny, because having depression and anxiety often disables your social skills, but I've been able to relate to people through running and being a leader.

Amanda recognises that she is still 'on that wave of mental health issues', but the point is that running has brought her a crucial support network. She is now part of the running community, and even if her fellow runners don't realise what is bubbling away beneath the surface, they help simply because they are there. Inevitably, Amanda hasn't a clue how far into the future her struggle for mental health will stretch, but she knows that running will remain a key way to keep her depression at bay. Her sights are set on a marathon. As she says, if she can do that, she can do anything.

I'm really happy that mental health isn't a taboo subject any more, but also sad that many people are suffering still. I wish I could scoop them all up and inspire them to run!

Cherissa Jackson

'Purging me from my grief and my sadness,
my anger and my pain.'

Captain Cherissa Jackson has become an important voice in the struggle to end the stigma still attached to post-traumatic stress disorder (PTSD) in the American military. Partly the stigma comes from a public that too often thinks: 'You are a soldier. This is your job. This is what you do. You are weak if you don't do it.'

Partly, though, the stigma comes from within the military itself, from servicemen and women who haven't been to war – from service personnel who haven't seen the sights, smelled the smells and lived through the horrors that Cherissa has herself endured.

Now retired, Cherissa served her country for 23 years as an Air Force nurse, surviving four deployments, three to combat hospitals. When her building was bombed in Afghanistan in 2011, she realised that she was tired of playing Russian roulette with her life. But by then the damage was done: PTSD was just waiting to take control of her.

Central to Cherissa's response, just as it was throughout her years of service, was to run – always her way, she says, of sweating out the horrors. The military trains its personnel to be in the best possible shape so that they can protect others. Cherissa came to realise that returning soldiers could use that same physical training to safeguard themselves in their own hour of need.

Cherissa makes it clear: running can never be the only solution, but it can certainly be a key part in the overall package as servicemen and women, damaged both mentally and physically, try to find their way back to some kind of equilibrium. For Cherissa, running was a crucial way of blocking out the horrors. She used it instinctively. Now she works to share her strength with those still looking for that all-important first step towards recovery. Part of her message is that exercise might just accelerate their return to mental health.

For Cherissa, it's all an extension of the impulse to care, which made her a nurse in the first place. Born and raised in Allendale, South Carolina, Cherissa was the fifth of six children. Her oldest brother served in the Navy. The military seemed a good career move – not least for the medical coverage it offered and the pay cheque that arrived every two weeks.

Just as importantly, it fitted in with the aspirations that Cherissa's parents encouraged in their youngsters. Cherissa's mother and father hadn't had high-school education themselves – which made them all the keener to impress on their children that they needed to make something of themselves. That they needed to leave Allendale, get a job, go to college or go into the military. All six responded. All six have got college degrees.

Cherissa graduated with a bachelor degree in nursing from the Medical University of South Carolina in December 2000 at the age of 29.

I have always had a caring and sacrificial spirit. Being the fifth of six children, I saw what my parents sacrificed for us, working in substandard jobs, the long, long hours just to support us all. I just knew that I needed to do something so that they didn't have to take care of me.

Cherissa's twin daughters, Anita and Ashley Lee, were born in 1994. By the time Cherissa gained her degree, she was going through a 'crazy' divorce. Nursing appealed to the caring side of her nature, but on a more practical level, with two young daughters to look after, it gave her a set of skills that would always be in demand.

Cherissa was commissioned as a nurse in the military in 2003. She continued her training at Wilford Hall Medical Center, a US Air Force medical treatment facility located in the grounds of San Antonio's Lackland Air Force Base in Texas. After two years, she was deemed ready and sent to Iraq in 2005 and then again in 2006: 'And then they said: "You are doing pretty good. We are going to send you again in 2011."'

Arguably, no training could have prepared her for what happened next.

Being in Iraq and being a nurse, well, I think you can sum it up in one word: unpredictable. In 2005, the war was on high alert. You just never knew what was going to come into the combat hospital. You had to live your life never knowing. We were at the Balad Air Base and you were talking about soldiers coming in with one or two or maybe three amputations, soldiers who were in terrible pain, terrible things, terrible injuries . . . and we were also taking care of the insurgents, the enemy that had been shooting at us.

Cherissa's instinctive response was to compartmentalise – to recognise that she could deal with only the particular problem in front of her. If the soldier died, the only option was to move on to the next casualty while the technicians took the previous patient away in a body bag. As Cherissa says:

The only thing you could do was stay in that moment. You didn't have time to dwell on it. You just had to keep going. And for me that worked until I was no longer doing it, but at the time, you knew you couldn't think about the death of one soldier. You had to be working to relieve the pain of the next. Compartmentalising my emotions meant that my emotions didn't get intertwined, which would have taken me out of the game as a good nurse. You get so overwhelmed, but at the same time you have to think critically because you have got to be a critical thinker if you are going to save someone's life.

Inevitably, there were colleagues who didn't cope and had to be sent back to the United States. They would break down back in their units, unable to hold it all together. However, Cherissa had every faith in her own ability to stay on top. She reasoned that if she could get through a crazy divorce and survive as a single mum, facing down all the financial hardships accompanying it, then she could certainly cope in a combat hospital. And she did. She applied that logic and willed herself to cope, helped by the crucial ally she found in running.

Running started way before I deployed. I knew when I was going through my divorce that I needed an outlet. I started working out in the gym really hard, and it was my escape. I would lift weights and do classes and do anything gym-related. It allowed me to have time not to think about the craziness at home, and then in Iraq, it was an important way to allow me to cope with the things that I was seeing – by having time not to have to think about them.

Some people run to solve their problems. Cherissa is clear: she was running to escape hers. Running was a way to switch off the sights and sounds; a way of forgetting that her life was in danger. When she ran, she purged herself of the horrors that piled up. In hindsight, she says it was a way of sweating out the PTSD she didn't yet know she was developing.

The year 2011 proved to be the crucial year. Cherissa's final deployment was to 'god-awful' Afghanistan. She was sent to Kandahar, 'the worst deployment that you could ever wish for . . . not that you would ever wish for it.' At the time, it was a city under fire; death and injury were ever present.

Cherissa was based on the outskirts of the city on the flight line for all the planes coming in and out; consequently, they were a target. At first it was random: 'The Afghanis never had accurate coordinates. They just fired rockets and hoped they would land.' But they struck lucky and hit the base, sending shrapnel everywhere.

Cherissa was off-duty at the time and missed the blast by two hours. But now the Afghans had their range, and the next night, when Cherissa was on duty, they knew exactly what they were doing.

We were in the tent, already patched up from the previous time, doing our mission of the day when all of a sudden we hear the alarm telling us of incoming fire. You have to drop to the ground for 10 seconds. The idea is that if shrapnel hits, shrapnel goes upwards and you get hit if you are standing up. And then after 10 seconds, we had to run to the nearest bunker.

And it was in the bunker – effectively a 'cement cave' – that Cherissa realised her military career was over.

We could hear the rockets going overhead, and I thought: What if one of those rockets came through the bunker? What if one of them penetrated? That would be my life. I just sat there and I prayed for what seemed like hours on end but was probably only minutes. I just said: 'If I get out of here, I am going to put in my papers.' And I did.

Ironically, Cherissa's decision to retire proved to be the way that she let PTSD into her life. It was back home in Maryland that it hit her, seizing its moment in the cruellest way.

PTSD didn't show its ugly face until 2012, when my daughters went off to college. I no longer had the busy life, was no longer getting them ready for classes. Being busy at home allowed me not to worry about it. But when my daughters went off to school in August 2012 and I was at home with nothing to do, that was when PTSD said: 'Hello! Here I am!'

And it hit Cherissa with full force. Insomnia. Hypervigilance. Anger. A sense of distance and isolation. Hypersensitivity and depression.

As the 'self-diagnoser' that she was, Cherissa recognised the signs of depression, but she put the depression down to being home alone without Anita and Ashley Lee.

But among the symptoms, there were also flashbacks to her time in combat hospitals. She was haunted by some of the servicemen she had treated and by some of the things they had said.

She remembered one particular soldier whose jaw was wired shut because of a facial fracture. He couldn't speak. Unusually, he was still awake, and because he was awake, he could see his injuries, including his own amputations and the injuries of his comrades on the unit. 'He was scared and unsure of surviving because he could see and hear everything around him,' Cherissa recalls. He needed to communicate. He and Cherissa did so by writing things down, and over the course of several hours, a strong bond developed between them, Cherissa being the only face he saw.

Then came the time for the soldier to be medevacked to Germany. Afraid, he asked Cherissa if she was coming with him. She told him that she couldn't, but that others would look after him just as well. His response was one that struck deep into Cherissa. He begged her: 'Please don't let me die . . . please don't tell my Mom . . .' – words that tormented Cherissa in her traumatised state back home. In reality, the serviceman was fine. He survived. But his words still assailed her.

Mostly the soldiers are sedated. They don't talk to you. But this one wasn't, and he was writing to me 'please don't let me die.' For me, it was like 'Wow, this is profound.' All these things that were going through this young man's head . . . this scared young man . . . And I just wished that I could have done more. I wished I could have gone with him. When someone is crying out for help and you are the helper, you want to solve that. I wanted to make sure that I was there for him. I felt I could have supported him.

From that point, Cherissa believes, a diagnosis of PTSD was as simple as it was inevitable. The girls left home in August 2012. Cherissa sought help in October. But it was on her own terms that she constructed her recovery.

Cherissa resisted medication. As she says, she didn't want to become a zombie on Valium and on the antidepressants she herself had been handing out. Instead, she resolved once again that exercise was her best retreat. Exercise along with a spirituality that has long sustained her. For Cherissa the distinction between the two is crucial.

Cherissa admits that she isn't a great churchgoer, but as she says, you can't survive four deployments without coming to the conclusion that there is someone up there looking after you. A comforting thought, which running helped sustain. Again, the running acted by blocking.

Running is my escape from life and from PTSD and from heartache and from difficult times. Running is escape. Spirituality is definitely not escape. Running does not solve anything. It does not solve what the real problem is. Running won't take away PTSD. But it is useful. It is like a Band-Aid. It allows me to stop thinking about the images and the noises and the sounds.

Cherissa won't ever claim to be cured of PTSD. She knows that the triggers are still there. It's a question of revamping her life so that she can find ways to cope. Helicopters are a trigger; so too are backfires. So are crowds – for the ghastly reason that crowds will always prove an attraction to a terrorist wanting to maximise impact.

Cherissa meditates and prays on a daily basis that today will be a day without any triggers. She knows to avoid fireworks. If she smells a smell she associates with the bad times, she forces herself to think of another one.

And in these ways she has found her own way to keep PTSD at bay – an approach she describes in her book, *At Peace, Not In Pieces: Powering Through My Pain* (Unlock Publishing House, Inc, 2016). In the words *At Peace* are Cherissa's seven powerful principles for coping with PTSD and trauma. The *a* of *At* is *a* for acknowledgement: recognising your PTSD or depression or suicidal thoughts for what they are. The *t* is transition, asking yourself: 'What are you going to do now? Are you going to stay here and wallow or are you going to carry on?' The *p* of *Peace* is for perseverance, recognition that it won't be easy as you navigate your way through your 'transitional space', steeling yourself to get through dark moments as you will yourself to stay on track. *E* is for engage, the fact that having decided to get out of bed, you now need to do so. *A* is for acceptance, the realisation: 'I am not perfect. I have blemishes and scars. One of my imperfections is PTSD'. The *c* of *Peace* is the courage that will get you there, and when you come out the other side, the *e* is for 'empower' – the stage that Cherissa has reached. The urge to empower others, and this is now the thrust of her life.

Having found her own way to cope, Cherissa is determined to offer to others the lessons that she has learned so painfully – so that they might learn them in a far kinder way. It comes back to the caring nature which made Cherissa enter the nursing profession in the first place. Having suffered herself, she is now intent on reducing the suffering of others.

On Veterans Day in 2015, Cherissa launched PTSFaces, a global platform that brings awareness of the treatment options for PTS (post-traumatic stress) veterans – an online one-stop shop providing support groups, partnerships, medical teams, survival stories and other resources for any veteran looking for support and assistance with coping with PTS.

I see and hear my fellow airmen and soldiers suffering and feeling trapped and alone, and I hope we can reach them. My purpose is to serve others and show them their greatness through obstacles they think are unbearable. We are all winners and if one person is changed by my story, I will have fulfilled my purpose.

In the meantime, Cherissa suspects that running will always be there to help her. Again, it's not a solution in itself, only ever part of the solution. But that's not to diminish its importance to her ongoing mental health. Running – and exercise in general – remain her most vital medicine. As she says, running and weightlifting helped her shed PTSD 'just like other people shed pounds'.

> *It all goes back to running being an escape. Running allowed me not to think about my divorce . . . not to think about my PTSD . . . not to think about being a single Mom. It was my way of escaping from reality. Alcoholics escape reality by getting drunk, and I would never advocate that! But running allowed me to get away, to feel the bugs on my face, to feel the sweat coming from my body and purging it . . . purging me from my grief and my sadness, my anger and my pain.*

Lynn Julian Crisci

'In my mind, you win when you reach the start line,
not the finish line.'

In 2006, Lynn Julian Crisci was performing as Pop Superhero, a Wonder Woman-esque stage persona and the embodiment of girl power. Eight years later, Lynn really was a superhero – though she would be the last to admit it.

When terrorists attacked the Boston Marathon on 15 April, 2013, the sheer force of the blast left Lynn with frontal lobe brain injury. A spectator that day, she was also left with severe post-traumatic stress disorder (PTSD), chronic lower back injury, hearing loss and extreme tinnitus.

A year later, she returned to the course as a runner. Many times she stopped and cowered alone on the pavement. Her 'PTSD brain' undermined her every effort to continue. And when the finish line finally came into view, Lynn had to be forced to stay on the course: the last quarter of a mile was exactly where the bombs had exploded right in front of her a year before.

But Lynn ran through it all. She ran through everything. She faced her fears and she completed one of the toughest, most painful marathons anyone has ever run. As she says, the marathon was her way of striking the word *can't* from her vocabulary.

Excruciating though it was, Lynn's Boston Marathon run was deeply, powerfully liberating. 'It set me back physically. But would I do it again one day? Yeah, like a shot!'

Lynn's long and painful journey began in 2006, in her Pop Superhero days. The character was a girl power mentor, a voice of female empowerment. Lynn wrote and performed all the songs for her band.

Her message was a powerful one: you can be anything and anyone you wish . . . even a Pop Superhero!

But tragedy struck when she slipped on an untaped electrical cable on the stage. She fell backwards, smashing her head. Ironically, everyone thought this was part of the act. Like 'a trained robot', she completed the set. She got the lyrics wrong. She got the guitar wrong. She announced one song and then played another. When she came off stage, her manager angrily asked if she'd been drinking. She hadn't.

Lynn was taken to the emergency room where she was X-rayed and told that she was lucky not to have broken a bone. They told her she'd feel like a truck had hit her in the morning, but that she'd be fine in four to six weeks.

In fact, Lynn had suffered significant brain and neck injuries. For the next three years, she was bed-bound or in a wheelchair. For the first year, severe vertigo left her virtually incapable of movement or sleep. Eventually, perilymph fistulas, holes deep in her ear canal behind her eardrums, were diagnosed, the result of the head trauma she had suffered. The operation to repair the holes left her with severe infections and multiple ER visits, and eventually hospitalised her again.

By the end of the year, Lynn finally started to get the traumatic brain injury treatments she desperately needed: home care, physical therapy, occupational therapy, vestibular therapy, ocular therapy and more. Slowly but surely, over the next three years, she learned to walk without a stick and began to get her life back. By April 2013, Lynn had done a dozen short films and had established herself as a Boston actress: 'Finally, I was excited about something, anything, again.'

However, in just 12 seconds, the Boston Marathon bombers were to wipe out six-and-a-half years of progress.

The Boston Marathon finish line is just around the corner from Lynn's apartment. She and her partner Doug loved to attend the race. In previous years, she'd been one of the spectators who'd get there early to 'secure their piece of real estate on the sidewalk', but by 2013, they'd resolved to do it properly. They got there early to reserve the closest pavement table at the only café on the finish line. Wooden walls, erected for the press, prevented them from seeing the finish line directly, but their table was the only one with a view of the 50-foot screen that was televising the finish.

At 2.49 p.m. the first bomb went off, about 30 feet (9 metres) away, immediately engulfing everyone in smoke. The year before, a transformer had exploded on the exact same street, cutting electricity to a major portion of the city – an explosion that blew five storeys high. The 12 seconds between the first and second Boston Marathon bombs were enough for Doug to say to Lynn: 'Another transformer blew . . . It's OK.'

In those 12 seconds, everyone froze – except Lil Stinker, Lynn's tiny, six-pound service dog, who'd never left her side throughout her six-year recovery. That day, Lynn was feeling great; Lil Stinker was sleeping on her lap, off duty. But as soon as the first bomb exploded, he immediately started scratching at Lynn's chest and face: 'He just wildly started doing his doggie version of slapping my face.'

After six or seven seconds of panic, Lynn 'squished' Lil Stinker against her chest so that he couldn't bolt. The primal part of her brain took over, the part that told her to run to safety, which meant into the café. She stood up – and was immediately assaulted by the second blast and its horrifying moment of realisation:

> *I knew we were being attacked as soon as the second bomb went off. You can believe one explosion is a transformer. There was no way to justify the second one in my mind. That was when I panicked and ran toward the door of the bar. I'm not sure if I ever consciously thought: 'That was a bomb'. Our 'lizard brain' takes over in terror and life or death situations – the smallest, oldest part of our brain that simply fights for the will to live. I was not thinking consciously at all, just taking actions to get to safety as I knew our lives were in danger.*

The immediate reality was the tsunami of sulphur-scented smoke suddenly swallowing up the pavement. Lynn couldn't see a thing and was gasping for air. All she knew was that her way out had to be through the café.

> *But bar patrons were blocking the entrance, frozen in place. I panicked, barking at them: 'Move! Move! Move!' I tried to get to the back of the bar,*

but it was jam-packed. People there had been drinking all morning. They didn't know what was happening. I think they saw me as a crazy or drunk woman shouting at them. But I scared them enough to move . . .

Then the real terror hit her: Lynn turned around and realised that Doug wasn't behind her.

That was worse than the bomb itself. People don't realise the trauma. Tens of thousands of people couldn't find their loved ones. Anything could have happened to Doug. When I finally found him in the bar, I just burst out crying.

Lynn then started directing people to safety, out of the emergency exit at the back of the building. The exit opened onto Boston's famous Newbury Street, which was a river of people – all heading towards the bombs, thinking the explosions had been fireworks. Lynn was crying, hyperventilating, urging people to turn back: 'They just thought I was crazy.'

When Lynn finally got back home, just around the corner from the finish, she shouted at the concierge to lock all the doors and not to let anyone out of the building. She was convinced they were under attack. The concierge chuckled. Then he saw the look on Lynn's face.

Minutes later, Lynn started to realise the full extent of her injuries. Too terrified to be alone, she went to a friend's apartment, where she tried to sit down. Searing pain ripped through her back and down her leg. Every sound existed as if she was underwater. All she could hear clearly was the painfully loud ringing in her ears.

It was only then that Lynn started to think 'consciously', only then that confirmation came. Her friend had turned the news on.

As for her injuries, Lynn felt that the emergency rooms that day were for those who were bleeding. She decided to wait until the next day to seek help herself – by which time the beds were all full and the doctors were all exhausted.

I was there for eight hours just begging for treatment. I couldn't sit right. I couldn't walk right. I was walking like a drunk. I was hearing like I was underwater. My head was pounding with pain. I was severely nauseated and vomiting. My mood swings, from anger to crying, ran continuously from one extreme to the other. Yet because I wasn't bleeding, there was no treatment offered. There was only a one-word diagnosis on my discharge paper: 'anxiety'.

After almost a year of trying to get help, Lynn was finally diagnosed with frontal lobe brain injury – a type of traumatic brain injury (TBI) affecting her ability to make life's little decisions and to realise their consequences. It left her with what she calls an unfiltered honesty, behaviour that was sometimes mistaken as rude and/or interruptive. In addition, her mobility was poor. She walked as if she had a muscular disorder. Her lower back pain was chronic, and she was terrified of falling. Compounding it all, Lynn was diagnosed with severe PTSD at a level comparable to military personnel on active duty.

Fortunately, this was the point that running crossed Lynn's path again. The Boston Marathon attack had set her back massively, but it was the Boston Marathon which now offered her a possible way to reclaim her life – for a second time.

The race organisers, the Boston Athletic Association, decided to offer injured survivors a bib to run in the 2014 Boston Marathon. Lynn was attending a weekly survivors' support group when the offer was announced to them in December 2013. Others in the group cheered with excitement, hugging each other. Lynn's immediate reaction was that she couldn't possibly run a marathon – she still had trouble walking. She rushed off to hide in the bathroom and cry, frustrated and depressed at being excluded, yet again, from something that seemed like it was going to be a validation for everyone else, but not for her.

But then I took time, before the next meeting, to think about all the possibilities. I decided that I could be bitter for the rest of my life or I could give it a go and just see what happened.

Lynn quickly hatched a plan: she would walk the 2014 Boston Marathon. She was already volunteering for the US Pain Foundation and decided to use her long, painful training for the marathon to highlight the plight of the millions of people who live in chronic pain. She wouldn't be able to run, but she would complete the course somehow. Suddenly she was a woman on a mission.

> *I told myself: 'You are not going to cry. You are not going to carry a chip on your shoulder.' It became my mantra. I told myself: 'Don't say you can't do this; eliminate that word "can't" from your vocabulary. It's not that you can't; it's just that you haven't yet figured out how to do it differently . . . yet!'*

Lynn started by simply walking on a treadmill. Still walking 'like a drunk', she was forced to hold on to the sides and slowly, very slowly, increase her speed. Eventually, she was power-walking. And then Lynn slowed it down again and took a leap of faith: she let go of the sides, faced her fear of falling, and walked on the moving treadmill – a key moment followed by an even better one.

As Lynn started to increase the speed again, something magical happened: she started running. It was slow, but it was most definitely a run – the point at which the former Pop Superhero, icon of female empowerment, felt empowered to join a group of fellow survivors who were also training to run the Boston Marathon. By far the slowest in the group, Lynn would often find herself running sections of the marathon course alone, and she always got lost. It was scary, but strangely it boosted her confidence.

The next lucky break came when Jack Fultz, winner of the 1976 Boston Marathon and now an inspirational running coach, volunteered to mentor the Boston survivors.

> *He gave us his personal training schedule. To him, it was just a file on his computer. To me, it was a priceless gift. Every day I would ask: 'What does Jack want me to do today?' I only met him a couple of times, but I would write down all my questions, and he would smile sweetly and ask: 'Now, what have you got for me today?'*

As she progressed, Lynn discovered that she was starting to look forward to running. It was calming. It was healing. During the first year of her recovery, Lynn's TBI and PTSD had left her prone to severe mood swings, either crying or lashing out as she hurtled backwards and forwards between the extremes a dozen times a day. Yet running centred her. The extremes met in the middle. She began to know peace again. Lynn was surprised how consistently she was able to increase her running distance, 'amping it up' according to Jack's instructions.

She had become 'a runner'.

I had never been a runner, but I wanted to be so badly. Letting go of the sides of the treadmill was like a metaphor for moving forward in your life. It takes intense courage to let go, but I was able to let go of my fear of falling because the prize for letting go was . . . running.

Running the Boston Marathon was always going to be one of the toughest days of Lynn's life. The fates told her so on the Thursday before Marathon Monday. She saw a policeman arguing with an angry person at the train stop on the finish line. Someone had decided to create 'art' by placing a fake bomb there and frightening the entire neighbourhood. Lynn's 'PTSD brain' now took over and told her to 'run, run, run'. She did and promptly tripped on the broken pavement, injuring her foot with just days to go until the marathon.

On marathon day, things got harder still. Lynn was starting as a mobility impaired runner. The meeting place was a mile away from all the other survivor runners. She was soon gripped by panic and sobbing uncontrollably. Doug was also running that day, on a broken foot that was not yet fully healed. He chivalrously walked her the mile to her tent, asked a stranger to look after her and walked another mile back to the other survivors. That stranger was Sarah Reinertsen, the first ever woman to finish an Ironman on a prosthetic leg. Sarah instantly offered support, but Lynn was already exhausting herself with her tears and her terrors.

Things soon got worse.

Lynn was in a tiny group of around 30 mobility impaired runners, starting well before the wheelchair races, the elite runners and the four corrals of 9000 runners each. She was terrified by the continuous, loud noise of the helicopters constantly hovering very low overhead, part of the race security. She was also triggered by the noise and the multiple strobe lights of the security trucks leading each new group of runners behind her. Crippling flashbacks repeatedly forced her to sit out her panic on the pavement before timidly moving on, shaking and crying the entire time.

Once the first corrals of runners started to come through, Lynn's panic slipped back to what she calls normal panic. The famous Wellesley girls, from Wellesley College, provided a huge boost at the half-marathon point. Tradition has it that the girls hug and kiss thousands of passing runners. Lynn was their first 'customer'. She hugged and kissed every single one of them before running on, recharged.

There was further encouragement at the notorious Heartbreak Hill, several hills where plenty of runners are forced to give up, exhausted. Consumed by panic again, Lynn didn't even know she was there until a spectator shouted: 'Congrats, you finished Heartbreak Hill!' Lynn wanted to kiss him too. She had new wind in her sails.

Then came another vital moment – one in which Lynn obeyed her instinct. She was limping badly from her foot injury of a few days before. Someone from a medical tent tried to remove her from the course, thinking she was too badly injured to continue. The medic insisted she would be allowed to continue after treatment, but Lynn's inner voice urged her to keep going. She did so, and at around mile 23, she found herself once again with her 'starting line angel', Sarah Reinertsen.

Sarah patiently pulled me onward, like I was her favourite pet. She continuously called back to me, saying: 'You can do it, sweetie! Come on!' as if pulling me on an invisible leash.

They turned left onto Boylston Street, at the end of which Lynn could see the Boston Marathon finish line . . . and also her apartment building. But PTSD, 'a terrible roommate', hadn't done with her yet. Tens of thousands of people lined the road; on both sides a roaring crowd was cheering the runners on. The problem was that in Lynn's PTSD-distorted mind, they were all screaming in fear.

I stopped running and started crying out for help from Sarah: 'Everyone's screaming! Why is everyone screaming? I've got to get home!' I thought something terrible had happened. As a runner, Sarah knew this was the happy cheering you get at the finish line. She kept saying: 'They aren't screaming, sweetie. They're cheering. They're cheering for you.' But I just kept saying: 'No, no, no, no, they are screaming! Please, just let me go home! I just live right over there!'

It was at that moment that Lynn nearly gave up. She couldn't stand it any more.

I could see my building on the other side of the finish line. I was saying: 'I live there! Let me go home!' Sarah said: 'You can't just go home! The finish line is right there!' The PTSD brain doesn't care about the 26 miles you just ran. The reptilian part of my brain was solely focused on its will to live. But thank goodness for Sarah. She said: 'See all the security officers? They will not let you off the race course. The only way for you to get home is to cross the finish line!'

Lynn trusted Sarah's kind smile. She now laughs at their finish line photos:

Sarah, the professional runner, is smiling cheerfully. I'm clutching her and bawling my eyes out like I am in an episode of I Love Lucy! *It's hilarious.*

It took another long year of healing before Lynn found those photos truly funny. Now, one hangs proudly on her wall. They are indeed hilarious, but they take nothing away from Lynn's achievement. In fact, the hilarity probably underlines its extent.

I faced my fears. When you face your fears, it's not about getting to the finish line, it's all about getting to the starting line. I am so proud of myself for making the commitment to learn to run, doing the painful training required for the task, and, finally, finding the courage to show up and honour my commitment. I am so proud of myself just for starting such an enormous, intimidating task. To me, it is not a matter of how you finish or when you finish. It's all about committing to moving forward with your life in some way. In my mind, you win when you reach the start line, not the finish line. I won as soon as I showed up and conquered my fears.

In the end, Lynn's instinct, at mile 23, was right. After she crossed the finish line, she was immediately taken to the medical tent. When they removed her compression sock, her damaged foot swelled up 'like a blowfish'. If Lynn had gone into that medical tent earlier and taken her sock off, she would never have been able to resume the race – a race which has been a source of strength for her ever since, in a life which remains chronically difficult.

The race set Lynn back physically, but the mental benefits have been immeasurable in terms of calmness, self-confidence and self-esteem.

Talking about what she survived is still tough. Hypervigilance and chronic anxiety are inevitable, but Lynn is clear: she wants others to know – and to be encouraged.

> *The bottom line for me is that talking about it is worth it! Every time somebody gives me a platform, a voice to speak to and for others with hearing loss, TBI and/or PTSD, I'm going to use it . . . Consequences be damned. Being given the chance to help countless others is a privilege and I am always grateful.*

Nearly five years on, Lynn still spends much of her time travelling between weekly doctors' appointments for specialist treatments and physical and cognitive therapies. The injuries linger on agonisingly, but so too do the hope and confidence she gained by completing the Boston Marathon.

Lynn finds huge purpose in volunteering and in advocating for others with her conditions. She is on the victim assistance council of Strength to Strength, a global organisation uniting victims of terrorism internationally. She is also a patient advocate for the Brain Injury Association of America and the Massachusetts ambassador at the US Pain Foundation.

Inevitably, Lynn looks at life differently now. She feels more present in the moment and more grateful for every little thing in it.

> *I am still angry at the bombers and all those who violently attack innocent civilians. But I simply know that holding on to that anger is like drinking poison . . . In the end, anger can kill you in the form of cancer and other illness. Let it go . . .*

The doctors' appointments and the chronic pain continue, but so too does Lynn's pride in all she achieved. Her response to the horrors of the Boston Marathon bombing was to become a marathon runner herself.

> *Whenever I think I can't do something, I tell myself: 'You finished the Boston Marathon . . . You can do anything!'*

Paul Shepherd

'My son would have become another fatherless child.'

One day, in January 2017, Paul Shepherd struggled to get out of bed. He forced himself to go to work, but the moment work was over, he went straight to an off-licence, bought a bottle of whisky and drank the lot. His hope was that the alcohol would make him sleep or – at the very least – push back thoughts of killing himself.

Neither happened. Instead, he walked to a remote stretch of beach in his hometown of Bognor Regis, West Sussex. It was ten o'clock at night. He was confident he would be alone. The beach was cold, dark and deserted. Just perfect for his grim intention. Listening to songs on his phone, the last sounds he thought he would hear, he strode into the water. Paul reached chest depth and willed himself to go further. His dearest wish was that in just a few moments, his battle against drink and drugs would be over and that years of pain and despair would simply float away.

It was then that something miraculous happened. Something intervened. Paul still has no idea what it was. Maybe it was pure chance. Maybe it was simply, as he says, the universe talking to him. But something certainly spoke to him, a voice in his head – a voice that turned him back to the beach.

Paul's life since that day has become a celebration of the moment that saved him. His brush with death brought him back to life – the turning point in his fight against the triple demons of alcohol, drugs and depression.

Paul traces his depression back to his school days when he was the victim of bullying, not by fellow pupils but by a teacher determined to belittle him as he struggled with dyslexia.

It was around the age of seven or eight that it was reinforced in me that I was no good, that I was nothing in the world, that I was bad; and that feeling never left me. As a child, you are looking at the teacher, thinking you are always wrong and the teacher is always right. I just accepted what the teacher was saying.

Paul was moved to another class, but inevitably the memories stayed with him. The damage was done and, coupled with his dyslexia, meant that Paul struggled both socially and academically. He left school with GCSEs but also with the feeling that he should have done much better than he did in his exams, which was when feelings of inadequacy and depression deepened. A possible job as a car mechanic fell through. Instead he went into engineering, quickly falling in with the 'wrong people'. Drugs and alcohol started to take over. Ecstasy and cocaine became his staples. He insists he wasn't addicted to the drugs, but confesses he was certainly addicted to the euphoria they gave him.

He was convinced the drugs made him happy and the alcohol even happier – a delusion that they made him the person he had always wanted to be: 'the cool guy, the guy that everyone likes and wants to be around'. The delusion persisted for years through a succession of jobs which, Paul admits, he would always sabotage the moment things started to go well for him. It was the classic downward spiral of depression.

I don't know what depression should feel like, but for me, it is a mixture of emotions. One second, I am feeling alone; the next, I am panicking about money or about my son. It is like a knot in your stomach. You have got so much going on in your head that you just want to scream and get rid of all the emotions. And so you end up being quite a solitary person because that is a way to cope, but that then makes you worse. It is a vicious circle.

Paul's response was to go into sales. He soon hated what it did to him.

You have to lose conscience. You have to be like a robot. You have got to pummel customers with product just so that you can earn a bit of money, and I realised that I was very good at making a quick buck. I was making lots and lots of money, so I was able to go out and get drunk more and do more drugs and have the lifestyle that I thought I needed. I rarely did the drugs during the week, but I would usually start drinking and drugs on a Friday and go right the way through to Sunday, when I would be on a massive downer. And that was my life. I worked, I drank and I took drugs.

For years, Paul remained in a relationship he didn't believe in, and his weight spiralled from 12 stone (76 kilos) to 16 stone (102 kilos): 'It felt like an obscene amount. I hated my appearance.' During the relationship, the one bonus was that he gave up drugs, but when the relationship ended, Paul resumed, trapped again as he hit the age of 30. Paul became a father in 2012, but soon after his son Leighton's birth, he and Leighton's mother split up.

For a while, Paul tried to be the father his son deserved. However, towards the end of 2016, his life spiralled dangerously out of control. In his depression, Paul has no recollection of buying his family their Christmas presents; in fact, he has no recollection of Christmas at all. Another relationship had failed; Paul was disorientated by working nights. He saw no way out.

Coming out of Christmas and getting back to normality, I could not shake off the low feelings. I was living in a bedsit. I hated work. I hated life. I was thinking I was at the point of either sink or swim, and unfortunately, I started to take the sinking route.

And so came that grim day in January 2017. After struggling through his shift in the food department of a chain store, Paul sensed he could take no more. He downed the whisky and waded chest-deep into the sea.

As far as I was concerned, it was game over. I had had enough. I could not drown out the thoughts, they were all I had. It was a horrible feeling, but you know when you are making the right decision, and I felt that I was making the right decision. In the most horrible of ways, I was convinced I was right and there was no other solution.

Then came the moment that changed everything – the moment that fate, fluke, call it what you will, took a hand. Suddenly there was a voice in his head – quite literally, as he was listening to YouTube on his phone – telling him exactly what he needed to do, pointing him back to the deserted January beach. At the very moment Paul steeled himself to walk out of his depth to his death, the song he was listening to finished, and in the random shuffle of YouTube, a documentary started – a documentary by the rapper Professor Green about losing his father to suicide.

> *And suddenly I saw it all from Leighton's point of view, a child losing his father. It just really hit me in the face. I stopped doing what I was doing and got out of the water and went back to the beach. I was freezing cold and soaked, and I just sat there and watched the rest of the documentary. I wanted to see it through. There were people talking about the problems I had been having.*

Paul doesn't think the moment was pure chance. Neither does he believe it was divine intervention. If there is a higher body that saved him, he is grateful. But he doesn't believe there is: 'Maybe it was the universe talking to me, I just don't know.'

All he remembers is the overwhelming sensation of relief pouring through him as he waded back to the beach. At the end of the documentary was a telephone number for CALM, the Campaign Against Living Miserably, a charity dedicated to preventing male suicide, the single biggest killer of men under 45 in the UK. Shivering, Paul called the number. The response was instant and understanding, precisely the voice he needed to hear. He had come back from the brink. The next day, he made an appointment to see his doctor – the crucial next step. Paul declined medication but accepted counselling.

> *And it was brilliant. The counsellor pushed me to limits that broke me. She angered me at points. And she got me through what I needed to get through.*

Just as significantly, Paul began to run. He had seen CALM's involvement with the London Marathon. He resolved to do the Bognor

Regis 10k in return for the support they had given him. He started the training, set himself the target of running a mile, managed just half a mile and returned home deflated. But the next day he was out there again. And again, the next.

I made four attempts to run that mile, but when I did, it was better than any drugs I have ever taken.

The next day he did 2 miles (3 kilometres). His response was to start to increase his goals and chase pace. Once he had reached 10 miles (16 kilometres), he set himself a new target: to run the 15 miles (24 kilometres) from the West Sussex village of Singleton back home to Bognor Regis. It was a decision that came on the back of a change in everything: attitude, diet, outlook, everything. Reaching 11 miles (18 kilometres) that day was a major landmark, pushing towards distances he had never done before. But then Paul hit the wall. The urge to walk was becoming irresistible, but he fought it.

Then I got to mile 12 and then hit mile 13, and then I started thinking I have done a half-marathon and I have only got two more miles to get home! And it was that passion, that drive, that sheer want for those two miles that took over. The whole thing gave me an incredible focus, just to get there. And I realised at that moment why I was running. I run for therapy. I have been through therapy. I understand therapy very well, but in that moment, I realised that there is no better therapy than running and exercise. It gives you that want . . . that desire to hold back the bad feelings and leave them behind.

Paul accepts that he could slip back into depression at any time. He has never feared anything in his life, but slipping back is now a very real fear. But he also feels that every mile he runs is a mile between him and his depression – and crucially that the distance between the two is something he can increase at any time, simply by running.

Running is giving me time to process things in the right manner. If you are planning a parkrun or a 10k or going up to a half-marathon, you have got to map it out and plan it, and it makes you structure your life. It makes you regiment your life. It gives you a backbone to everything you do. Sport is great. Any sport is great, but there is nothing like running. You feel like it is you against the road, you against the woodlands, you against no one, just you against you, and the only person you have got to beat is yourself. And that means it is complete freedom. When I am running, I am thinking nothing, and it is the best feeling in the world. You settle into the run, but then I let go and let my body do what it wants to do, what it has got to do . . . and I just enjoy it.

Possibly it's symbolic, but Paul confesses there is nothing he likes better than running up a hill. The steeper the hill, the longer the incline, the better the experience.

One particular memory endures:

I got to the top of a hill, and I could see for miles. I just thought Wow! And for the first time in forever, I just naturally smiled. I just felt so happy, so euphoric. And I just thought: This is why I run. There was no one else around. It was just me in this moment for me. I took a photograph of me on this hill and wanted to save this moment. I ran home, and I still had a smile on my face. I ran faster and harder than I have ever run. These are the moments no one can ever take away from you. It was a moment like seeing my child for the first time. It was like me in the right place at the right time and me just being the me that I want to be.

Support from CALM remains a foundation in Paul's life – a life he considers a new life in every respect, given back to him at the age of 37. They will phone him just to check how he is. And he is happy to tell them, just as he is happy to tell anyone who asks. As he says, he held it all back for far too long and far too damagingly. He nearly lost his life as a result, but he has come back a new person – more sociable, more appreciative of friends and family, more conscious of the moment and much more inclined to cherish it.

A blissful moment came when Leighton joined him for the last 100 metres of a 10k run.

Without running, I realised I would have become just another statistic and my son would have become another fatherless child. I look at him now and he is pretty much the angel on my shoulder. When I took him to school for the first time ever, I was thinking I could so easily not have seen this. Instead, I now feel that I want to be the best role model for him in everything. I want him to run!

In April 2018 in Brighton, just 15 months after that awful night in Bognor Regis, Paul completed his first marathon.

Bryn Hughes

'I was thinking if I allow myself to die,
then evil will win.'

When Bryn Hughes joined the prison service, he and the six other recruits were told straight away that within a year every single one of them would be assaulted. One of the trainees left at that point. To Bryn's mind, the training officer had said exactly the right thing. Bryn and his colleagues would be going into their new career with their eyes wide open.

And so it was when Bryn's daughter Nicola joined the police force. Bryn, who served 25 years in the prison service, wanted to make sure that she knew exactly what she was doing.

> *I had that conversation with Nicola so that she knew that she would be involved in fights, so that she knew she would be spat at, so that she knew she would be sworn at. I explained it all. I made sure that she didn't go into it with rose-tinted glasses. I didn't want her thinking it would be fast cars all the time chasing criminals. I wanted her to know what it would really be like.*

Looking back, Bryn suspects that seeing him come home every day in uniform was an influence on Nicola's decision. It was a decision that pleased him. The police force seemed to offer a good career, and he was confident that Nicola's prospects were good. She was 19 when she applied and nearly 20 when she joined Greater Manchester Police in August 2009. Bryn was proud of her; he knew she had all the right qualities to succeed.

> *I know all parents – well, 99 per cent of parents! – will always think that the sun shines out of their children's backside, but Nicola . . . well,*

I wouldn't say that she was different. I wouldn't say she was special. But she just had something about her. I always felt that she was wise beyond her years. She was intelligent. She was clear-headed. At times, she could be naïve and a typical little girl, but most of the time, it was like she had already been around the block before. She knew a lot of things. She could talk to people. She could reason with people. She could argue. She could show her vulnerable side, but she would also show her very positive side, and she just always loved helping people.

It wasn't long before her superiors in the police force picked up on all the special qualities she had. Bryn treasures a handwritten letter from her superintendent praising the compassion and consideration she had shown to a couple in their 60s when the wife's mother died. Typically, Nicola went back on a second visit to check they were OK. Typically too, she personalised the death report. Instead of giving an address for the place of death, she wrote simply 'at (name's) home'. The couple wrote to thank her for her kindness and sensitivity, saying just how much easier she had made a horrible time. Word reached her superintendent. His response was that handwritten letter. No one could have guessed just how precious that letter was soon to become.

Less than a month later, Nicola was dead.

On 18 September, 2012, Greater Manchester Police constables Nicola Hughes and Fiona Bone were murdered in a gun and grenade ambush when they responded to a hoax 999 call in Mottram. Unarmed, the two of them walked into a brutal, cold-blooded trap. Prime Minister David Cameron described it as an 'act of pure evil'.

Bryn, who was working at HM Prison Wakefield at the time, was driving home when he got a call from a police officer who identified himself as a detective chief inspector from Oldham. The officer told him he was waiting in his car outside Bryn's house. Bryn repeatedly asked what had happened. The officer kept saying that he needed to see Bryn in person. Bryn started to suspect the worst. His thoughts racing, he instinctively knew that if Nicola had been injured, the DCI would have been telling him to hurry to the hospital. But he wasn't: he was simply saying that he was waiting for Bryn outside his home and needed to see him.

I was saying: 'Tell me what has happened!' He was saying: 'I will tell you when you get here.' Eventually, I said to him: 'Don't you dare tell me she's dead!' He said: 'There is no easy way to say this.'

Bryn hasn't a clue how he coped. There are certain moments he remembers in sharp, vivid focus. Others of which he has no memory at all. He likens it to driving home: you get there and you wonder how on earth you did it. Bryn would get from Tuesday to Thursday or from Saturday to Monday on complete autopilot.

Inevitably, the double murder was massive national news – a double-edged sword, as Bryn recalls. It meant plenty of support and comfort, but it also meant there was no escape from the sheer horror of it all.

There was no let-up. The press were ringing and trying to find you, even to the point where the undertakers had to have a list of approved people that could go to the Chapel of Rest. There were certain elements of the press trying to get to see Nicola there.

And then there was the funeral. The very last thing you ever expect to do, as Bryn says, is to organise your own child's funeral, and yet this again was on the grand scale, a personal tragedy lived as a national event. The police chaplain commented that Manchester Cathedral 'can hold only 850 people', and there was Bryn thinking *850 people is a phenomenal number of people*. But it was packed, and the decision was taken to put up big screens so that the vast crowds, gathered outside, could also pay their last respects.

At the service, Sir Peter Fahy, chief constable of the Greater Manchester force, paid tribute to Nicola's great sense of humour, her huge amounts of energy and her initiative. He told the mourners: 'Nicola in her dedication and professionalism in the way she carried out her duties showed that policing is not about muscle but is about reason, restraint and intelligence.'

Fine words which carried comfort, but as he navigated his way through his own grief, Bryn found himself thinking that he wanted to give something back. Conscious of all the support he had received, he began to realise that he needed his own act of commemoration.

Bryn had been sporty at school, and he was a regular at the gym at work. It was natural that his thoughts turned to running. Six or seven months before, he had watched a television programme on the North Pole. He'd been thinking he'd run a marathon – 'not the best decision I have ever made!' And so the two strands of thought converged in his mind. He resolved to run the North Pole Marathon. The idea was to show his gratitude for all the kindness the family had received – and also to honour Nicola.

Bryn admits to a fair amount of naïvety in the decision he took.

It was the typical thing, having seen people running marathons, of thinking: Well, how hard can that be? I thought all I would have to do was train for it.

True, to an extent. But Bryn's challenge was that he hadn't exactly picked the most straightforward of marathons. Dubbed the world's coolest marathon, the North Pole Marathon only ever has about 50 people running it – a reflection of its sheer toughness.

Bryn started his training in earnest. The marathon is run as 10 laps of 2.6 miles (4.1 kilometres). Conveniently, there is a reservoir on Saddleworth Moor which offers a 2.6-mile lap. Bryn hit the trails, but it was hardly the North Pole. So he also got in touch with the sports department at Leeds University, where there is a climate chamber. Bryn hit the treadmill in temperatures of –25°C (–13°F) – crucial preparation for the temperatures he would soon be enduring.

But as he says, the climate chamber brought false comfort. You can always step out and warm up in the office when necessary. Bryn quickly realised there would be no such comfort when he ran the race for real in April 2014.

Runners fly out first to the staging island at Svalbard, halfway between Norway and the North Pole. The temperature was –28 to –25°C (–18 to –13°F) in Svalbard when Bryn got there – coldness that nothing can prepare you for. It dropped to –42°C (–44°F) at one point at the Pole.

Adding to the difficulty is the fact the race takes place in 24-hour daylight. Bryn completed the course in 11 hours, 5 minutes. He started at around 11 a.m. and finished towards midnight, but the only way he knew it was nearly midnight was that the temperature had dropped still further. The cold is unrelenting and inescapable. Your head freezes.

Your sweat freezes. Everything freezes. You go into a heated tent for a drink, but then you step outside again, and the cold hits you once more as you slog on against all the odds.

In 2014, heaping hardship upon hardship, there was a psychological blow on top of all the difficulties. The laps were shortened, which meant that there were suddenly more of them, 12 rather than 10. In the coldness, Bryn's iPod had stopped working by lap three. He was among the slower runners, and inevitably he found himself running alone for most of the race. Alone with thoughts of Nicola.

I would not say that you are processing things. But you do start to think. You think: What would Nicola be doing? What would she be saying to me? How would her life have gone? It wasn't like I was doing a marathon because I was doing a marathon. I was doing it for a very different reason. I was doing it for Nicola. A lot of the time, I was constantly thinking about her.

However, with every step, he was heading towards trouble. By lap nine, everything caught up with him.

'Us old athletes talk about the wall,' Bryn says. His was an emotional wall – and he hit it square on. Along the route there were armed guards to protect the runners from the polar bears, but after nine laps, with most of the other runners having now crossed the finish line, the guards were much less in evidence. All Bryn could see was an ice shelf and how inviting it looked.

I just thought: If I take my jacket off and lie down over there, it will all be over in a minute. I just thought I would never wake up. All the pain, all the suffering, would have gone. And I just thought to myself: That's what I want to do. But then I started thinking about my son Sam. How would he react? How would he cope? And I even started thinking about the race organiser, Richard Donovan. I started thinking it wouldn't be fair on him. And also, I could hear Nicola shouting. She was shouting: 'Carry on, Dadzilla, carry on!' She always called me Dadzilla. She was shouting 'Come on, Dadzilla!' And then I was thinking, if I allow myself to die, then evil will win, and evil will win all the time. I thought I am bigger than this. I am stronger than this. I have got a purpose.

That purpose was the PC Nicola Hughes Memorial Fund. It became a charity just weeks before Bryn left for the North Pole. It was waiting for him when he got back, its aim to commemorate Nicola's life by supporting other families coping with the cruellest of bereavements.

The fund's mission is to provide learning opportunities and pre-employment skills in the form of support through grants or services to children (under 21) who have suffered the loss of a close family member through a violent crime such as murder or manslaughter. Bryn finds himself only too well placed to understand the specific challenges such youngsters will meet. Importantly, he understands what help they need.

We have seen the devastating effect this has on people and that how we, as adults, cope in the aftermath is different to how children cope. We would like to help them to try to rebuild their lives and look towards the future – to be able to stand on their own two feet by continuing with education where financial situations may have changed or start that course which will enable them to gain employment.

As Bryn says, it's a tragic but special connection. He cherishes the times a bereaved child emails him with thanks. There is a special understanding. Bryn and the youngsters he helps don't need to explain their grief or their emotions to each other: they just know. Their shared suffering brings them together in the tightest of bonds. And in return, their simple words of thanks make a world of difference to Bryn.

In support of the fund, Bryn's aim is to run a marathon on each continent, ideally by 2022 or 2023. To that end, in November 2016, he ticked off America when he completed the New York City Marathon. His aim was to ensure a representative of every single one of the country's 43 police forces ran the race that day. He didn't do badly: 31 police forces were represented. Gratifyingly, but slightly frustratingly, several others have since said to him: 'If only we'd known. . .' In some instances, internal communications within the various forces were the problem.

Even so, the end result was that Bryn, who lives in Huddersfield, West Yorkshire, was able to present a cheque for £40,000 to the National Homicide Service – a massive achievement. PC Nicola's Fund will pay for specialist counselling for children. Bryn is now hoping the initiative will continue through central funding.

Another money-raiser for the PC Nicola Hughes Memorial Fund, typically expressed through running, is the annual Run to Remember – a virtual event that invites people to run 100 days at two miles per day. Beginners can join at Day 50 and run one mile per day for the remaining 50 days. Under-16s can join at Day 75 for one mile for 25 days. The year 2017 was the fourth time the event was run.

In 2016, David Cameron, on the day after he left the office of Prime Minister, unveiled a memorial to murdered PCs Fiona Bone and Nicola Hughes, telling their families: 'They are lights that will never go out.' The PC Nicola Hughes Memorial Fund will make sure the lights will always burn bright.

And so life goes on.

Bryn was forced to retire from the prison service in 2014 because of post-traumatic stress disorder (PTSD), something that still creeps up on him. There are still triggers, but thanks to eye movement desensitisation and reprocessing (EMDR), he no longer thinks that every ambulance he hears is carrying Nicola's body. He has worked through the trauma of seeing his daughter in the mortuary. He has come a long way. For the most part, Bryn is able to say he's strong now. His achievement has been to ensure that evil hasn't triumphed.

> *I think sometimes what would Nicola be saying to me: 'What on earth are you doing, Dadzilla?' We used to do karate, and I would always be trying to beat people. And she used to say to me: 'Dad, you are not Peter Pan!' I think she might be saying that now and laughing. But I also think she would be proud. . .*

Stephanie Foley

'Then we did as Sarah did – we ran with all our Hart!'

Something didn't feel right from the moment Stephanie Foley got up. Her intention was to go for a run, but on Thursday, 14 June, 2012, she just couldn't find the motivation to get out there. She still can't say why. She got ready, she put her running shoes on, and she looked out of the window at the glorious sunshine in Russell County, Kentucky. She would be working late that evening. She knew now was her only chance to run if she was going to run that day. She even found herself thinking it would be a perfect day to hit the pavement.

> *But still, my heart wasn't in it for some reason. There are just times you choose to give in to that odd feeling – that's exactly what I did. Instead, I fixed my coffee and sat on my back porch enjoying the beauty of the morning before work.*

Tragically, it was a beauty that was soon to be brutally shattered.

Stephanie's father, Larry Bennett, the County Sheriff, came by. He told her he was on his way to join the search for Stephanie's friend, Sarah Roberts Hart. Sarah had gone running with her sister Elizabeth early that morning, but 31-year-old Sarah, a mum of three and in the early stages of pregnancy, hadn't felt well. Telling Elizabeth to carry on without her, she turned back to return to her car. Now she was missing, last seen alive at around 5.30 a.m.

Stephanie's thoughts raced. Was there some sort of mistake? Had Sarah got a lift from someone else? This was small-town Kentucky, a place where people knew each other. A place where bad things just don't happen.

Fighting her anxiety, Stephanie went to work. But the worry niggled away – even though the route Sarah and Elizabeth would have taken that morning was along a stretch of main highway with a pavement beside it. It was the route most runners in town took on a regular basis simply because it was safe. It wasn't remote. There were no alleys. It was well lit and well travelled.

By lunchtime, however, the horrifying truth had emerged. In a town almost without crime, in a town so unthreatening, Sarah had been murdered – strangled and hidden by the roadside, the cruellest end to a life that had touched so many. Ryan, the high-school sweetheart who became her husband, was a widower. Their young children, daughters Avery and Addison and son Archer, had lost their mother. A small town in rural Kentucky – 'the type of town where you practically know everyone and everyone knows you' – was in shock. Stephanie had lost a friend in a million.

As Stephanie says, some of her greatest and strongest friendships have developed through running. At first, she ran with her father, the great encourager. Stephanie saw it as the perfect opportunity to have quality time with him, plus she needed a healthier lifestyle. They began running together in the spring of 2000, and other runners joined them. Her father suggested they train for a 10k. Then came a half-marathon, a marathon and a mini triathlon, always new goals emerging.

It was at this point that Sarah Roberts Hart became part of the running group.

We would meet in the evenings during the week to run. Sarah had a couple of young girls and would bring a stroller to push her youngest daughter while she ran. Sometimes we'd all take a turn pushing the stroller or come alongside and help her push. It was a fun running group. We ran, we laughed, we cried, we challenged each other, we encouraged each other, and sometimes we even hated each other – but only briefly – especially when running up a hill!

Sarah was a pharmacist and would have to work some Saturdays. If she drove past her running friends, she would sound the horn in encouragement. However, when she was well into her third pregnancy, she had to cut back on the running. Life was just too busy.

When I think of Sarah, I remember her as a person who deeply loved her husband and children. She enjoyed photography. And – which surprised me — she was a good hunter. This college graduate, Mom, wife and pharmacist could hunt a deer better than any man. Sarah was the type of person who seemed to have it all together — the ability to maintain a demanding career, take care of her family, include friends in her life, run and still enjoy other hobbies. She had a very full life! When we would meet to run, time passed so quickly because we spent most of the time talking. Sarah would share funny stories about her children and her husband. She never failed to talk about her sister Elizabeth. Sarah would tell us what they were going to do when Elizabeth came home from college. She loved her family and she loved her life.

And now, suddenly, in the most brutal fashion, she was dead. Nothing made sense as the questions crowded in on Stephanie. Who would dare do such a thing? How could this horrible tragedy happen to such a wonderful person? What would life be like now? Would the running group stop running? Suddenly, for the first time ever, Stephanie felt unsafe and unsure as a runner. Would she ever be able to run again?

It was such a frightening thought for me as running is a huge part of my life. I literally plan my life around being able to run. If there's one thing that brings the most satisfaction to me, running is it.

In every respect, Sarah's murder struck at the heart of the community. As Stephanie says, it was personal for almost everyone in their small community.

Our entire town grieved deeply. They grieved for her husband and three young children. They grieved for her sister and her parents, and they even grieved for her friends. People who did not even know Sarah learned of who she was and fell in love with her.

Sarah's story spread across Kentucky and into other states, and it wasn't long before people were wanting an outlet for their grief. They needed to channel it into an event that honoured and celebrated Sarah. Stephanie's father Larry received a call from Sarah's father, Wendell Roberts. Wendell told him he had been contacted by a company called 3 Way Racing, asking if the family would be interested in hosting a run in Sarah's memory. Larry told Wendell to contact Stephanie and their other friend, Ashley Bennett Hart, Sarah's sister-in-law. Stephanie set about the task immediately, identifying the two essentials: the event had to reflect who Sarah was and it had to bring about good. With 3 Way Racing, she started to try to identify a venue that would accommodate perhaps a few hundred runners.

> *Sarah died 14 June, 2012 and somehow we set a race date for 11 August, 2012. When I think about that now, my mind just cannot comprehend how in the world we pulled it off in such a short amount of time. There was so much we had to accomplish.*

Fulfilling the twin aims, they decided that proceeds from the race would help fund scholarships for graduating seniors from Russell County High School, where Sarah had graduated, who were majoring in pharmacy or a medical field.

The next tasks were to choose a route and come up with a logo. They managed both with an increasing sense that the event was an event meant to be. They traced and Googled various routes and mileages and found the best route traced an 'odd heart shape – but definitely a heart'. The race gained its title, again subtly honouring Sarah. It became **Run With All Your Hart** (RWAYH), to which Stephanie and her co-organisers added a verse from Hebrews 12:1: 'Let us run with patience the race that is set before us'.

As for the logo for the race shirts, the design came from one of Sarah's cousins.

> *We actually took an imprint of the foot of Sarah's son Archer and the hands of each of her daughters, Avery and Addison, and made an angel.*

A graphic design company turned the imprints into a printable logo. The T-shirts were donated by Fruit of the Loom, which had a factory in town, just half a mile from where Sarah was murdered. As Stephanie says, every aspect of the planning and every element of the race simply fell into place, perfectly timed within the tightest of frameworks.

People were volunteering. Donations were coming in like crazy. Restaurants were offering free food and discounts on race day. Businesses and churches were providing everything they needed. They didn't even need to ask. Police and emergency personnel were on board, willing to do whatever Stephanie and her friends thought of and didn't think of. Music groups were volunteering to have a concert. DJs were volunteering to provide entertainment. TV and radio stations were hosting interviews and promoting the race. An entire community was coming together.

Stephanie is in no doubt exactly what was happening.

I must tell you with all assurance: God's hand was in every detail of this race because we alone could not have accomplished this task. We're not that great and I had never planned an event other than a kids' birthday party. I take no credit in any form or fashion.

Another piece slipped into the perfect picture the race was forming when the route came out at four miles – a mile for each of Sarah's children, the three living children and the baby who died with her. Sarah's husband Ryan named him Alexander. The mile markers incorporated a photograph of the child they celebrated: Avery, Addison and Archer. Baby Alexander was the angel in the logo.

A 1.5-mile (2.4-kilometre) route for walkers who did not think they could make a 4-mile (6-kilometre) distance was added, and a Facebook page and website were set up to promote the race. The likes grew as they prepared to open race registration. They were expecting around 500 runners, a figure rapidly reached and exceeded.

Stephanie spent a huge part of each day taking registrations. More race shirts were needed. Emails were pouring in, and so too were donations, specifically to allow families to take part who might not be able to afford the registration fee. At no point did Stephanie and her friends have to ask for help.

I loved how our community pulled together not just for themselves but to lend some help to others they may never know.

People from other states and countries were saying they wished to take part somehow. With demand growing, the race team opened up a virtual run option where people could register and run on the same day, at the same time, wherever they were. Remarkably, the race ended up with participants from every state in the USA plus seven other countries.

On the day, hundreds of people ran virtually. More than 2900 people turned up to run in person – a result that raised more than $70,000 for the Sarah Roberts Hart Scholarship Fund. The crowds that filled the campus of the Russell County High School Auditorium/Natatorium Complex were unbelievable, Stephanie says. The main highway had to be shut down for the race. The traffic was detoured, with the runners stretching a quarter of a mile across the four lanes of KY Highway 127. Meanwhile, the walkers walked their 1.5-mile route.

It was an astonishing day. And an astonishing celebration of Sarah.

> *It was more than just a race. It was an amazing tribute to a beautiful friend and her son. It was a day that was filled with tears and laughter and appreciation for life – the life of Sarah and how her death touched thousands of people. Running and walking that day brought healing. On 11 August, 2012, all the participants and spectators and volunteers stood outside in Russell Springs, Kentucky, holding hands lifted up to the heavens as we prayed and thanked God for the life of Sarah and prayed for healing and forgiveness. Then we did as Sarah did – we ran with all our Hart!*

In May 2014 Christopher Allman was sentenced to life for the murder of Sarah Hart. He was 6 foot 6 inches (1.98 metres) tall to Sarah's 5 foot 5 inches (1.68 metres), 190 pounds (86 kilos) to Sarah's 120 (54 kilos). Allman admitted an eight-count indictment in exchange for a life sentence with no possibility of parole.

Meanwhile, remembering Sarah's life rather than her death, Run With All Your Hart went ahead again that year, repeating the success of its 2012 debut and its 2013 return. Still celebrating good rather than recalling evil, the race returned for a final time in 2015. However, by 2016, the Hart and Roberts families felt it had fulfilled its purpose. They issued a statement on the race Facebook page: 'This year we've decided to remember and celebrate Sarah's life privately and quietly. This event has helped us with our healing but we believe it is time to suspend the event.' However, they promised that the scholarship fund would continue to benefit students from Russell County. They also expressed their hope that everyone would continue to honour Sarah's memory and 'run with patience the race that is set before us'.

Which is precisely what Stephanie has done.

Running took Sarah to her death, but for Stephanie, running will always be about life. She continues to run for the sense of personal achievement it brings. She runs for fitness, both mental and physical, and she runs for the friendship it fosters – not least the cherished friendship she shared with Sarah.

Stephanie runs at least four days a week, but it is not about being the best. It is about enjoying the challenge and making the challenge fun.

> *I plan my life around running. I plan trips to run, vacations to run and weekends to run. My running group and I seek out new routes to run, new events to participate in and how we can inspire each other to do our best. If you're a runner, you'll always be able to find friends. If I go on vacation, I search for running groups – because I know I have friends no matter where I go.*

It is not about being fast, it is about going the distance. Stephanie has run one marathon, one mini triathlon and more than 30 half-marathons and 4 x 200 relay races, plus more 5k and 10k races than she can count. It is about self-discipline, about being able to motivate herself and about overcoming the mental challenges that threaten to defeat us all.

Inevitably, the tragedy of Sarah's death has shaped Stephanie's running. She tells someone her route in advance and keeps to it. She runs with a group, not necessarily at the same pace, but always with the awareness that they need to look out for each other. She also runs with her dog Roxie, a Weimaraner.

> *The key to our healing was to not allow the tragedy of Sarah's death to keep us inside our homes. But rather, Sarah would want us to be smart runners, enjoying life and overcoming the fear.*

Getting back out to run after Sarah's death was a testament to their shared belief that they will overcome; that they will always run the race that is set before them. As Stephanie says, they are smart runners now.

But that morning in June 2012 will always haunt her:

I often think back to the day Sarah was murdered. I was prepared to go run. I would have run the exact same route Sarah ran. Generally, we met each other along the way in the wee hours of the morning. And, that day, I would have been running alone. Sometimes I think I could have been the victim. Maybe that's why my urge to run wasn't there that morning. Then other times, I think maybe I could have helped Sarah if I had gone for my morning run. What would have been different about that day? So many questions . . . But I can't allow the what ifs in life to overtake me. I must accept the reality, as hard as that may be. Once we accept it, we find ways to heal, forgive and hopefully, help others along the way.

The Finish Line

'A group of people I have come to admire hugely.'

What if? What if indeed.

The gun goes. For a few seconds nothing happens, a little lull before the 26.2 miles ahead of us all. Then the shuffling starts. Imperceptibly, the shuffling becomes a jog, which just as imperceptibly becomes a run, timed to perfection, 10, maybe 15 steps from the start line. We gain momentum as we pass over it, each of us pressing – in that instant – the button on our watch, which will time our marathon over the next however many hours it will take.

It's a release. There has been a traffic delay. The start was put back, but no one seems to mind. It heightens the anticipation – and makes it all the more pleasurable as we finally start to lengthen our stride. But not too much. I haven't hustled to get to the front, I want to be mid-pack. I want to be sucked into the race, but not too quickly. My mind needs it, but I am not confident I have got the legs. I start gently, and for the first time ever, I relish the fact that it is so easy to find yourself cabined, cribbed and confined at the start of a marathon. There is something reassuring about it. I am hemmed in, but hemmed in by precisely the kind of people I want to be hemmed in by.

We are all looking straight ahead. There is nowhere else to look as determination kicks in and takes over. But I know we are all conscious of each other in our mass getaway. I feel a little wobble in my knees and the slow trickle of a gentlemanly tear. Bloody hell! I have done it. I am back where I want to be. Back at the start of a marathon.

Even after all these days, after all these nights, my overwhelming reality is that pavement in Cape Town, more real than any reality that comes from the present moment. It's a pavement I feel like I am never going to leave. I'd always assumed that we control our minds. The stabbing has shown me that the very opposite is true. It's now brutally, endlessly clear: *banishing a thought* is a pipe dream. *Perish the thought* is a myth. Our minds think what they want to think – and mine is still locked in thoughts that this is where I am going to die.

Logic doesn't come into it. I can tell myself repeatedly that my attacker hadn't intended to kill me. I can tell myself time and again that my wounds weren't ever likely to be fatal. But then the reality kicks in. I was bleeding profusely. What if I hadn't been found?

What if? What if indeed.

If I hadn't been found, then my attacker's intentions would have been utterly immaterial.

And that's the obsession that plagues me – an obsession punctuated by endless unanswered questions. How come I didn't see the knife? Why didn't he just finish me off when I pulled him to the ground? Or did he drop the knife when I toppled him? Was that what saved me? I am never going to know.

And that's what I'm thinking. Because it's what I think all the time.

But as I look around, I look at runners who know nothing of my circumstances, just as I know nothing of theirs. All I know is that they accept me unquestioningly as part of this wonderful shared experience that lies ahead, just as I suddenly, desperately, want them to be part of my landscape on this slightly chilly morning.

I think of the runners I have interviewed for this book, ordinary people who have shown themselves to be amazing people; people who would never have known the strength they possessed if adversity hadn't plonked itself in their way. If adversity had not suddenly been there, huge, immovable, lowering, immense and obscene.

So what did they do? They found the strength to run round it, under it, through it, up and over it. With strength, decency, self-awareness, compassion and sheer humanity, they steeled themselves, told the world: 'See you on the other side' – and they got there.

They have faced death, terrorism, savage attack, the depths of depression, the appalling grip of addiction. They have faced it all, and their instinct has been to find the resolve to carry on. Forwards is the only way out. Running has been their only way to go.

And with this run, I am going to join them, a group of people I have come to admire hugely.

Some have run to confront their demons; some to block them out. Some have run to connect with their trauma; some to escape it. Some have run to skirt round their vicious circle; some to shatter it and, by shattering it, to escape.

They have recognised that running can't ever be everything; but they have run because they know that running will always be something. Some have run thousands of miles; some just a few. Distance matters less than the act of getting out there and embracing the benefits which start to stack up when we start to walk and when a walk becomes a run.

In writing this book, I have been amazed at every turn by just how open these runners have been, just how willing to tell their tales, just how eloquent and brave they are. And just how conscious they are of what running is and what it has meant to them. As so many have said, nothing else would have done: it simply had to be running.

And I find that fascinating. It's a promise, a gift.

Our pace quickens as we leave the edge of Worcester behind us and launch into the countryside for the first of the two big loops that will eventually bring us back to where we started. And it is the space that strikes me; running is giving me space. I look at my watch, and I realise that it is also giving me time. All the time I need. As much time as I want as I run my race against the thoughts I can't dismiss.

I am running with the reality of my stabbing horribly, brutally present at the forefront of my mind. I am not talking memories. Memories are the things we let go and watch as they drift into our past. No, this is reality, 100 per cent in my present tense, painful and horrid.

But suddenly there is a crucial difference. I am running surrounded by hundreds of other runners who will get me there because they are going to get themselves there. We are all in it together, and that's the glory of our undertaking. The race is about finding space. It is about finding time. But it is also about connection.

And I think of the great American runner Kathrine Switzer, who so famously and so beautifully said: 'If you are losing faith in human nature, go out and watch a marathon.' Never have her words felt truer. With every step, I am feeling safer.

The marathon isn't putting a plaster on my wounds. It is doing something much more subtle than that, accelerating a process which began when I went for my first post-stabbing hobble more than a year ago. The marathon is tilting my world view back to a place where I can accept that I am not turning cartwheels that I survived; that stupidly, infuriatingly, I can't stop thinking: *Shit, I could have died.*

Running is giving me back a world view where there is no need to feel guilty that I don't feel boundless gratitude for having been spared; a world view where I can start to accept just how hard I have found this past year.

It is helping me see that all I can really do is to keep going. KBO, as Winston Churchill used to say. KBO; *Keep Buggering On.*

I am never going to know what the knife looked like, whether he dropped it or simply chose not to kill me. Nor will I ever know how many other people he stabbed that day and how many other people he has stabbed since.

I will never know whether he is still alive. Surely you can't do what he did with impunity every time? I can never know – though I can guess – what would have happened if Steven hadn't stopped, just as I will never know why my mind still smoulders at what happened when surely I should be rejoicing at still being here.

But I do know I am always going to run, because running has changed my perspective. Running is my freedom. Running is me. Running is the best expression of me. And I smile as the miles start to add up.

Fiona is out there on the route, a route we researched the day before. She's there at 17 miles all alone, standing there and supporting me, just as she has done pretty much for all my marathons. And I do something I have never done on a marathon course before. I veer across and kiss her. Later, she tells me that the chap behind me also veered across and jokingly asked whether he was going to get one too – the kind of quip which takes us to the heart of running, the spirit it engenders, the connection it gives us.

OK, I know. I always get desperately pretentious at the mere thought of a marathon. But the fact is that running elevates the soul. My soul, at least. And I love the tired old cliché – a cliché which endures because it is so manifestly true. The only person you are running against is yourself – unless, of course, you are at the elite end of the race, which I'm patently not. For the rest of us, we are running with each other, and that's a heart-warming distinction.

I cast my mind back to the day four years before when, less than a quarter of a mile into the Portsmouth Coastline Marathon, I stupidly ran smack into a lamppost, broke my nose and gashed open my forehead. I wish I had a fiver for every runner who said to me, over the next 26 miles, 'Are you alright, mate?' or 'We are with you, my friend'. The runners ahead of me – and there were plenty of them – even made sure that St John Ambulance were ready and waiting when I finally crossed the line.

And that's what running is all about. It is about togetherness and it is about healing. And that's why I am running here now. It has been a terrible year. I crave the healing that only running can give, and I know that it is flowing through me now.

I look at my fellow runners again and I ponder that wonderful convergence of the individual and the collective. We start as individuals and we run as individuals, but mid-race we have all been subsumed into a panting sweaty mass of heaving humanity, across mile after mile of Worcestershire countryside. Gorgeous! I love the sweat. I love the effort.

Yet within that collective we will remain individuals. We are running with the others, but running against ourselves – and outrunning the demons that assail us. I wonder just how many other runners this morning are running to regain their equilibrium just as I am.

I thought I was running to say a big fat 'sod off' to the guy who knifed me. But I realise it is much more positive than that. I am running so that I am no longer the *guy who got stabbed* but the *guy who has just added to his tally of 30 marathons*.

And as I cross the line, 30 becomes 31, and I can't even begin to tell you how good that feels. I was stuck on 30 for too long, a horribly round number that suggests a target set and a target achieved. Thirty-one is a much better number . . . a number which is crying out to be turned into 32 . . . and then 33. A number which suggests that I am not done yet.

As the great Dean Karnazes says, running is about finding your inner peace. I am now restoring mine – just as the people I have interviewed for this book have restored theirs.

If you don't shed a tear at the end of a marathon, you haven't fully reaped the benefits of its long and warm embrace.

At the end of the Worcester Marathon, I slump on the grass. I feel empty. I feel happy. I squint into the sun, which has just come out. It's too bright for my tired, slightly tearful eyes. I close them and feel the sun's warmth on my face. Bliss! I am a runner again. I can't say I am complete. But I am as complete as I am ever going to be, and that is enough.

Postscript

'Better Things'

Six months later, I round off the year with the glorious Portsmouth Coastal Waterside Marathon. Marathon number 32 was the New Forest in the September. Number 33, a week before Christmas, is Portsmouth, 13.1 miles (21 kilometres) with the sea on your right, after which you turn around for 13.1 miles with the sea on your left. Wonderfully pointless. A race in fact where the pointlessness is the point of it – and the beauty.

But it is also a race that brings four of the finest race-side signs I have ever seen.

The first is: 'Smile if you're not wearing pants!' I force a straight face. It is a big day, so I am wearing my stab-day pants as a guarantee that all will be well. I can't fault my logic. No one is ever going to get stabbed twice while wearing the same pants, are they? They make me feel like a middle-aged, rather damaged, past-his-sell-by-date Superman, but a Superman nonetheless. No one is going to get me again. They are my defence against the Dark Arts.

Sign number two is the beautifully meta sign, which simply reads: 'Motivational sign'. Not much you can say to that.

Rather more obvious, and rather more inspiring, is sign number three: 'Tough times pass. Tough people endure'. That's what this book has been about. It feels like an endorsement of all I have been writing. It quickens my step.

But best of all is the sign much closer to the finish, which is this book in a nutshell: 'Life isn't about waiting for the storm to pass . . . It's about learning to dance in the rain'. A phrase which makes perfect sense the moment you realise that running is the best dance we've got.

A couple of minutes later, I find my perfect dance partner.

Suddenly, I stop. Overwhelmed. Exhausted. Unable to put one foot in front of the other. It feels like I will never move again – until a passing runner (and plenty are passing at this point) taps me on the shoulder and says: 'Come on, mate, not far to go.' I take it as an invitation and run the final 0.2 of a mile alongside him.

I remember his number. I could look up his name. But I prefer not to, I would rather not know. He is, and will always be, *the runner who got me over the line*, a runner who could have been any one of the hundreds of thousands of runners I have run alongside in 33 marathons around the world. He stands for them all and sums up precisely why I love runners – and running.

This is what running does, and he did what runners do. It's as simple as that.

And to cap it all, my random MP3 shuffle of my all-time favourite songs launches into the perfect number just as we cross the line together. I'd been hoping for 'Start Me Up' or 'Don't Stop' by my gods, The Rolling Stones. Instead, it is 'Better Things' by The Kinks.

I know you've got a lot of good things happening up ahead.
The past is gone, it's all been said.
So here's to what the future brings,
I know tomorrow you'll find better things.

Better Things indeed. For me, I hope – and, above all, for the remarkable people I have interviewed for this book. They led the way. It was my privilege to follow. It has been my honour to get to know them.

Appendix:
The Science Behind the
Transformative Power of Running

'Science is illuminating what I instinctively feel to be true.'

For many millions of us, *I run because it makes me feel happy* is the sentence that says it all. It's as simple as that. There's nothing more to add.

Except these days there is plenty we can add if we want to.

In recent years, a growing weight of evidence has emerged which underpins that sensation of simply 'feeling better' with solid scientific research. Feeling better is no longer merely observational or anecdotal. Behind it is a connection between exercise and mood that is ever more clearly understood. Research now offers a validation for the things we as runners instinctively know to be true.

When I go for the counselling that has helped me since the stabbing, I park my car two miles away and run to the session. It gets me in the zone. After the session, I run a big loop back to my car, seven miles of intensity, running as fast as I can. The running takes me back to where I want to be – in every sense. Running and therapy go hand in hand.

My running is unthinking on session days. It is instinctive. I am listening to my body. But it's reassuring to know that the science now exists to explain the message my body is giving me. Science can give context to the things we unthinkingly do as runners – and it is perhaps this fact above all which has prompted a remarkable increase in public awareness when it comes to the physical and mental health benefits that running can bring.

Exercise is something that modern medicine actively promotes. Scientists, for instance, now tell us that running can play a part in our recovery from post-traumatic stress disorder (PTSD). I know for certain they are right. Why else was I secretly so pleased that it was impossible to find a parking space at the hospital and that I had to look elsewhere, further away?

In 2015, the National Center for Biotechnology Information in the United States published a study entitled *Exercise Enhances the Behavioral Responses to Acute Stress in an Animal Model of PTSD*. The study looked at the effects of endurance exercise on animals' behavioural response to stress. Some animals ran on a treadmill. Some didn't. All were exposed to predator scent stress (PSS). The sedentary animals were observed to have a greater incidence of extreme-behaviour responses, including higher anxiety. Exercise-trained animals exposed to PSS, on the other hand, developed a resilience to stress.

In another 2015 study, The University of Texas looked at human responses. The researchers focused on levels of brain-derived neurotrophic factor (BDNF), a protein in the brain associated with learning and survival instincts. It is key to the way we react to danger – and is typically found to be low in people suffering from PTSD. In the study, one group of PTSD sufferers jogged for 30 minutes before their therapy sessions. The other group did not. With time, those who ran exhibited an increase in BDNF and a decrease in PTSD symptoms. The study's inevitable conclusion was that running could help alleviate PTSD.

But clearly, as this book has shown, running's benefits go far beyond PTSD. When we talk about the mental health benefits of running, we can talk far more generally about the sense of equilibrium that running can create and encourage. Britain's National Health Service is categoric. It places exercise specifically among the treatments that can be used as alternatives to antidepressants. Research by the NHS suggests that regular exercise may even be more effective than antidepressants as a treatment for mild depression:

> *Exercise helps boost levels of chemicals called serotonin and dopamine in the brain, which can lift your mood. Exercising on a regular basis can boost self-esteem and confidence, which can help to relieve symptoms of depression.*

The NHS stresses that the exercise needs to be enjoyable. Otherwise it is simply self-defeating. More important still, it needs to be proportionate. Our levels of exercise must reflect our age and our physical condition. If they do so, then the National Health Service is clear: to stay healthy, as adults, we should do 150 minutes of moderate intensity activity every week, a level of activity especially useful for people with mild to moderate depression.

'Any exercise is better than none. Even a 15-minute walk can clear your mind,' the NHS tells us. My yardstick, when the children were small, was that if I hadn't been for a run, I would often hear myself asking them to go and fetch something for me; if I had been for a run, I simply fetched it myself.

It comes as no surprise, then, that British mental-health charity Mind keenly promotes exercise as one of its paths to well-being. Hayley Jarvis, Community Programmes Manager (Sport) at Mind, is determined to encourage people to see the possibilities in exercise rather than to stumble at the hurdles that seem to stand in our way.

As Hayley says:

We know that having a mental health problem can make getting active more difficult. The thought of joining a running group when you have bipolar disorder, depression or OCD can stop you in your tracks, but a mental health problem doesn't have to prevent anybody from getting active.

In 2016 Mind warned that women with mental health problems who are not exercising because of bad experiences with physical education at school are putting themselves at greater risk of poor physical and mental health. Some 85 per cent of women with mental health problems do not participate in sport because they don't feel confident in their sporting ability – a finding Mind is determined to address. Supported by Sport England and the National Lottery, Mind launched a new physical activity project, Get Set to Go. Mind is clear: we can often improve our mental health problems through physical activity.

It is fascinating to see both government and health authorities increasingly recognising that responsibility falls to them in this area of our lives. The need to act was underlined in *Start Active, Stay*

Active (published in the UK in 2011 and updated in 2016), a report on physical activity for health from four chief medical officers. The report described inactivity as a silent killer. Addressing health professionals, it cautioned them against the danger of allowing physical activity to be seen as 'everybody's business', an approach that could result in no one actually taking the lead: 'This must not happen; physical activity is a win-win intervention which can help to achieve multiple objectives across public health, transport, the environment, education, healthy ageing, childcare and social care'.

It concluded:

We know enough now to act on physical activity. The evidence for action is extremely strong, and we have reached a unique UK-wide consensus on the amount and type of physical activity that is needed to benefit health. This new approach opens the door to new and exciting partnerships and will help to create a more active society.

However, perhaps the biggest breakthrough in terms of public debate came when the 2017 Virgin Money London Marathon, one of the world's most popular marathons, adopted Heads Together as its charity of the year. It proved the perfect way to get the UK talking about mental health.

Heads Together, a campaign which aims to 'change the conversation about mental health', has set out to demonstrate the beneficial power of conversation – of talking about our mental health problems and sharing our experiences with each other. Thousands of runners wore Heads Together headbands to show their support for the world's first ever mental health marathon. It was a day when the stigma surrounding mental health issues took a massive and very public battering.

Charlie Engle, interviewed in this book, based his Icebreaker Run – a 3,100-mile relay across America in May and June 2016 – on the connection between running and mental health. Before setting out, he said: 'We named the expedition the Icebreaker Run because we intend to have a running conversation with people across America as we run from coast to coast.'

Also in the United States is Still I Run, a community with a powerful voice. Its runners run for their health, to raise awareness of mental health issues and also specifically to stop the stigma that surrounds the difficulties they face. 'If we don't talk about it because we feel ashamed, then we continue to suffer alone and in silence,' the community argues:

Because one of the best ways to combat anxiety and depression is through exercise and running, we're combining the two. Still I Run is our take on the famous Maya Angelou poem 'Still I Rise'. Though we may feel defeated and deflated, we can fight the good fight and get out and be healthy, both physically and mentally . . . together.

The charity Anxiety In Teens, founded in 2006 in Minneapolis, works along similar lines. Its vision is 'comfort and certainty at every young adult's fingertips'. Its OutRun Anxiety 5K events attract thousands of walkers and runners to come together to support teens with anxiety and other disorders.

I have spoken to plenty of runners who have felt a significant sense of release as a result of their running – the fact that running gives them the confidence to talk about how they are feeling. Tackle stigma, and there is a sense of liberation. Campaigns and charities worldwide are encouraging precisely that openness on a national and international level; running is proving a key way to give people the confidence to open up.

Dr Ross Dunne, consultant psychiatrist for later life with the Greater Manchester Mental Health NHS Foundation Trust, can put the science on the bones of what happens when we run, and why it makes us feel better. As he says, much of the evidence we have about how running affects different cell types in the brain is from animal studies – for the simple reason that 'human runners are understandably reluctant to give up their brains for study'. However, at a cellular level, mammalian brains are similar enough that we can make inferences about what might be going on in humans from exercise studies in smaller mammals that run, like mice and rats.

Dr Dunne explains:

Running enhances the birth rate of new neurons in the central nervous system. In several types of experiments, running in animals has been found to increase the rate at which new nerve cells are created in an area called the dentate gyrus, which is embedded in an area of the brain known to be important in mood and memory – the hippocampus. In other studies of animals with experimentally induced PTSD-like symptoms, scientists have found less new neuron formation in the same area. This might be one of the mechanisms by which running improves PTSD symptoms. PTSD symptoms can be thought of as an over-generalised fear, caused by a trauma. Such over-generalised fear has to be learned – and can be un-learned. Increasing new neuron generation in the dentate gyrus may help un-learn the fear.

Running thus brings benefits, and those benefits create their own momentum. But as Dr Dunne explains, it is crucial to retain a sense of proportion. As he says, for very depressed people, sometimes getting out of bed is a marathon. It requires every ounce of drive and willpower:

People who don't understand depression infer that depression itself is sort of a 'lack of willpower'. It isn't, any more than allowing your cancer to spread is a lack of 'self-control', an idea you hopefully find idiotic. Nonetheless, small steps towards 'behavioural activation' can be achieved, and with every step, the person with depression re-learns that they have control of at least a corner of their illness, at least a portion of their life.

Dr Dunne stresses it is vitally important that people are encouraged not to aim too high. As he says, there is no point in engendering failure and reinforcing the depressed person's belief that they are 'worthless' and 'good for nothing'. Any defeat will be magnified and overgeneralised by what he calls the 'dun-coloured glasses through which the world appears in depression'. It is far better to set small achievable goals, which can be reflected upon and built upon. The benefits then accumulate:

After some time, there is a greater sense of an 'internal locus of control' – the idea that at least some of my stressors can be managed by me, that I am not merely a pinball in a machine.

It is a powerful image. My problem has been PTSD, not depression. But it seems to me that Dr Dunne completely nails it. Thoughts of my attacker converge with memories of my blood; visions of it pooling mingle in an endless rerunning of that day; all the while I am playing a tediously counterproductive *what if* game that I can't stop playing. It all leaves me feeling buffeted amid the bells and buzzers as an evil Pinball Wizard racks up his highest score. But if I run, I reclaim something essential. Running is me reasserting me, and I am grateful to science for giving me the vocabulary to express it. Running is helping me snatch back my internal locus of control. I love the expression. Science is illuminating what I instinctively feel to be true.

That sense of increased control is a key part of the attraction and indeed the benefit of running – as is the sense of peace and connection that running can so often foster. Many runners practise running as a form of mindfulness. I certainly do. Again, Dr Dunne can help to explain the science behind it:

> *Running is a meditation. Alright, maybe not right at the start or when recovering from injury. As you heave your way up the first hill in six months, it certainly doesn't feel very Zen. However, if we examine the things you do when you run well: focused attention on breathing and avoiding unnecessary movements, a focused awareness of signals from your body (which often seem to be heightened), an awareness of your perceived effort, and an acute awareness of your surroundings, these are all things that are described by expert meditators.*

The absolute global experts on meditation are Zen Buddhist monks, who often spend years perfecting breathing technique and concentration. From this practice, as Dr Dunne explains, Western medicine has derived a secular practice called mindfulness, which enhances relaxation and can be useful in PTSD, anxiety and depression.

> *The Marathon Monks of Mount Hiei in Japan run, jog and walk their way to enlightenment, exercising the same fine control while moving over uneven ground. Their walk-jog-run is undoubtedly a meditation and may explain why running, like mindfulness and meditation, brings relief to those dealing with depression, trauma or bereavement.*

Psychiatrist Dr Amit D Mistry, who is part of the Royal College of Psychiatrists' Sport & Exercise Special Interest Group (RCPsych SEPSIG), has a special interest in the relationship between elite sports, exercise and mental health. He is currently working with Public Health England's Physical Activity Clinical Champions Scheme to promote the benefits of physical activity within the mental health setting.

He too underlines the role exercise can play in treating depression: 'There is robust evidence demonstrating the antidepressant effects of aerobic exercise in major depressive disorder.' In its clinical guideline CG90, the UK's National Institute for Health and Clinical Excellence (NICE) recommends physical activity as a first-line option for mild to moderate depression. Offered under a structured group physical activity programme, with a competent practitioner, this should typically consist of three sessions per week of moderate duration (45 minutes to 1 hour) over an average 12 weeks.

As Dr Mistry says:

It can benefit older adults too with major depressive disorder, although we need to factor in physical health co-morbidities as these can lower anti-depressant effect. Older adults do better in group settings rather than exercising on their own. However, in view of its physical health benefits and antidepressant effects there are many calling for exercise to be given greater priority within NHS mental health care.

Again, it comes back to mindfulness. Dr Mistry finds running to be 'a form of meditation due to its repetitive nature'. As he says, it overlaps with meditation/mindfulness in that it encourages concentration, contemplation and relaxation.

Harvard Health Publishing, part of the Harvard Health School, adds even more weight to the arguments. It labels exercise an 'all-natural treatment to fight depression'. One in 10 adults in the United States struggles with depression, but antidepressant medications aren't the only solution. Research from the Health School shows that exercise is also an effective treatment:

Exercising starts a biological cascade of events that results in many health benefits, such as protecting against heart disease and diabetes, improving sleep and lowering blood pressure. High-intensity exercise releases the body's feel-good chemicals called endorphins, resulting in the 'runner's high' that joggers report. But for most of us, the real value is in low-

intensity exercise sustained over time. That kind of activity spurs the release of proteins called neurotrophic or growth factors, which cause nerve cells to grow and make new connections. The improvement in brain function makes you feel better.

Also in the United States, Mayo Clinic, which has major campuses in Arizona, Florida and Minnesota, firmly backs exercise as a response to depression and anxiety: 'once you get motivated, exercise can make a big difference.'

As the Clinic explains, exercise releases feel-good endorphins, natural cannabis-like brain chemicals (endogenous cannabinoids) and other natural brain chemicals that can enhance your sense of well-being; it can also take your mind off worries so you can get away from the cycle of negative thoughts that feed depression and anxiety. It can also help you gain confidence, get more social interaction and cope in a healthy way.

Doing something positive to manage depression or anxiety is a healthy coping strategy. Trying to feel better by drinking alcohol, dwelling on how you feel or hoping depression or anxiety will go away on its own can lead to worsening symptoms.

In this way, running – and exercise more generally – has come to be seen as having a positive role in suicide prevention. Paul Shepherd, interviewed in this book, is the living proof. The Campaign Against Living Miserably (CALM) is an award-winning charity dedicated to preventing male suicide, the single biggest killer of men under the age of 45 in the UK. In 2015, 75 per cent of all UK suicides were male. It was CALM that urged Paul to take up exercise – a moment he recognises as a turning point. His debut marathon in April 2018, just 15 months after the awful night when he attempted to take his life in the icy waters off Bognor Regis, is the measure of the remarkable recovery he has been able to make.

The American Foundation for Suicide Prevention (AFSP), the leading national not-for-profit organisation dedicated exclusively to understanding and preventing suicide through research, education and advocacy, undertakes similar work in the United States. Significantly it promotes exercise through a programme of walks. As the charity says, its Out of the Darkness Walks are proof that when people work together they can make big changes in the world. They are AFSP's largest fundraiser; crucially, the walks also 'unite those who have been affected by suicide and create communities that are smart about mental health'.

In Australia, too, exercise is seen as an important way to tackle a truly horrifying statistic: suicide is the leading cause of death for Australians aged 15–44. Every day, around eight Australians kill themselves – a figure more than double the national road toll.

Anytime Fitness Australia, the biggest fitness community in the country, was determined to help change the statistics by promoting a treadmill run. They asked members to get involved by walking, jogging, running or dancing to keep the treadmills moving for 24 hours. Almost 300 of its clubs took part. Search #AFATreadmillChallenge on Facebook and Instagram.

The initiative was in support of Suicide Prevention Australia (SPA), which aims to work 'collaboratively to develop a community that knows how to ask for help and how to give help'. SPA organises a series of stadium stomp events at Australia's key cricket grounds: the Adelaide Oval, the Gabba in Brisbane, the MCG and the SCG. Each is a mass stair climb, celebrating 'health, fitness, fun, community and [giving] back to the causes you are passionate about'.

Running has also been shown to be beneficial in addiction recovery. AlcoholRehab.com, a resource for information concerning substance abuse, alcoholism, mental health and addiction treatment options, offers a section specifically on why running might help.

Aside from the benefits to cardiovascular health, the plus of strengthening our bones and the advantage of simply getting in shape, the site advocates running as a way to relieve stress, improve our sense of well-being and boost our self-esteem. Meeting people is another knock-on benefit.

Specifically for people in recovery, the site encourages running as a way to make positive use of any free time that comes with becoming sober. It also fosters the mental strength needed in recovery. In addition, running can undo some of the physical damage caused by alcohol or drug addiction, and it can also open up new and more health-conscious social networks away from people who are still drinking or using. It will also promote self-esteem. AlcoholRehab.com notes:

Simply speaking, people run because it makes them happy. Those individuals who recover from an addiction deserve plenty of happiness in their life, and this is one way to make that happen.

In the United States, Linda Quirk (*see* pages 79–85) is an expert in the field of helping former users on their path to recovery. She sets out the challenges and benefits clearly in an August 2014 blog:

To get clean, addicts often have to sever most of the emotional relationships from their former lives, and the loneliness can be overwhelming and relapse-inducing. Unfortunately, getting sober often has losing odds, but it can be done with support. And exercise.

Recovery can take advantage of the crossover between the urge to run and the urge to take drugs, as Linda explains:

Why we run and why we become addicted to drugs have something in common: dopamine. Dopamine is one of about a half dozen neuro-transmitters in the brain (out of about 50 discovered to date) that play a key role in addiction. Dopamine is responsible for pleasure and is released in the brain when we do things like eat chocolate, have sex, do drugs or run. Research has shown that exercising animals are less inclined to tap a lever for morphine and it's likely that humans experience similar effects, which is why exercise often plays a key role in recovery at treatment centres. Running and other exercise release dopamine and can provide a natural high that has the potential to help addicts overcome drug and alcohol cravings.

In all these ways, running can reconnect us, whether we are suffering from PTSD, depression or addiction – or indeed bereavement, as the stories of Eleanor Keohane, Anji Andrews and Lisa Hallett have so movingly and powerfully shown in this book.

The important point is that running has brought them a sense of community, and I am with them every step of the way in that respect. One of the most distressing aspects of being stabbed has always been the wall that it puts between me and everyone else: the feeling, irrational and unhelpful, that no one can possibly understand what I went through that day. Through this book, I have connected with people who have been through similar and worse; running has been our common ground. These interviewees are my community.

And it is in this context that it is tempting to see the massive rise of parkrun. parkrun organise free, weekly, 5km timed runs around the world.

Of course, many parkrunners run from a starting point of complete happiness; they start positive and finish even more so, revelling in all the health benefits of simply being out there and being part of something. But among the parkrunners are plenty of people who run for the strength it gives them in their own personal darkness. Sujan Sharma in this book is the perfect illustration.

The first parkrun saw 13 runners gather in Bushy Park, Teddington, UK in October 2004. By 2018, there were around 1300 timed 5km parkruns around the world every Saturday, with around 600 in the UK alone. Current figures suggest 110,000 people will be parkrunning in the UK on any Saturday, 230,000 globally. And with six to eight new parkruns starting in the UK each week, the growth is remarkable.

parkrun spread to the United States in June 2012 with the first running of the Livonia parkrun in Michigan, though it has been slower to take off in the States than in other countries. Quite why is difficult to determine. There have been plenty of suggestions, including a relative lack of accessible parks, an already overcrowded running market and perhaps, quite simply, society itself. But there is no doubting the determination of the USA's devoted parkrunners to overcome the obstacles and to use this relatively small starting point as the basis for rapid growth.

In Australia, it has been a different story. parkrun began on the Gold Coast in April 2011, and in 2017, 48 new locations were launched in Australia. By mid-2018 there were more than 130 venues across the country, with the prediction that around 50 more would be added by the end of the year.

Community psychology is Paul Morris' particular interest: an area of study that aims to use our understanding of psychology to benefit and support the community. Its aim is to prevent distress before it actually happens. For his doctorate in clinical psychology, Paul discovered that parkrun was effectively community psychology in action.

parkruns are open to everyone; they are free, they are safe and they are accessible. Pleasant parkland surroundings are a key part of the attraction, as is the fact that parkrun encourages people of every ability to take part, whatever their levels of experience. In other words, parkrun creates a community where mental well-being is given every chance. This is running that isn't about distance; running that isn't about competitiveness and speed. It is running that is all about togetherness.

As Paul says, go along to a parkrun and you will see people embracing so many of the things underpinning good mental health. You will see people encouraging each other. And you will see an equitable world where there is no distinction between the slower runners and the faster runners. As Paul says, parkrun is community psychology in microcosm.

For his research, Paul focused on parkrunners and parkrun volunteers who had experienced mental health difficulties. He discovered that the running itself was part of a wider package. More important than the running was the sense of community. Paul was able to look at the sense of achievement that comes from running, but also at the sense of achievement that comes, just as importantly, from contributing to the event – whether organising it, supporting others or simply chatting with fellow runners on the day. This is a fundamental part of the friendliness and warm welcome at the heart of parkrun.

Paul, who completed his doctorate in clinical psychology in the autumn of 2017, discovered a direct link between parkrunning and improved self-esteem, improved confidence and improved mood. As he explains, one of the biggest problems facing those with mental health issues is that they can feel isolated. parkrun brings them into a healthy, positive environment with significant knock-on benefits. It is free; almost anyone can do it; and the distance is achievable. For those suffering anxiety and depression, parkrun offers an activity which is inclusive, friendly and safe.

Not the least of its benefits is a very real sense of contributing, something people can take with them into other areas of their lives. They feel better because of parkrun, and they can take that improvement with them into their home life. Increased self-esteem through parkrun can mean increased confidence elsewhere. As Paul says, it is an experience that people can feel positive about.

> *The benefits of volunteering with parkrun are reciprocal. People are putting something back into something they are taking out of. They are giving back to something so that they can keep it going so that they can continue to use it.*

It is the perfect circle, and therein lies the beauty of running. It is the great connector, the great solver of problems. It offers safety and inclusivity, a sense of value and a sense that we are giving as well as taking.

And the great news is that science can help us understand it.

There are those of us who will always regard running as an art, but it is yet another vindication of running's great power for good that science is increasingly taking it seriously and telling us of its benefits. Hardened runners will inevitably feel that science is simply dressing up all the things that we already instinctively know, but there is no doubt that a solid scientific understanding of running will help spread its warm embrace even further.

And as we run, we know it won't be long before we see another runner. And that's when we will exchange the nod that says it all. The nod of recognition and community. The nod of support and solidarity. I love what Alastair Campbell says in this book, that nobody now looks at a runner and thinks: 'Poor guy, must be so lonely'.

We can talk about serotonin, dopamine and brain-derived neuro-trophic factor when we talk about running. And why not? It's all good validation. These are things it is interesting to know.

But do they make running any less magical? No, they certainly don't. I would say that they make it even more so. They almost capture it, but not quite.

Running is fun but hard work; it is draining and yet enriching; depleting and yet deeply restorative; sobering and yet intoxicating. It is individual and yet collective; it is sweaty and yet beautiful; it is art and, yes, it is science too. Running is accessible and yet so often remarkable;

it is prosaic and yet poetic, a challenge and yet a delight; and perhaps above all it manages somehow to be both freedom and connection.

How can we possibly ever explain it entirely? All I know for certain is that I would never have coped without it.

Which is why I return again and again in my mind to Dean Karnazes' beautiful words that open this book. We can talk about neurons, the hippocampus and the dentate gyrus, but for me, it is Dean's beautiful phrase that sums it up best: 'the splendour of a spirit in motion'.

Splendour indeed.

Running sets our spirits soaring. No wonder we feel better when we run.

Acknowledgements

It's not an easy thing for a chap to admit, but I suspect there have been times in the past couple of years when I haven't exactly been the easiest person to live with. And yet from the moment I FaceTimed from South Africa to say: 'Err... I've been stabbed', my wife Fiona has been utterly unswerving in her love and care and concern.

I am not sure I would want to live with someone who leaps out of their skin at the slightest, sudden, unexpected noise as I still do, but Fiona has accepted my new and rather odd normality in the same way she has always accepted my running. Thank you. You have been amazing.

Massive thanks also to our children Adam and Laura, medical students both, fantastic human beings too. We are immensely proud of you and thrilled that your beautiful caring natures are taking you both into the caring profession.

My thanks also to my parents, Graham and Juliette. I don't think I have ever been happier to see anyone than when you turned up to meet me at the airport after my ill-fated trip to South Africa. I could barely stand. I hurt all over. I still shiver at the thought of that awful journey home; I still go wobbly when I think of my relief when I saw you both waiting for me at arrivals.

As for my friends, it would be impossible to repay the debt I owe you.

When I think of the support you have shown me, I start to understand why I have never for a moment wished the stabbing hadn't happened. It underlined, double underlined and triple underlined that I have got some fabulous mates, all with hearts of gold.

I am a little horrified when I think of the hours you have listened to me droning on and on about my South African adventure. I am bad enough when I talk about cricket. Awful too when I kick off about The Rolling Stones.

But with the stabbing, I know I have talked and talked and talked, my way of coping. And I know I lost the filter that should have cut out some of the more gruesome details. It has been my nature to niggle away at what happened, to agonise over the *what if*s and to search for answers I can never possibly find. My friends have all responded with astonishing kindness, compassion and understanding – and also a total lack of judgement. Gary, John, Ian, Steve, Helen, Vicky, Jo, Hazel, Brian and Sophie in particular. Fabulous people. Very, very dear friends indeed.

And in the immediate aftermath of the stabbing, Tony looked after me amazingly in Cape Town. You wrapped me up in warmth and kindness when I needed it most. Truly a friend in a million. Your strength and decency counted for everything in those first few days.

My thanks also to my father-in-law, Michael. Michael started marathon-running at the age of 69 because he was fed up with seeing my finishing photos on the wall of our downstairs loo. He went on to achieve far more in his running career than I could ever dream of: in terms of medals and age-related times, he has lapped me time and time again, and he is still running strong at the age of 86. Michael, you are a genuine running mate.

You have been superstars, one and all. Thank you too to Ros: endless patience, endless insight, endless kindness.

And Kate too. I still squirm in embarrassment at my overreaction in your kitchen: my moment of sheer, stupid, unspoken terror when you, a dear friend of 25 years standing, picked up a knife as you quietly, unthreateningly, did the washing-up. I am so sorry, Kate. But again, I can't truly regret it. You saw that I needed help. Your encouragement was a turning point – as was your encouragement, a couple of months later, in the writing of this book. It came, as so many of our best conversations do, over a pizza in Chichester.

Thank you too to Matt Lowing at Bloomsbury, a fine runner himself and a superlative editor. Thank you, Matt, for seeing beyond the book I originally submitted and opening the door to the book I needed to write. This book truly took off with your vision.

I also owe a huge debt of gratitude to the remarkable people I have interviewed in these pages. People I approached out of the blue, people who responded with warmth, openness and kindness when I asked them to share with me – and with you – their tales of adversity.

I am still jumpy; my memory has been poor since the attack; my concentration is often abysmal; I long for an unbroken night's sleep, even as the third anniversary approaches.

I cope. And I cope because I run. But I cope too because of the people I have spoken to in this book. You have been my guides. I have learned from you all, each and every one. You have inspired me. Fantastic people. Good people. Brave people. Ordinary people who have braved extraordinary events and have come out running the other side.

Thank you all, Caroline in particular. Your gentle wisdom and your patience with someone relatively new to trauma have been invaluable. You have helped me massively. Your kindness has been very real, very immediate – despite the thousands and thousands of miles between us. The sweetest of voices from the other side of the world.

But my biggest thanks inevitably go to Steven. How could I possibly thank him enough? The fact that he stopped for me was the warmest of comforts in the sleepless nights that followed my stabbing. I saw the worst in man. Very quickly, I saw the best. How decent. How brave. How very human in the very best sense of the word. It's perfectly possible that I owe him everything – a thought I am proud to carry with me for the rest of my days.

References

Runners

Hanny Allston
    www.hannyallston.com.au
    https://findyourfeet.com.au
    www.findyourfeettours.com.au

Anji Andrews
    www.facebook.com/anji.close

Alastair Campbell
    www.alastaircampbell.org
    www.headstogether.org.uk
    www.bloodwise.org.uk
    www.time-to-change.org.uk

Liz Dunning
    www.runlizzierun.com

Caroline Elliott
    www.youtube.com/watch?v=Fmjd3JZMgXk
    www.facebook.com/caroline.elliott.39

Charlie Engle
    www.charlieengle.com
    www.charlieengle.com/blog
    www.charlieengle.com/runningman
    www.facebook.com/charlie.engle.12?ref=br_rs

Ana Febres-Cordero
    www.facebook.com/ana.o.fc
    www.deconstructingstigma.org

Theresa Giammona
www.answerthecall.org

Lisa Hallett
www.wearblueruntoremember.org
www.youtube.com/watch?v=Z54PKRSS67c

Bryn Hughes
www.pcnicolahughesmemorialfund.co.uk

Cherissa Jackson
www.cherissajackson.com

Kate Jayden
www.facebook.com/kate.jayden

Lynn Julian Crisci
www.BostonActress.org
www.PopSuperhero.com
www.uspainfoundation.org
www.stosglobal.org
www.biausa.org
www.baa.org
www.alwaystri.com

Dan Keeley
www.dankeeley.co
Twitter, Facebook and Instagram are all @IamDanKeeley

Eleanor Keohane
www.facebook.com/TheHospiceRunningClub/

Carolyn Knights
www.facebook.com/carolyn.knights

Sandra Laflamme
www.organicrunnermom.com

Emma Malcolm
www.rethink.org

Jason Nelson
www.facebook.com/nosajnoslen
www.sirensofsilence.org.au

Bryn Phillips
yeovilmarathon.co.uk

Linda Quirk
www.runwell.com
www.caron.org

Jessica Rigo
www.chescohalf.com
www.facebook.com/jessica.gasslerrigo

The Schneider Twins
www.autismrunners.com
www.robynkschneider.com
www.amazon.com/Silent-Running-Family%C2%92s-Journey-Finish/
    dp/1629370916/ref=sr_1_1?ie=UTF8&qid=1421981319&sr=8-1&keyw
    ords=silent+running+autism (or search 'Silent Running Family')
www.rtsnp.org
www.achillesinternational.org

Daniele Seiss
www.facebook.com/dani.seiss
https://danirunner.wordpress.com/

Sujan Sharma
www.mind.org.uk
www.youtube.com/watch?v=pSR2-Y1XL48

Paul Shepherd
www.thecalmzone.net

Danny Slay
www.hope24.team-hope.co.uk
www.hope-for-children.org

Serena Wooldridge
www.facebook.com/serena.wooldridge

Don Wright
www.facebook.com/ERACECANCER

Organisations
The American Foundation for Suicide Prevention (AFSP): afsp.org.
Anxiety in Teens: anxietyinteens.org
Anytime Fitness Australia: www.anytimefitness.com.au/treadmillrun
Mayo Clinic: www.mayoclinic.org
Mind: www.mind.org.uk
National Health Service (NHS): www.nhs.uk
Still I Run: www.stilliruncommunity.com

Bibliography
AlcoholRehab.com: http://alcoholrehab.com/addiction-recovery/running-in-recovery/

At Peace, Not In Pieces: Powering Through My Pain, Cherissa Jackson (Unlock Publishing House, Inc, 2016)

Exercise Enhances the Behavioral Responses to Acute Stress in an Animal Model of PTSD: www.ncbi.nlm.nih.gov/pubmed/25699481

Harvard Health School: www.health.harvard.edu/mind-and-mood/excercise-is-an-all-natural-treatment-to-fight-depression

Linda Quirk: http://runwell.com/blog-post/running-can-curb-addiction-and-ease-recovery

Running Man, Charlie Engle (Simon & Schuster, 2016)

Silent Running: Our Family's Journey to the Finish Line with Autism, Robyn K. Schneider (Triumph Books, 2015)

Start Active, Stay Active: www.sportengland.org/media/2928/dh_128210.pdf

The Non-Runner's Marathon Trainer, David A. Whitsett, Forrest A. Dolgener, Tanjala Mabon Kole (McGraw-Hill Education, 1998)

University of Texas: https://alcalde.texasexes.org/2015/07/ut-researchers-running-may-help-treat-ptsd/

About the Author

Phil Hewitt was brought up in Gosport, Hampshire, where he attended Bay House School. He later gained a first-class honours degree in modern languages at the University of Oxford, where he also completed a doctorate in the French theatre of the early 20th century. Phil joined the *Chichester Observer* in 1990 and became the newspaper's arts editor four years later. He is now also arts editor for all the *Observer*'s sister papers across West Sussex, including the *West Sussex Gazette* and the *West Sussex County Times*.

Phil lives in Bishops Waltham, Hampshire, with his wife Fiona. Their children, Adam and Laura, are medical students at the University of Newcastle.

A keen runner, Phil has completed 34 marathons, including London six times, Paris three times and Portsmouth four times, as well as New York, Berlin, Dublin, Rome, Mallorca, Amsterdam, Marrakech and Tokyo. In June 2018 he was proud to run the Yeovil Marathon, created by Bryn Phillips, who was interviewed in this book.

Phil is also the author of *Keep on Running, In The Running, Chichester Remembered, Chichester Then and Now, Gosport Then and Now, A Chichester Miscellany, A Portsmouth Miscellany* and *A Winchester Miscellany*. You can follow him on Twitter at @marathon_addict.